SUPERLEARNING

* "Superlearning—Super reading!"
  Gannet News

* "A fascinating book . . . outlines breakthrough techniques which show how to use body, mind and creativity as one, to leap from learning to Superlearning."
  Santa Cruz Sentinal

* "Superlearning—a blueprint for achieving excellence in *any* field."
  New Age Journal

* "Eminently readable, one of the most popular books about learning written in years . . . conveys basic self-help methods for accelerated learning . . . the authors deserve an A + for their wizardry."
  Frontiers of Business Education

* "I started using Superlearning techniques for Spanish; once I mastered the exercises, I found they improved my interviewing, my writing, speechmaking and just about everything else involving my memory."
  Charlayne Hunter-Galt, Journalist, MacNeil/Lehrer News Hour

SUPERLEARNING

SUPERLEARNING

Sheila Ostrander
and Lynn Schroeder
with
Nancy Ostrander

DELACORTE PRESS/CONFUCIAN PRESS/NEW YORK

Printing history:
Delacorte Press/Confucian Press, Inc.
Seventh Printing 1980
Delta
Tenth Printing 1985
Dell/Laurel
Seventh Printing 1985

IBSN: 0-385-28952-9

Printed in the United States of America

Mail Order Edition
Superlearning Inc.
450 Seventh Avenue
New York, New York 10123

Contents

SECTION III — SUPER-RAPPORT

SECTION IV — EXERCISES

APPENDIX

SECTION I
SUPERLEARNING

Chapter 1
Your Potential Quotient

"We are just beginning to discover the virtually limitless capacities of the mind . . ." says Dr. Jean Houston, president of the Association for Humanistic Psychology.

Mathematician Dr. Charles Muses puts it this way, "The potentials of consciousness remain well-nigh the last reachable domain for man not yet explored—the Undiscovered Country."

Dr. Frederic Tilney, one of France's outstanding brain specialists, declares, "We will, by conscious command, evolve cerebral centers which will permit us to use powers that we now are not even capable of imagining."

Dr. Richard Leakey is involved in digging out humanity's three-million-year history. The potential for the human race, he feels, "is almost infinite." And, George Leonard, from his perspective as an education expert, concludes, "The ultimate creative capacity of the brain may be, for all practical purposes, infinite."

We've just barely begun to realize the potential of a fully powered man or woman. The idea is becoming very vocal in the upper echelons. It's supported by people as various as theologian-scientist Teilhard de Chardin and mind-drug explorer Dr.

Timothy Leary. And these potentials move out in all directions. According to psychologist Patricia Sun, we are at the point of developing "talents we haven't got words for." Neuroscientist and engineer Dr. Manfred Clynes has determined from hard scientific research that we are at the stage where we can develop new emotions, genuinely new states we've never before experienced.

We've cracked the cocoon, we're being told. We can start shaking out our wings; it's time to claim our birthright. We can be so much more than we are. It's a seductive idea. And it always has been, because almost everybody has a secret, though few admit it. We feel there's something special about ourselves. Maybe it hasn't quite burst forth, maybe others don't quite see it, yet it's there, something special that sets us a little apart. Now, it's beginning to look as if all those unrealistic, stubborn human feelings are right. We are special—or could be.

If we're going to grow into these potentials, waiting, it seems, just beyond reach, we have to have ways of doing it. And that's been the obstacle. Too often we can imagine how lab animals feel pushed on by little shocks, running faster and faster through their maze. Old fashioned trying harder isn't the answer. But perhaps trying a different route is.

We need new ways, more efficient and less stressful ways of getting to these potentials. We need to learn how to learn. That's what this book is about, learning how to learn better and without stress. The kind of learning that makes you feel good while you're doing it. This book is also about how you can apply this learning skill in a great many areas of your life.

The various learning systems covered are drawn from many sources. They come from the work of innovative doctors: the Bulgarian Georgi Lozanov, the German Johannes H. Schultz, the Spanish Alfonso Caycedo; they come from the long-tested science of yoga and from contemporary physiology and psychology. They come too from the accumulated experience of creative, accomplished individuals, from golf stars and ski champions to top American executives.

Various as they are, all of these systems share a common viewpoint, a holistic viewpoint. They see you always as a whole person. Whether you are trying to learn French, to play tennis, or to make good business decisions, these systems work on the principle that you have a logical mind, a body, and a creative mind. In other words, they use left brain, body, and right brain in concert.

In the past decade, complex research into how we think has turned into the pop concept of left brain/right brain. To over-simplify, the theory is that the left side of our brain has to do with logical, rational, analytical thinking. The right side is concerned with such things as intuition, creativity, imagination. Whatever you're doing, holistic learning methods try to insure that you're neither half-witted nor disembodied. The point is to keep the left brain, body, and right brain from working against each other and hamstringing your abilities. Going further, holistic learning aims to have these three work together to allow you to use the full power of your being.

What happens when you do get yourself together is the difference between learning and superlearning. As many people are finding, there's a quantum jump in your ability to accomplish. Compared to the way most of us have been grinding along, this new approach is literally superlearning.

It might help to think of an orchestra: brass, percussion, and strings. When the horns are featured, the drums and violins don't try to pound and saw against them. Nor do they go rambling off on their own. They play in concert. Logical mind, body, creative mind—you may be focusing with one, but because you are a whole person the other parts are there, are in resonance. They can create disharmony. Or, they can play in concert. Usually in our efforts to learn, we've separated ourselves into pieces. Superlearning works to put Humpty Dumpty back together again so he can see what he can become.

Discovering just how much one can do is almost unsettling, as a group of Bulgarians found when they got involved with perhaps the most striking, far-reaching learning system in this book. They heard it was a way to learn and remember vast quantities of information, quickly, effectively and, it was claimed, with less effort than any of them thought possible. In the mid 1960's, these fifteen professional people, men and women from twenty-two to sixty, gathered in a warm, sunny room in the Institute of Suggestology standing on a shady side street near the heart of Sofia. They were to take part in an experiment that they weren't at all happy about.

"Nothing can come of this," a woman doctor complained to the architect beside her as the group arranged themselves in a circle of easy chairs. Others chimed in, an engineer, several teachers, a judge. "We should give up now. It's a waste of time." No one could offer much hope. The teacher arrived; she too was having trouble shaking the feeling that she'd been asked to do the impossible.

Still, there they were and they began. As the class members shuffled through pages of material, the teacher started reading French phrases in different intonations. Then, stately classical music began in the background. The fifteen men and women leaned back, closed their eyes, and embarked on developing hypermnesia, more easily called supermemory. The teacher kept reciting. Sometimes her voice was businesslike as if ordering work to be done, sometimes it sounded soft, whispering, then unexpectedly hard and commanding.

Shadows began to darken in the room, it was sunset, yet the teacher kept on, repeating in a special rhythm French words, idioms, translations. Finally, she stopped. They weren't through yet; they still had to take a test. At least the class members weren't as keyed up. Somehow during the session their anxiety had been smoothed, the usual kinks relaxed. But they still didn't hold much hope for decent test scores.

Finally the teacher told them. "The class average is ninety-seven percent. You learned one thousand words in a day!"

One thousand—they knew that was like learning almost half the working vocabulary of a language in a few hours. And they'd done it effortlessly. Men and women wheeled out of the institute feeling ten feet taller, feeling as if they'd just had a fundamental encounter, for the extra-dimensional beings they'd met were themselves.

Usually in such courses, people learn 50 to 150 new bits of information a session. This was an experiment. To Dr. Georgi Lozanov, the originator of the method, it helped prove something he suspected: The human ability to learn and remember is virtually limitless. Lozanov and his colleagues in Bulgaria and the Soviet Union call this "tapping the reserves of the mind." To the people who've tried, it's more like suddenly coming into a large legacy. They see themselves differently. Possibilities open up. They begin to grow into a larger notion of who they are and what they can do.

This sort of rapid-learning system can be used to learn any kind of factual information. It is left-brain learning. How can the logical mind suddenly perform with almost stupifying ability? It can soar because the body and right-brain abilities are in harmony, are lending their support, are playing in concert. In all the learning methods in this book, no matter which part of the whole is featured—left-brain, body, right-brain—the others are there, harmonizing and supporting. That's why they are holistic learning systems. These systems can be used to learn chemistry, languages, or history. They can also be used to learn to shine at a business meeting or to give one's best performance on the tennis court. In Dr. Hannes Lindemann's case, all he wanted to do was put his feet on stable ground, on the Western shore.

A decade before the Bulgarians were coming to the unsettling realization that they could all perform like "geniuses," Hannes Lindemann, a German medical doctor, embarked on a different kind of feat. Launching his one-man sailing canoe from the Canary Islands, he swung the bow of the canvas boat west; he was going to the new world. "West," Lindemann told himself, "west." The command even echoed and took form in his dreams. For seventy-two days and nights, he sailed on, sitting upright, like a lonely pea in his canvas shell. He could sleep only in snatches, there was almost no room to move about. On the fifty-seventh night, he got a break in routine. He capsized and lay on the slippery bottom of his canoe until dawn. Over a hundred other men had tried this type of crossing. All had failed. But Hannes Lindemann stepped onto the western shore at St. Martin in the West Indies and wound up smiling from the cover of *Life*. Not only did he survive, he did so in robust shape. He had learned, for instance, how to control circulation to protect parts of his body; he didn't even develop the saltwater sores that invariably fester under such conditions.

"I succeeded," Lindemann says, "thanks to autogenic training." He'd been taught this holistic method by its originator, Dr. Johannes H. Schultz, and believes, understandably, that he proved its soundness under the most overpowering circumstances. Autogenics and its many current adaptations are concerned with harmonizing all the forces of mind and body so the body can perform at its best. It also can help heal body and mind and give the kind of all-around, bounding health that few enjoy or even expect anymore.

Not many people are going to wager their lives on a learning system as Dr. Lindemann did. But tens of thousands have proved these superlearning systems to be successful through their own experience. Plenty of scientific tests back these methods, but in the last few years things have begun to happen that don't really need any abstruse test to interpret. As you'll see, there's a lot of proof in flesh-and-blood performance. In the USSR, thousands of adults learned a language in twenty-four days. In Switzerland, skiers returned from the Olympics with gold and silver medals. In Bulgaria, children came home from their ordinary schools on their ordinary streets having learned in a month what usually takes half a year. In France and Spain, everyday people discovered they could mentally control their bodies and regulate their health. Some learned to release themselves from pain, without drugs. U.S. business people found intuition could help make the decisions that doubled profits. And when superlearning methods were used to help rehabilitate the blind, blind people started to tell the sighted about things the sighted couldn't see.

Superlearning methods always see you whole, in the round. They have something else in common that's harder to explain because it isn't straightforward. When you begin to operate more as a whole, seemingly inexplicable things can happen. A woman studying French suddenly finds her sinus trouble has disappeared; a man learning chemistry realizes his intuition has accelerated. An athlete doing body training techniques finds his concentration improved in academic exams. As obstructive divisions dissolve, all areas of the person can be strengthened. It's similar to light striking one facet of a crystal, soon it lights up another and another.

This ricochet effect rearranged the life of Georgi Lozanov (Lo-*zan*-ov), a doctor and psychiatrist, who didn't set out to be an educator. He did set out, following the old adage, to study the nature of man, of the human being in all its potential. Like just about everybody else, he concluded that we're only using a fraction of our capabilities. Lozanov devised ways to open the reserves of the mind and, as a doctor, put them to work to improve the body, to heal mental and physical disease. But in investigating what the whole human being can do, he couldn't help being drawn into creative and intuitive areas. Then still investigating, almost by necessity, he became one of the leading parapsychologists in the communist world. At the same time, Lozanov realized that with his new techniques, the average person could develop supermemory, could learn factual information with unheard-of ease.

It is paradoxical that Lozanov is world famous for developing a system of factual learning; the path he first took seemed to be leading away from the typical Western overemphasis on factual thinking. But paradoxical is a left-brain word. It is paradoxical to the logical mind. From the more encompassing holistic point of view—it figures.

In a sense, superlearning adds by taking away. The programs are geared to help dissolve fear, self-blame, cramped self-images, and negative suggestions about limited abilities. They try to flood away the many blocks we handicap ourselves with and release the unobstructed personality. It's not so much that superlearning gives you something new; it gives you something you already have—yourself. That's why it can be so very powerful. This centered, unobstructed self, this radiant self, as educator Paula Klimek calls it, knows. It seems to be plugged into a wider consciousness that knows how to accomplish almost anything.

Success in learning, sports, business, and relationships is rewarding. People also seem to find another kind of reward in superlearning—one more involved with doing than winning. There is a feeling of harmony one sometimes gets, of riding along on the full wave of one's being. It's a total satisfaction of itself, the kind that comes when you feel the bat connect solidly with the ball, when you really understand a difficult concept for the first time, when, for a moment, you find yourself wholly in tune with another person. It's lighting up alive, for that moment —joyously alive.

Joy of learning is something you hear about in superlearning courses. For most of us learning hasn't always been a catapulting, joyous experience. But perhaps in the nature of things it was meant to be, because learning is growing and growing is life. One of the most common reports from those involved in superlearning courses is that as you get into the course, you start to feel good—good about yourself and good about others.

Perhaps one reason for feeling good is that superlearning deals with your potential quotient, not your intelligence quotient. For practical purposes today, our potentials seem limitless. As we limber up and own more of ourselves, it's beginning to look too as if IQ may not be as fixed as we thought.

Arthur Young is a philosopher and inventor; Charles Muses is a mathematician and a cosmologist. Not long ago, they collected the views of some of the seed people of our time, pulse takers and concept changers, in a book called *Consciousness and Reality.* In their preface they wrote, "It is the moment of evolutionary truth for the race, and what man does with that moment will be more important than the events of the previous millennia."

As we've said, to be more than we are is a sweet old idea, but there is perhaps a deeper reason why these new learning methods are beginning to quicken around the globe. It has to do with the historical moment. We're running out of gas in more ways than one. We seem to be running down in the old tracks in all areas of society. A few years ago, word came out of the Soviet Union that they were attempting to train their cosmonauts in precognition—the ability to foreknow, to see the future. Cosmonauts are traveling so fast, one scientist explained, that they have to know beforehand what's going to happen, just to keep up. A lot of us are beginning to get that feeling.

Horse-and-buggy learning isn't practical in a jet-speed age. If we could look down from Olympus, we'd probably see that we've just about streamed past the jet age too. We want to stay part of our world, to feel the center isn't out there, somewhere, treadmilling us along. To make the decisions, to have the equanimity and the capabilities we need, it is quite probable that now is the time to open up those further, rarely used circuits of ourselves. We're told we only use about ten percent of our brains. The rest of it must have been built-in for a reason. As Dr. Frederic Tilney says, we will consciously evolve brain centers that will give us powers we can't even imagine now.

This book presents some of the ways a great number of people have used to start reaching those reserves of mind and body. The first and major section deals with factual learning and remembering—left-brain specialities. The second section deals with the body, with physical performance and health. The third section deals with intuition, creativity, and so-called extrasensory abilities—right-brain activities. The whole book has to do with imagination. Napoleon worked out his battle strategy in a sandbox because, he said, "Imagination rules the world."

To get yourself started, imagine what you could do if your

ability to learn and remember increased five to fifty times. That's what the following section is about in detail. It's a holistic approach. If you follow this superlearning route to expanded memory, you may find that you're also re-membering and re-collecting something else—yourself.

Chapter 2
Supermemory

A ruggedly built, sandy-haired man in his sixties with a perpetually wrinkled forehead walked quickly to the back of a large auditorium crammed with scientists. It was at Dubna, near Moscow, the Soviet Union's major atomic research center, and the prestigious audience included many world-renowned Soviet physicists.

This man, Mikhail Keuni, an artist, was going to show these famous physicists how to do math. "Cover that huge blackboard with circles," he told a volunteer on stage at the front of the room. "They can intersect. They can be inside one another. Draw them any way you wish."

As physicists spun the board around for Keuni to glance at, the audience laughed. It was totally white with circles. Keuni's eyes scarcely blinked. In two seconds he called out the total: "167!"

It took the Soviet Union's foremost brain trust over five minutes to do the calculations necessary to verify Keuni's instant and accurate answer.

Forty-digit numbers went up on the board and Keuni could recall them and calculate with them faster than a computer.

After his demonstration of numerical memory and wizardry, Keuni received a letter from the scientists at the Joint Nuclear Research Institute: "If we weren't physicists, then it would be extremely difficult to verify that man's brain is capable of accomplishing such miracles." (Dubna, April 12, 1959.)

Mikhail Keuni possesses the gift of supermemory, that is, what allows him to do instant math faster than a calculator. It also allows him to learn with extraordinary speed. If something registers on Keuni's mind once, he can retrieve it whole, without straining or trying hard. He can retrieve whatever he perceives. This superlearning ability stands him in good stead when he tours foreign countries to demonstrate his unusual abilities. He's never at a loss for words. In less than a month, for instance, he became completely fluent in Japanese. Then when tour plans were changed, he was said to have mastered Finnish in a week.

Is Mikhail Keuni an evolutionary freak? Does he have a unique set of brain cells? Or is supermemory a basic human potential? Is it something any of us could light up, at least in part, if we knew how?

That was a leading question in our minds when we landed in the Soviet bloc countries in the summer of 1968 to attend the first Moscow International Conference on Parapsychology. Among others, we were going to talk to a Bulgarian scientist, Dr. Georgi Lozanov, who had investigated a number of people with extraordinary mental abilities like Keuni's. Lozanov had come to claim that supermemory was a natural human ability. Not only can anyone develop it, he said, but one can do so with ease. To prove his point there were supposedly thousands of people in Bulgaria and the Soviet Union who were well on their way to acquiring supermemory of their own.

We first heard of this new route to learning in Soviet bloc newspapers. "A Method That Can Transform Education," "Hidden Channels of the Mind," ran the headlines. "It's Possible to Learn a Language in a Month," said *Pravda*. The *Bulgarian Evening News* proclaimed, "Parapsychology Can Be Applied in Education." As press reports and scientific papers began to accelerate through the sixties, they grew steadily harder to believe. At first, Bulgarians and Soviets were supposedly learning 100 words of a foreign language in a day. Then it was 201. Next there were claims that people had learned 500 words in a single day. Then research data came out saying 1,000 words had been learned in a day by a Bulgarian group.

The claims didn't stop there. This system, we read, speeds up learning from five to fifty times, increases retention, requires virtually no effort on the part of the students, reaches retarded and brilliant, young and old alike, and requires no special equipment. And, people testified, not only had they learned a whole language in a month, or a semester of history in a few weeks, they had rebalanced their health and awakened creative and intuitive abilities while they were learning their facts.

Almost anyone will tell you such things aren't supposed to happen. One of the authors knew it more strongly than some from first-hand experience. One of Sheila's degrees is in education, she trained in languages and had also spent some sixteen years studying music. (And music was said to be a key element in this learning system.) The Bulgarian claims sounded preposterous. Yet they kept appearing with favorable comments from reputable scientists and institutes. In the mid 1960's Sheila started to correspond with researchers at the Institute of Suggestology in Sofia, which is directed by Dr. Lozanov; she began translating papers on this new method from other Slavic countries.

In these accounts, writers invariably mentioned a basic contention of Soviet physiologists: We use barely ten percent of our brain capacity, yet we can learn to plug in to the other ninety percent; we can, as they put it, learn to tap the reserves of the mind. Dr. Lozanov, it appeared, had uncovered some of the biological secrets that lead to expanded potentials. He had coordinated them into a system that let people use *both* body and mind at peak efficiency to literally develop supermemory and thus to speed learning.

Lozanov called his learning system suggestopedia. It is just a branch, though a very vital one, of a much larger subject embraced by his institute: suggestology. Suggestology is a holistic "ology" that weaves together a bundle of techniques to help people reach those reserves of mind and body. Suggestology attempts to get the body and left-brain and right-brain abilities working together as an orchestrated whole to make people more capable of doing whatever they're trying to do. Even before it was applied in factual learning, suggestology was used to heal disease and control pain, it was used in psychotherapy, and it was used to help people open up their intuitive and so-called extrasensory abilities.

One didn't have to be a social visionary to imagine what a system that speeds learning five to fifty times might do for teaching basics, for head-start programs, for job retraining, and for everyone's ability to keep up and expand generally. If it was true. If it would work in America. We knew about the Slavic secrecy reflex when it comes to explaining almost anything to foreigners. But we didn't realize just how complicated it would prove to piece the supermemory system together. We didn't know either that almost a decade would pass before this extraordinary system would be properly tested in American classrooms.

Bulgaria had been closed to Westerners until the beginning of the sixties. When we arrived in 1968, we were full of curiosity about what had been going on there. On the streets of the five-thousand-year-old capital city, Sofia, elements of past and future human consciousness intermingle. Minarets of ornate mosques keep watch above buses, taxis, and rush-hour crowds as they jostle past remnants of ancient Roman baths and street-level rooftops of secret underground churches used during the six-hundred-year Turkish oppression. Not far from the hub of the city stands the massive St. Sophia Church—for fourteen centuries a refuge for human longings and aspirations. A few blocks away stands a different kind of center for human aspirations, a space-age center of the mind, headquartered in a pleasant, three-story, charcoal-gray building surrounded by rose gardens—the Institute of Suggestology and Parapsychology.

In such an ancient country, it would not be so hard to shuttle back and forth in time as a kind of "archaeologist of consciousness" to bring to the contemporary world the lost knowledge and techniques of more ancient eras. In a way, this is what Dr. Lozanov has done in putting the old techniques of supermemory into a modern, scientific format.

Dr. Lozanov greeted us in his office. Like the brilliant flowers in the garden outside, the room was awash with bright, vivid colors. As we'd already discovered at the conference in Moscow, Lozanov had a "holistic" sense of humor and a "cosmic" laugh like the Maharishi of TM fame. A lithe, compact man with warm brown eyes and a great cloud of curly, graying hair, he could be as kinetic as a handball one minute and deeply serene the next. "Suggestology can revolutionize teaching," he asserted. "Once people get over preconceived ideas about limitations, they can be much more. No longer is a person limited by believing that learning is unpleasant; that what he learns today he will forget tomorrow; that learning deteriorates with age."

He grew philosophical, "Education is the most important thing in the world. The whole of life is learning—not only in school. I believe that developing this high motivation—which comes through the technique—can be of the greatest importance to humanity."

"What exactly is the technique of suggestology?" we asked. To create this new "ology," Lozanov and his co-workers had drawn from an almost dizzying array of specialities: mental yoga, music, sleep-learning, physiology, hypnosis, autogenics, parapsychology, drama, to name some. Suggestology's deepest roots lay in the system of Raja Yoga. "There is really nothing new about suggestology," Lozanov explained. "The *application* is the new thing."

Lozanov's suggestology is basically "applied" altered states of consciousness for learning, healing, and intuitive development. The same mechanisms of mind that lead to supermemory (and thus to accelerated learning), can also lead to ESP and voluntary control.

From his medical practice and from his probing of people with supernormal abilities like Keuni's, Lozanov became convinced that "both history and experimental data show that humans possess vastly larger capabilities than those they now use."

In the weeks that followed, we learned more about Lozanov and his intriguing discoveries. Though just in his early forties then, he was one of the country's most outstanding medical men. He believes he was among the first, if not *the* first psychotherapist in Bulgaria after the war, and he was physician to the families of some of the ruling elite of the country. As we'd observed when we met him, he seemed to be the kind of doctor who could make you feel better just by walking into the room.

Lozanov himself was from the old intelligentsia. Both his parents were professionals—his father was a history professor at the university and his mother was in law. He completed his medical and psychotherapeutic training in Bulgaria. With no previously entrenched psychiatric tradition to counter, he was able to be innovative and eclectic in his approach. He then went on to complete a Ph.D. at the University of Kharkhov in the USSR. His thesis dealt with suggestology and how his discoveries about supermemory and parapsychology could be applied to education.*

We had endless questions. "What is supermemory all about? How did you get interested in it? How did a medical doctor switch over to education?"

Lozanov revealed he'd uncovered some fascinating lore about the origins of supermemory. It was almost as if the "how-to" of expanding memory had been handed down in ancient

---

*To clarify two frequently used terms in this book: *supermemory* is the English translation of the technical term "hypermnesia" meaning "unusually exact or vivid memory," or virtually semi-photographic memory. *Superlearning,* used specifically, refers to an eclectic system for accelerated learning of factual data resulting from westernized, modernized techniques for developing supermemory. Superlearning is also used generally to refer to all the learning systems that work holistically to develop reserves of mind and body.

times as a fail-safe measure in case of some major holocaust. "Yogis needed hypermnesia," he said. "Certain yogis did nothing but memorize all the sacred writings so that if some colossal disaster occurred, and all books and recorded knowledge were destroyed, so long as even one yogi lived, he would be able to restore all the lost knowledge from memory."

Was the technique of supermemory a legacy of some sophisticated, long-lost civilization that had suffered a holocaust? It had earmarks of the Atlantis legend about it. Lozanov's research showed supermemory was known in other countries too, in the most ancient communities. "The Maoris in New Zealand," he said, "were also trained in the same supermemory methods used by the Indian Brahmins. In modern times, Maori Chief Kaumatana could recite the entire history of his tribe covering forty-five generations and over one thousand years. It took the chief three days to recite it all and he did not use any notes."

Lozanov enthusiastically recounted to us a recent trip he'd made to India. "I studied yogis at many different centers. At the Institute of Sri Yogendra in Bombay, I met Yogi Sha. After doing daily exercises for a year, he developed 'supermemory.'" Yogi Sha, a lawyer, could instantly recall many eighteen-number columns, effortlessly remember the name and day of the week for any date in a given century, and remember photographically the arrangement of scores of objects he'd barely glimpsed. There were dozens of people in India who'd developed hypermnesia (supermemory) through these ancient yoga techniques, Lozanov observed.

"There are many different ways to develop supermemory," he points out. "The exercises used by these yogis wouldn't be suitable for mass application in schools" so he had studied them and developed his own techniques. Lozanov did not have to go all the way to India to encounter yogis or people who could demonstrate supermemory or do instant math faster than a computer. There were plenty in Bulgaria. And Lozanov himself had practiced Raja Yoga for twenty years.

Most people know about Hatha Yoga, which involves physical exercises and the assumption of various positions. Raja Yoga, mental yoga, is less well known. "Raja" means royal or ruler, and Raja Yoga has to do with ruling or governing the mind. It is considered by its practitioners to be the "science of concentration" and involves techniques for altering states of consciousness, methods of training in visualization, concentration practice, and special breathing exercises. Raja Yoga claims it has a set of techniques that allow people to develop "siddhis"—powers that include the various supernormal abilities supposedly latent within us all: a photographic "supermemory"; instant-calculating; extraordinary mental abilities; pain control; and the whole range of paranormal abilities from eyeless sight to telepathy.

Lozanov determined to put all these claims to the test. Could he find a scientific basis for them? He studied people with paranormal abilities from instant-calculating to telepathy and brought a host of yogis into physiology labs to scrutinize every aspect of their training methods and results.

The spectacular physical accomplishments of Bulgarian yogis —one out of every seventeen Bulgarians practices yoga—leads one to speculate about their mental accomplishments. In one film demonstration, we saw a yogi prone on a table. Suddenly, he seemed to rise horizontally several inches into the air and almost hovered over the table. "This isn't levitation," Lozanov clarified. "He has learned to use the muscles in his back for a type of horizontal jump." The Sofia Yoga Center is considered by yoga expert Professor S. Goyal of India to have the fullest curriculum of all the centers he knows. He reports, "The greatest attention is paid to breathing, controlling one's consciousness through concentration, and meditation."

Lozanov's research convinced him that, in a sense, we already have supermemory. The problem is we can't recall what we store away. "The human mind remembers a colossal quantity of information," he says, "the number of buttons on a suit, steps on a staircase, panes in a window, footsteps to the bus stop. These 'unknown perceptions' show us the subconscious has startling powers." He believes that the brain, freed from all distractions that hamper its functioning, resembles a sponge able to absorb knowledge and information of all kinds.

The brain research of Dr. Wilder Penfield of the Montreal Neurological Institute backs up this idea. It shows that, in effect, we have a kind of natural built-in "tape recorder" in our heads. Penfield performed brain operations on patients who were conscious under local anesthesia. Using a very weak electric current, Dr. Penfield stimulated certain brain cells during the operation. Every patient reported a word-for-word "playback" of long-forgotten conversations, songs, jokes, childhood birthday parties—things that had only been spoken *once* in their entire lifetimes—all perfectly recorded. A patient might, for instance, recall standing outside a farmhouse on a summer morning. He would hear music from the radio, smell the odor of manure, feel a breeze.

Dr. Penfield theorized that *every* experience—sight, sound, smell, and taste—registers as a particular pattern in the brain and that this pattern stays on long after the experience is consciously forgotten.

For the purpose of remembering things we are trying to learn, the goal would be to try to find a way (other than Dr. Penfield's "gentle electric current") to "trigger off" recall of what we have recorded in our minds.

Dr. Lozanov agrees with Penfield that we record all the data brought us by our senses of sight, sound, smell, and taste. But he goes further. He thinks we are also constantly recording information perceived intuitively and telepathically or clairvoyantly. "Higher sense" perceptions play a role in what we pick up and remember. "There's nothing supernatural about expanding memory or receiving telepathic information," says Lozanov.

Supermemory and Sleep-Learning

The capacity seems to be there. The trick, of course, is to recall, to bring into consciousness information imprinted in our brains. Why had Lozanov decided to create his own system? "There are other techniques around right now that seem to 'trigger off' supermemory," we said to him. "Sleep-learning, for instance."

With sleep-learning, people in America have reported learning languages in a month, and mastering a variety of factual material. TV star Art Linkletter learned Mandarin Chinese in only ten nights of sleep study. On one of his shows years ago, he chatted in Chinese with the Vice-Consul of China who stated that Linkletter was perfectly conversant in the elegant Mandarin dialect.

Bing Crosby and Gloria Swanson are reported to have used sleep-learning to memorize lines and lyrics. Opera singer Ramon Vinay sleep-learned the opera *Carmen* in time for a performance he had to give at La Scala. For a while, sleep-learning made a lot of headlines across the United States.

The Russians, who pioneered sleep-learning, have used it extensively for years. Dr. Lozanov also delved into sleep-learning. He even devised something similar for psychotherapy—the "whispering method." But he rejects sleep-learning as a way to supermemory. Why? First and foremost because the learner is not conscious and in complete control of everything going on. In sleep-learning, too, stress can create a barrier to learning that may take weeks to overcome. A relaxed, slowed-down state of body and mind is necessary for successful sleep-learning; but often people sleep in such a state of tension that learning is blocked. Moreover, sleep-learning requires a lot of special equipment, which is cumbersome and awkward, Lozanov points out.

After clambering through a maze of wires and electronic devices ourselves to try out sleep-learning, we could attest to that. One of the authors found another difficulty with it. Every night in her sleep she dismantled the sleep-learning equipment until it was beyond repair.

Sleep-learning is a misnomer, actually. The learning doesn't take place *during* sleep. The tape of the material you wish to learn is turned on by a timer during the *reverielike* phase just as you're drifting off to sleep, and just as you're waking up. This principle is the basis of the enormously successful Suzuki music method by which even very young children learn to play musical instruments well. A recording of the music that they are to learn is played to the children just as they are falling asleep.

Despite Soviet success with sleep-learning, there were many drawbacks to magnifying memory this way. Some researchers worried about health hazards. Others found enigmatic happenings. Some people might require weeks of listening to sleep tapes before beginning to learn anything. Others had experiences similar to sensing Dr. Penfield's probe. The tape recorder clicking on would trigger complete recall of a lesson heard weeks before. They lacked conscious control of the memory-triggering mechanism.

One night Lozanov uncovered something else about sleep-learning. Two groups of students were going to have their daily lesson reinforced with sleep-learning. As they snoozed, Lozanov unplugged the speakers for one group. The next day, *both* groups scored at a higher than usual learning level. Just the *suggestion* that they would learn better had triggered memory recall for one group.

Lozanov believes there are a number of "suggestive" elements that can trigger off memory recall. His goal in studying systems such as hypnopedia (learning through hypnosis) and hypnosopedia (hypnosis plus sleep), was to find out how a learner can remain fully conscious and take over the triggering controls of his own mind and memory.

Supernormal Powers and Health

After years of experiments, Lozanov concluded that the basis of supermemory and supernormal yogic powers could be termed *suggestion*—a topic well explored in Slavic psychology and one that lent itself to physiological research. Lozanov included in the category of suggestion a number of things most of us aren't used to thinking of as *suggestive:* rhythm, breathing, music, and meditative states.

Just as biofeedback in America was taking the mystification out of yoga techniques for body control, Lozanov began physiological research to de-mystify and modernize yoga techniques that develop memory control and other mental abilities. "The 'miracles' a yogi achieves spring from the trained use of thought or suggestion," he says. "The yogi can anesthetize himself through thought. He can consciously command inner body processes. The interplay of his thoughts with his body can determine health, peace of mind, and longevity."

Quite naturally, Lozanov first began to use suggestology in medicine and psychiatry to develop voluntary control of the body. At the Trade Union Sanatorium at Bankya, a typical group-healing session begins with Lozanov explaining how the mind can help heal the body. Then in his calm, melodious voice he tells the relaxed but fully awake patients, "Relax! deeply, deeply . . . there is nothing troubling you. Your entire body is fully relaxed. All your muscles are at rest." He does not try to remove any specific symptom but follows the yogic principle that deep relaxation erases tension and fear. After about twenty minutes of positive suggestion while the patients relax, Lozanov concludes, "You feel completely well. You are able to overcome all difficulties."

Then a singer begins with a melodic recitation of well-loved poetry. "It's important to fix your sights on an elevated goal to stimulate you toward creative pursuits," says Lozanov. The healing suggestions seem to catch the attention of one's innermost thoughts, according to the patients. According to Lozanov, "It's not so much healing as it is teaching the art of living." Sanatorium officials testify that it works and cite numerous case histories of people being cured of functional disorders of the nervous system, neuroses, and allergies.

The first waves that suggestology made on a wide scale rose from its use in pain control. In the summer of 1965, a fifty-year-old gym teacher asked Lozanov to instruct him in suggestology so he could undergo major surgery for a very large inguinal hernia without any anesthetic. Televised and filmed, this operation became graphic evidence to an international medical congress in Rome in September 1967 of the power of suggestology. It was a little too graphic for some people when we had the film shown in the United States. Nonmedical members of the audience seemed to suffer more than the patient when his belly was sliced open and he lay there joking about the clicking of the instruments. Bleeding was at a minimum, and according to hospital director Dr. M. Dimitrov, "This man healed much faster than usual." Lozanov and attending doctors hastened to clarify that this was not hypnosis, it was a new form of voluntary control. That's why Bulgarian newspapers claimed a medical first.

Although Dr. Lozanov was interested in human potentials generally, it was something that happened in his psychiatric practice that led him to concentrate increasingly on supermemory. People were consulting him who suffered from what he came to realize was apparently a common, but unnamed, disease. After dealing with numerous cases, Lozanov gave it a "proper" name. Should you ever be laid low, you can explain you have *didactogeny*, illness caused by poor teaching methods. Overpressed students were collapsing under stress. They were developing a panoply of tension diseases and neuroses.

Lozanov speculated, if you could have painless surgery, and painless childbirth, why couldn't you also have the painless birth of knowledge? If techniques derived from Raja Yoga took the pain out of surgery and childbirth, why not also try them to take the pain out of learning?

Students suffering with exam anxiety were given suggestology treatment. They immediately noticed a major improvement in memory as well as lowered tension. A welder attending night school reported that after suggestology he could recite an entire poem in class after seeing it only once. "It's a miracle," he told Lozanov. He'd always had trouble remembering what he learned.

ESP, Supermemory, and Learning

In his search for ways to open the reserve circuits of the mind, Lozanov was convinced that body, mind, and intuition are all intertwined holistically in the learning, memory, and communications process. How does a great actress move us and influence us so powerfully? How does a charismatic politician influence us? How does a great teacher influence us? He became convinced that not only do we hear the *words* the actress, politician, or teacher says, but we also perceive and are influenced by things we pick up from them at an intuitive level. We constantly perceive on two levels, he says.

Moreover, he was beginning to find that the same yoga techniques that open up supermemory and heal the body also open up many of the mind's other latent powers, like clairvoyance and telepathy. If this happened we would be picking up even more of these intuitive signals from other people. Therefore, he felt it was important to know something about parapsychology in connection with any kind of expanded learning system.

"Parapsychological phenomena can be applied in pedagogy," Lozanov announced to the *Bulgarian Evening News* in 1964. What might have sounded astonishing in the United States did not come as much of a surprise in a culture as ancient and steeped in hermetic tradition as Bulgaria. That there is a psychic side of the mind was taken as a matter of course. Bulgaria for centuries was the focus of the Western occult tradition. During the tenth century, Bulgaria became the center of the Cathars, a religious movement following the Gnostic tradition. Gnostics held that one should get direct knowledge, or "cosmic consciousness," of divine principles on one's own, rather than arbitrarily through church and priest. To do this, one had to develop what we would call psychic abilities through various secret techniques.

From the Renaissance on, the country teemed with occult movements and societies dedicated to psychic development. Mystic and esoteric practices have filtered down into the daily life of the eight million inhabitants of Bulgaria today. Little wonder, says Christian Godefroy, French ESP expert, that proportionately, Bulgaria has more clairvoyants, more psychic healers, more telepathists, more seers than virtually any other country. This has made the Bulgarians especially interested in understanding the scientific basis for these happenings.

"It was just a natural part of our lives," one Bulgarian educator told us. "We did awareness exercises and meditations every day, just as a matter of course."

With such a culture, it was not unusual that Bulgaria became the first country in the world to nationalize a prophetess. The famed blind oracle of Bulgaria, Vanga Dimitrova, was put on the government payroll as a "natural resource" of the country. It would be like having the late Edgar Cayce nationalized by the U.S. government.

Vanga, who lives in the town of Petrich near the Yugoslavian border, is consulted daily by dozens of people—from local farmers to top government officials. She finds missing people, helps solve crimes, diagnoses disease, and reads the past. But her greatest gift is prophecy. More than anything else, Vanga is known for her ability to foretell the date of one's death.

For more than ten years, Dr. Lozanov studied Vanga to try to understand how such psychic perceptions come into the mind. He set up a complete physiology lab in Petrich, paid for by the government, to chart all the case histories and the different conditions that affect psychic perception—why it's good one day and bad the next. What facilitates it, what blocks it.

He tried to understand the "why" of cases like this: Vanga was consulted by a pregnant woman from a village in south Bulgaria. "The child you are carrying will be killed when it is little more than an infant," Vanga told her. She described the house where the future killer lived.

"It did happen," says Lozanov. "Afterward the militia arrested the killer in the house that Vanga had pointed out."

Lozanov's very first encounter with Vanga unveiled aspects of psi perception that were later to play a role in developing his ideas about how people's minds reach out and pick up information in the learning process. "I'd heard so much about Vanga that when I was in my twenties I decided to go see for myself," Lozanov explains. "A friend from the University of Sofia went with me."

The two young researchers pulled their car off the road before the outskirts of Petrich and started walking. They didn't want anyone to have a straw of information about them. Lozanov suspected Vanga might have spies spread around the village to tip her off about new arrivals.

"We lined up with hundreds of others," Lozanov related, "and waited a full three hours before inching to the head of the line. We didn't even talk to each other. Why should we give any listeners clues? Finally it was our turn. My friend, Sasha, went first. Vanga told him his first and second name. Then she told him where he was born and described the second floor corner apartment where he lived at that time. Next she told him his mother's name and identified the disease she suffered from. She told Sasha the date of his father's death and named the illness that had killed him. She gave Sasha all this information as if she were reading it from a book. Then she said, 'You've been married seven years, but you have no children. You will have a child one year from now.' This happened exactly as she had predicted.

"Then it was my turn. As I came through the door Vanga said, 'Georgi, why have you come? You want to test me. You're too early. You will come again some years from now.' She seemed to imply that serious scientific study of her prophetic talent might be possible at that time. I didn't say anything; instead I tried my first experiment," Lozanov says. "Using all my willpower and the little telepathic ability I possess, I imagined that I was another man, a man I knew very well. She began to foretell, but it was wrong. And she told me so. Then she said, 'Go, I can't tell you anything.' "

Lozanov points out, "My being able to block Vanga is a very interesting thing. It was the first bit of assurance I had for my hypothesis that Vanga gleaned what she told visitors from their own minds, telepathically."

Vanga's charted clairvoyant score over the years is said to be at the eighty percent level. Rumors fly that the Bulgarian government was offered a fabulous sum of money by a private German institute to buy the prophetic services of this woman, that jet-set celebrities such as Jackie Kennedy have tried to consult her, but that she refused all to continue working with the Suggestology Institute.

Though nothing is said about it publicly these days, because of shifts in political policy, Bulgarians tell us that this work of the institute has continued quietly. There is still a plaque on Vanga's house reading: "Scientific Co-worker of the Institute of Suggestology."

At the Medical Postgraduate Institute where he first started working, Lozanov devoted half his time to studies in telepathy, clairvoyance, and eyeless sight—the paranormal ability to sense colors and printed figures with the skin. He tested over sixty-five different sensitives trying to understand how they were able to reach into greater pools of information than most of us. How did they make such information conscious? How did they reach through time?

Lozanov found that certain things tend to happen in the body when sensitives used their paranormal abilities. It was claimed that with Raja Yoga exercises one could engender specific rhythms of body and mind that open links to greater awareness. There seemed to be a connection between what the sensitives were doing naturally and what Raja Yoga is said to do. Lozanov tested various methods said to develop psi. He had success with telepathy. Then he used his new method to try to train blind children in skin sight. It worked too (see Chapters 15 and 16).

Suggestology "can improve the parapsychical performance of an individual or an entire group. . . . Faculties of telepathy and clairvoyance can be cultivated and developed by suggestology," Lozanov reported in 1966 at the International Congress on Parapsychology in Moscow. Just as advocates of Raja Yoga had claimed, he found ancient techniques did develop supermemory, self-healing, and psi abilities.

Training people to develop these paranormal powers, he further confirmed his idea that as awareness increases, people pick up added intuitive information that can help or hinder the learning process.

He also became increasingly aware of the importance of the suggestive elements from the culture in developing potentials. The acceptance of Bulgarian culture gives people the permission to allow psi abilities to come into play, he observed. American author-educator George Leonard, who conducts seminars to develop psi for athletes, agrees. He reports that what he's doing, in effect, is creating an environment where people have permission to use their natural powers.

Lozanov noted something else, too, in these experiments. Intuitive and psi information comes into the mind rapidly and automatically the same way supermemory data does. It seemed as if ESP and supermemory might operate on similar mental mechanisms.

Suggestopedia Begins

So far Lozanov had scientifically researched Raja Yoga, sleep-learning, and parapsychology. From his findings, he now had a jigsaw puzzle of methods to fit together into a whole, holistic way to learn. (For fuller explanation, see Chapters 4 and 5.) The system he envisioned would have two parts: a session for developing supermemory while people are fully conscious; a new way of teaching to go with it. Teaching would include psychotherapeutic methods such as self-image therapy and affirmations. The whole system would enhance the whole personality. It would feature learning without stress. It would be a teaching method that would not bring on illnesses, but instead cure them (see Appendix).

From all the evidence, people seemed to be able to reach supermemory and learn much faster than usual when they were in a slowed-down physical state as in sleep-learning or hypnopedia. Even those born with supernormal abilities seemed to switch into this relaxed state when they worked their wonders. As body rhythms calmed, the mind grew more effective. How could one reach this state without being on the edge of sleep or in trance? How could one do this when fully conscious? Yoga and a common communist medical technique have some answers.

In Bulgarian health sanatoria music therapy is often used. Patients with heart trouble or hypertension, for instance, are treated with music that has a very slow, steady beat. This calms the body. Even a tape of rhythmic clicks beating at forty to sixty beats a minute was found to slow down body and mind rhythms. To strengthen memory, Lozanov would use music. He would start with slow movements of classical Baroque music, music that has a steady beat about once per second, sixty beats per minute. Music rather than sleep or hypnosis would calm the body so the mind could begin to realize its waiting potentials.

It was appropriate that the idea of using music as the bridge to reach the reserves of mind should come from the country of the legendary musician Orpheus of Thrace, a land that is now part of Bulgaria. Orpheus had used music as a means of charming both nature and living creatures.

Once people are in this calm learning state, what is the best way to feed them the information they want to absorb and remember? Yoga said rhythmic presentation was the answer. Lozanov found a specific rhythm that seemed to synchronize well with body and mind rhythms. As with sleep-learning, he broke data up into brief fragments or short phrases. A phrase would be spoken every eight seconds. In sleep-learning the same five minutes of data might be repeated thirty-six times a night. With their new system, the Bulgarians found that little repetition was needed. Teachers added different intonations to break the monotony of the steady rhythm.

A slowed-down presentation of material was also found to be the secret of better learning by UCLA researcher Dr. Willard Madsen. Working with retarded youngsters, Madsen found that when he slowed the *pacing* of presentation to a relatively longer interval, the low-IQ children learned almost as efficiently as their bright counterparts. The rhythm seemed to act as a resynchronizer for out-of-synch internal rhythms and thus improved memory.

Small learning experiments began with the musical memory method. Lozanov started students with "de-suggestion," one of the psychological elements of his method. This is self-image therapy. "We are conditioned to believe that we can only learn so much so fast, that we are bound to be sick, that there are certain rigid limits to what we can do and achieve," he told them. "We're all bombarded constantly, from the day we're born, with limiting suggestions." The first step, he explained, is to get over these limitations in thinking. That way, we can learn faster and release our inner potential.

He had students do deep-relaxation exercises to get rid of tensions. They were shown how to do Raja Yoga breathing exercises for improved concentration. Then a teacher took over the class and taught a language lesson. Next came the supermemory concert session with the "suggestive" elements of altered state, music, and rhythm. Students relaxed as they listened to the stately music designed to slow body and mind rhythms. Over the music they heard vocabulary phrases read in a slow-paced, strict rhythm.

The next day, these students took a test. It was amazing. They remembered almost everything. They seemed to have memory control. And they didn't have to be asleep or hypnotized to do it. The students were fully awake and aware all the time. It was a genuine breakthrough. People had never been able to acquire supermemory while awake. Lozanov knew he was on to something.

As Lozanov predicted, the supermemory sessions seemed to enhance awareness generally. Students were even more likely than others to pick up some of the teacher's emotions or attitudes. If the teacher felt depressed, or thought the students were stupid, or that the method wouldn't work, students might realize it, and this would affect performance. Lozanov calls this by a cybernetic term—"signals from the second level." To handle this, part of the teaching method involves creating a positive, authoritative, supportive atmosphere. The teacher's behavior is also organized so that nonverbal cues like gestures, tone, and facial expressions are directed toward increasing students' motivation and self-confidence. Rapport between student and teacher is important. (See Appendix.)

In the early sixties, Lozanov announced publicly that he could improve a person's memory more than fifty percent with suggestopedia. Shortly thereafter, he announced that with this tension-free learning system, students easily learned a language in a month and a year later showed very high retention. It worked for old or young, brilliant or retarded, educated or uneducated. On top of it all, the method appeared to improve health and cure stress-related illnesses.

This was enough to ignite a fuse in other professionals. "There are no such memory reserves in humans," skeptics protested. Suggestopedia brought so many diverse fields together, specialists were baffled. Teachers didn't grasp the psychotherapy; musicians didn't understand the medical side; doctors didn't follow the pedagogical part. The controversy spread through the daily papers. Lozanov was attacked and investigated. An official government commission set its sights on suggestology, something that could have unnerving consequences in countries like Bulgaria.

Commission members met in a large room at a major Sofia hotel. They had agreed to try out this preposterous scheme and abolish it if it didn't work. They found themselves seated in lounge chairs under subdued lights, with quiet music playing. It didn't seem like a place to get down to work.

"Relax. Don't think about anything," the teacher told them. "Just listen to the music as I read the material."

The next day, chagrined commission members discovered that even though they were sure they'd learned nothing, they did remember. When tested, they could easily read, write, and speak from 120 to 150 new words absorbed in the two-hour session. In the same way, the grammar rules were painlessly absorbed. At the end of several weeks, despite many firm beliefs that they couldn't learn a thing in this effortless fashion, they emerged fluent in a foreign language they'd not known before. What could the government commission report?

In 1966 the Bulgarian Ministry of Education founded the Center for Suggestopedia at the Institute of Suggestology. With a staff of over thirty specialists in education, medicine, and engineering, the institute taught regular classes with suggestopedia while at the same time doing physiological and medical research in its labs to see what made rapid learning and super-memory tick.

Suggestopedia class graduates were frequently brought back for further tests. How much did they forget? Did the health benefits last? Not only had they learned much faster, but they didn't forget. Six months later retention was still eighty-eight percent. Twenty-two months later without any intervening use of the new language, retention was still 57 percent. Students returned on their own, too, to say how much their emotional well-being had improved from the courses.

People of all ages and all walks of life came to evening courses at the institute after a long, full workday. They arrived tired, and sometimes with headaches.

"The meditative sessions leave you feeling great, wonderfully refreshed and invigorated," students asserted. "There's no strain at all," they testified. "You don't get tired mentally or physically."

Monitoring equipment revealed that during the concert session, students' bodies showed a pattern similar to certain kinds of yoga meditation said to refresh and restore the body. Body processes slowed down to a healthful, optimum level; brain waves slowed to the refreshing alpha level. Students reported that even their headaches disappeared during the sessions with the musical memory method.

How far could the mind expand once it started to open up? It seemed just as easy to learn one hundred words as fifty. Classes of volunteers were formed. In a single session they were taught fifteen lessons from a French textbook covering five hundred new words. Immediately afterward, they were given a test, and three days later, another test. Results were excellent —extraordinary. "All the words had been retained," Lozanov says.

On an average now, people learn eighty to one hundred words a day in accelerated-learning courses. The world's largest language school, Berlitz, says that two hundred words after several days (thirty hours) of intensive "immersion" learning is considered successful. Unfortunately, the forgetting rate has been almost as rapid with these high-pressure methods.

With the Bulgarian approach, 500 words a day was just "Mach 1." By 1966, a group learned 1,000 words in a day, and by 1974, a rate of 1,800 words a day was charted. In 1977, Lozanov reported, some tests showed people capable of absorbing even 3,000 words per day.

Unlike sleep-learning in which as many as thirty-six repetitions of the same five or ten minutes of material may be required, suggestopedia needs few repetitions. Much more information can be learned in a shorter time. Presenting material at a rate of around four-hundred data-bits an hour, the only limitation seems to be the number of hours in a day. When you read the reports you begin to get the feeling that right now, someone, somewhere must be setting a new rapid-learning record.

What are the outer limits, then, of the mind's potential? Once you learn to open your mind, Lozanov finds that the capacity to remember seems almost boundless—there is no apparent cut-off point.

Initially, the institute taught languages because progress was easy to measure with word counts. Lozanov, of course, was not trained as an educator. Alexo Novakov, an outstanding teacher, musician, and actor, developed much of the language work. He prepared full-length programs equivalent to two- or three-year language courses (six thousand word vocabulary and complete grammar). Students were graduated in three months. Gradually, courses began in all fields from math to physics to biology.

During our 1968 trip to Bulgaria, we toured the institute's loungelike classrooms featuring circles of easy chairs, examined its well-equipped labs, checked out the special electromagnetically shielded rooms used for ESP research, and inspected the library and translation department. We met staff members, scientists, and teachers. "We're still exploring, still experimenting, still changing the method," Franz Tantchev, the institute's information officer, said, summing up what others had told us. "Every day we discover new things about how suggestopedia works."

We didn't know exactly how it worked, but we were beginning to be convinced that something real, something genuinely exciting, something way beyond another new wrinkle in educational technology was happening in Bulgaria.

We gathered, too, that the Soviet Union was deep into suggestopedia. The Soviets have always been interested in rapid-learning systems. After the upheavals of the First World War and the Russian Revolution, the Soviets wanted to help their then largely illiterate populace catch up with Western industrialized countries. They turned to relaxopedia, hypnopedia, and later sleep-learning, and hypnosopedia. Apparently many of their best learning centers were now using the Bulgarian suggestopedia. We heard that other Soviet-bloc countries were also planning to use it.

As we said good-bye to Dr. Lozanov, he remarked he hoped his rapid-learning method might eventually be used in America. "An astrologer once told me my 'Venice' is in Gemini, and that means good relations with America," he joked.

"That's 'Venus,' " we said with a smile.

Lozanov laughed good-humoredly and went on quickly to say that unlike the students at his institute, *he* did not have the advantage of suggestopedia for languages! He was too busy working and jetting to other countries to supervise suggestopedia centers.

We left Bulgaria with the impression that we'd be hearing more of this enormously dedicated man who believed the benefits of the Bulgarian findings "should be given to the world and not kept for the benefit of just a few."

We had scarcely gotten back to America, when suddenly, in 1969, though few Bulgarians were permitted to travel to the West, Dr. Lozanov arrived in New York. " 'Venice' in Gemini," he said triumphantly at Kennedy Airport.

"That's 'Venus,' " we joked. Something was certainly working for him.

On this and subsequent visits he made to America, we viewed numerous films on suggestopedia and suggestology, read his thesis and many of his other publications, and saw the presentations for UNESCO and the Ford Foundation.

In 1970, our book *Psychic Discoveries Behind the Iron Curtain* came out here and abroad, and our report on Lozanov and how supernormal powers of the mind could be applied in education spurred literally thousands of people from all over the world to contact us. Teachers, students, businessmen, private individuals, converged by the hundreds on Sofia to visit the Institute of Suggestology—so many, in fact, that the Bulgarian government set up restrictions.

An Evolutionary Leap?

It's now been over two decades since Dr. Georgi Lozanov began his first experiments with his musical memory method to open the reserves of the mind and to develop supermemory and rapid learning. Suggestopedia is used today by thousands of people in Soviet-bloc countries and is rapidly spreading through many Western countries. In addition to the regular courses at the Institute of Suggestology in Bulgaria, many special experimental courses have been conducted over the years at various schools and centers. And a host of international conferences on suggestopedia have been held in numerous countries.

As of 1976, there were seventeen public schools throughout Bulgaria that had been using Lozanov's method for all subjects for several years. Supposedly, out of the scores of children in these Bulgarian schools, *every one* was a virtual prodigy. Supposedly, first graders read advanced stories. Third graders did high school algebra. Everyone covered two years of school in four months. Children learned to read in a matter of days. The "supposedlys" began to soar off into the wild blue yonder. Everyone had fun. Everyone loved learning. Everyone was creative. Nobody failed. Sick children cured themselves in this new process of learning.

Dr. Cecilia Pollack of Lehman College, New York, was able to get into a Lozanov school because of high government contacts she had in Bulgaria. She observed classes in school number 122 in Sofia, an ordinary school, in an ordinary neighborhood. She watched nine-year-olds eagerly solving abstruse algebraic equations far beyond the capabilities normally expected of the best third graders. She saw first graders after four months of school fluently reading and discussing folk tales usually of a third-grade level. All grades in the school had completed two years' curricula in four months. It was an "incredible phenomenon," she reports.

"But where are the failures?" she asked, thinking of those at home who could not master basics. Surely slow learners and failures were separated off somewhere.

"There are none," school officials replied. They didn't believe IQ was innate or inflexible. Should any child lag, he or she was immediately helped to reach required standards. This kind of global education stimulates the whole person; it not only develops the child's mental powers much faster, they said, but also frees creativity and delight in learning at the same time.

"These appeared to be schools without failures," Pollack reports. She came back talking about "prodigious implications." Lozanov's system, she said, has "opened a world of exciting new possibilities for human development. . . . He will have pointed the way toward educational possibilities leading to the enhancement of knowledge and the enrichment of the human personality, far beyond what we now consider possible."

If even part of what they told her is so, it is a stunning development. In 1977, at a conference in Iowa, Lozanov hinted of new developments. The one-time *experiments* to learn five hundred foreign words in a day were supposedly now *regular* everyday practice in certain language courses. Canadian government observers indicate they saw classes learning four hundred words a day. In 1976, Swedish educators visited the Bulgarian schools and confirmed math results—third grade at sixth grade level.

Ivan Barzakov, a recent Bulgarian defector, taught briefly in the Lozanov schools and was at the institute for a couple of months. He claims the reports of phenomenal results are true. "The whole point is to create miracles in education," he says. Barzakov confirms the drive for secrecy that winds around mind-expanding programs in Bulgaria and the USSR. Few of the staff were privy to the whole program, yet they did see the end results. Secrecy also pervades training teachers in the method as well (see Appendix).

Over the years, even the Bulgarian government had trouble believing that their children were blossoming so variously. Over the years, suggestopedia underwent new rounds of skirmishes and attacks. The government again mobilized forces to investigate. The Ministry of Education sent teams to examine academic standards; the Ministry of Health sent doctors and psychotherapists to investigate students' health; the Ministry of Culture sent experts to check on the various arts used widely in courses. Long-time critics of Lozanov were hand-picked for the investigative teams, to be sure the commissions would be tough.

In 1976, at a major national conference, the Bulgarian government ministries unveiled their reports and their judgment. The President of Bulgaria and top party officials were present. Suggestopedia *did* achieve as reported. It was to be expanded.

"We shall be applying the system all over the country in a very short time," Lozanov announced in 1977.

Because of conflicting reports, just how extensive the use of suggestopedia is in the USSR can only be estimated. There are centers from Moscow to Leningrad to Kharkhov in the Ukraine. Mosfilm, the major Soviet film company, prepared a documentary on suggestopedia for regular movie theaters, to encourage even wider use of suggestopedia by the public. Outstanding results with suggestopedia at the prestigious Moscow Foreign Languages Pedagogical Institute were headlined in *Pravda* as early as 1969. "It's possible to learn a language in a month," they enthused. That there's extensive military involvement with suggestopedia would appear obvious. The major 1974 Moscow conference on suggestopedia was closed to Westerners, but one U.S. observer who managed to slip in reports the large audience included military personnel in uniform. Some were evidently from the Frunze Military Academy in the Kirgiz Republic near the Chinese border.

Students from the University of Norilsk in the Arctic Circle to the University of Novosibirsk in Siberia are using suggestopedia—at the rate of about ten thousand Siberian students annually. Joseph Goldin, Vice-Chairman of the Soviet Academy of Science Commission for Development of Human Potential, says suggestopedia will be used for Moscow Olympics interpreters. Centers in Leipzig and East Berlin report long-lasting ninety percent-plus retention achieved by hundreds in suggestopedia courses. There are still more students involved in Hungary and other Soviet-bloc countries. Soviets are promoting suggestopedia in Africa too.

Does this mean that a communist world brimming with

prodigies is on the horizon? If it does turn out to be a brave new world at least it's less like Huxley's and Orwell's vision of the future and more like Shakespeare's, one filled with people like the adventurers in *The Tempest,* who suddenly were seen and saw themselves in a new light. Perhaps the Bulgarian school-children will one day be credited with a further accomplishment—showing us what the human norm really is. Once the "conspiracy" of limitation lifts, so does the ceiling on human capabilities. Perhaps we are beginning to see what the unobstructed personality can do.

One of the world's greatest violinists, Yehudi Menuhin, who was a child prodigy (Carnegie Hall debut at age ten), says he always felt that he was in no way different from other children. Menuhin, a long-time practitioner of yoga, feels these are normal human abilities and in his case came from sheer exuberance of life. Besides, he says, "Children are generally underrated."

Genius doesn't belong to the special few, but to everyone, in the view of Pandit Gopi Krishna. "We must investigate the biophysical basis of genius," insists this former government official and leader among Kashmiri Brahmins. He has prompted scientists in such centers as the Max Planck Institute to look into time-honored Hindu yoga techniques that supposedly fuse the energies of your body and your mind. From fusion comes light. The whole person lights up, becoming what we call a genius and a spiritually developed person, the Pandit says. This potent act of getting ourselves together is, according to Gopi Krishna and many others, the next evolutionary jump of humankind.

The techniques that expand memory also appear to be capable of opening additional circuits in the mind that lead to the expansion of many human abilities. While it is far from a panacea, and not suitable for everyone, it may well be one answer, a practical, workable, even enjoyable answer to our needs.

If we continue trying to cope with world problems and the "information overload" in areas from world economics to government with our present limited abilities, we'll never catch up, Lozanov thinks. Unless we switch on additional learning circuits in the human brain, he feels, progress could come to a standstill.

We need multiple levels of knowing for modern decision-making, says Dr. Jean Houston, 1978 president of the Association for Humanistic Psychology, yet education is geared to the nineteenth century. "In order to respond to the problems and complexities of our time, we need the full complement of known and unknown human capacities," she says. ". . . the only way to develop our human potential is to break through this [narrow] range and integrate a wider spectrum of human consciousness."

Chapter 3

Jet-Speed Learning Takes Off in the West

Thirteen-year-old Timmy rested on a comfortable rug on the floor of a Georgia classroom, along with ten classmates. Mentally, he visualized a set of picture patterns he'd devised for his own, personal relaxation program. "My head feels like a marshmallow . . . my eyes are like Nerf balls . . . my arms are like spaghetti. . . ."

Quiet music began in the background. He heard his teacher's voice, sometimes businesslike, sometimes a whisper, sometimes commanding, rhythmically reciting various words from his reading list.

Now in the seventh grade, Timmy had undergone almost seven years of reading instruction, and two years of remedial reading training. Still, he could not read. His teachers' report classified his reading problem as being "as intractable as could be imagined."

Suddenly in only a few weeks of these concert sessions, tests showed Timmy zooming ahead some eight months in reading ability. Students with the greatest learning problems in DeKalb County were trained in this and similar programs at the Huntley Hills Elementary School, near Atlanta. They gained more than a year's reading ability in under twelve weeks. It was something like a four-to-one speedup in learning.

In the eighth-grade science class at the Woodrow Wilson Junior High School in Des Moines, Iowa, another scenario unfolded. Dr. Wilbur Shure, "renowned scientist" as played by Jack (a fourteen-year-old farm boy), outlined to a fellow "scientist" classmate how they'd search for phosphates on a small Pacific island they were exploring. With teacher Charles Gritton as director, the previous day's science material came dramatically alive.

Next, the class listened to a record by an Austrian chamber music ensemble. They relaxed at their desks and breathed rhythmically in time to the music—in two, hold four, out two, and repeat.

Gritton said, in varied intonations paced with the music, "Iron. Symbol Fe. Strong as Iron. Mercury. Symbol Hg. As the days get warmer, the mercury rises." There were fifty words in all.

On the quiz that followed, Jack checked his results. He found one mistake. Though he was an average student in other classes, this was his *first* mistake in five weeks of this new science course. None of the students missed more than two. They were excited and proud of their new-found skills. In another class, on their own, they were offering popcorn to the "poorest" student to encourage him to do better. (He had all of three mistakes.)

Four days into the course, all 115 of Gritton's eighth-grade science students had reached a ninety-seven percent average— and they were staying there.

In a Persian garden, under the shade of a Persian thorn tree, three Americans sat glumly over lunch in the Rose-Garden Self-Service Restaurant. "What are we going to do about learning Persian in a hurry," they asked each other. They would be in Iran for a number of months, and it was hard to get around without knowing the language.

"I have an idea," Texan Doug Shaffer said to the other two, a husband and wife team who'd just arrived in Iran to teach in the English Department at the University in Mashhad. He'd heard about the Bulgarian rapid-learning method and had just received a set of instructions. Why not try it?

"It'll never work for *me,*" scoffed the wife. "I've tried every kind of language method and nothing works."

After a lot of persuasion, and with much skepticism, she agreed to try some self-teaching sessions. She and her husband relaxed and breathed in time to Baroque music while Doug Shaffer read English phrases and an Iranian friend read their Persian translation aloud to them. They used the required slow pacing of eight seconds a phrase.

In three weeks, "results were truly spectacular," Shaffer reported in 1977 from Ferdowsi University in Mashhad, Iran. They'd learned Persian amazingly easily. "It works, and works well," Shaffer maintained.

At Iowa State University, students learned a whole semester of Spanish in two weeks—seven times faster than usual, and they had fun learning. In Washington, D.C., students learned Latin in a fraction of the usual time. In California, students learned a Slavic language three times faster. The U.S. Navy Atlantic Fleet Training Center in Virginia reported good results with an accelerated-learning project.

Jet-speed learning through music has finally gotten off the ground for Americans. At schools and colleges and on their own, many Westerners are beginning to come into some of the benefits of supermemory and their own expanded potentials . . . the kind of benefits many Soviet-bloc people have been enjoying for twenty years.

Untangling the Method

Why did it take us so long? The reasons are as convoluted and laced with subplots as a Byzantine intrigue. But they boil down to misinformation, misinformation on a grand scale rising from communist politics and Western bungling. Because of communist politics, Westerners had great difficulties finding out exactly what the method is and how to use it. Because of Western administrative bungling, people were misled into believing the system could not be adopted for North American use. Unfortunately, the intrigue has more than historical interest because it is still going on and even seems to be increasing on the international level.

Though it is hard for most of us to realize, politics is involved in *everything* in communist countries from nuclear physics to contract bridge. Of the hundreds of Westerners who rushed to Bulgaria and asked to see some students in a classroom, many didn't realize that their simple request put them into at least a low-grade spy scenario. The Soviet Union and satellites had taken up suggestopedia in a big way; and the Soviet military also appeared to be involved with its use. It grew obvious that one authority or another wanted to keep certain parts of the steps to supermemory and vastly accelerated learning to themselves.

Soviet bloc governments can be very touchy about anything to do with the superpowers of the mind. In 1977, for instance, a Moscow scientist gave *Los Angeles Times* reporter Robert Toth a scientific report on some Russian parapsychological research. The KGB (Soviet Secret Police) immediately arrested Toth and interrogated him for days. He was accused of receiving "state secrets"—material on telepathy. Not until President Carter intervened was he let go. Such events in Moscow cause rumbling all through the bloc, and Bulgaria is considered the satellite least independent of the USSR.

A friend of Dr. Lozanov, Dr. Milan Ryzl, a Czech biochemist, formerly of Prague, explains the difficulties scientists often have in those countries when they research mind powers. Ryzl developed a successful system to train people to develop ESP through hypnosis. Immediately the Czechoslovakian government became very interested in his work. He noticed he was constantly being followed by Czech secret agents. His scientific reports and manuscripts were stolen. Eventually, he was asked, in rather forceful terms, to spy on his scientific colleagues in other countries. The authorities made it very clear that they were interested in the development of parapsychological techniques for espionage purposes. Ryzl asserts that the government exercised such control over his life he had no choice but to comply. Finally, he realized he did have another choice and he defected to the United States in 1967.

Dr. Ryzl's is a typical account of what can happen under such political regimes. Any particular pronouncement made to Westerners has to be checked out pragmatically to see whether it's correct—not just taken at face value. Most, or probably all, mind-research institutes have a spy who reports on colleagues. Naturally researchers tend to be very secretive and often don't tell each other what they're doing, let alone Westerners. Staff members sometimes don't get to see what their colleagues are doing; they are not supposed to fraternize with Western visitors or go out to lunch or dinner with them, unless an "observer" goes along too. Dr. Lozanov and his staff have never talked freely or openly about the specifics of their work dealing with supermemory. When Lozanov lectured in the West, he discussed mainly the psychotherapeutic teaching side of rapid learning.

In 1974, Edward Naumov, a foremost Soviet parapsychologist, whom we all knew, was arrested and sentenced to a labor camp. His "crime" consisted of fraternizing too freely with Westerners, despite the so-called scientific exchange agreement between Russia and the United States.

The words "and Parapsychology" are now gone from the title of the Institute of Suggestology in Sofia. On a radio show with us, Lozanov felt he had to say he'd never known his research subject, Vanga Dimitrova. The ESP background of suggestopedia has been deemphasized.

When the USSR issued an edict in 1971 that yoga is "hostile to our country," not to mention "bad for your health," the Bulgarians insisted there was no Raja Yoga involved with suggestopedia, though the data was published in Lozanov's thesis. Even before yoga became politically taboo, when we were in

Sofia in 1968, workers at the institute claimed never to have researched yoga, until we showed them the published reports of their own work. By 1977, yoga was *in* again, and Lozanov discussed it at a conference on supermemory in Iowa. That old Russian standby, sleep-learning, suddenly went under wraps again, too, a few years ago. Scientific data on its new directions are not being let out.

The Westerners who jostled for position to watch suggestopedia classes in Bulgaria found little on the surface to *see*. The classes of twelve students sat in a circle in comfortable reclining chairs that looked a bit like airplane seats. In the background, music played. The teacher spoke in different tones and when it was over, everyone knew everything.

The secret must be in the chairs! some said. One Canadian university spent over $10,000 on special beanbag chairs for rapid learning in the hope they would lead to instant bilingualism for students. Nothing was spelled out to Westerners. Conference statements were vague. The *Suggestology Journal,* published by the institute, was abruptly cut off from circulation in the West.

Finally, thanks in part to the untiring efforts of Dr. Jane Bancroft, Associate Professor of French at the University of Toronto, and a long-time friend of the authors, an effective way to open supermemory got under way in the West.

Dr. Bancroft, a specialist in languages, with graduate degrees from the Sorbonne and Harvard, had also trained in music. In 1971, she helped the authors arrange for Dr. Lozanov to come to Canada to lecture at the University of Toronto. Before she headed to Bulgaria for an international conference on suggestopedia and four weeks of research, she extensively studied the authors' files, read Lozanov's thesis, boned up on Raja Yoga and sleep-learning. We had brought back the bare bones of the system, but there were still some missing points needing clarification.

One day, while Dr. Bancroft was at the Institute of Suggestology, she was inadvertently swept into a class with a group of visiting Soviets. She taped this demonstration as well as those for Westerners. Back home in Toronto, she replayed the tapes. As she'd begun to suspect in Sofia, the versions shown the Russians and Americans were different, though it was hard to detect on the surface. The Soviet Union would hardly be spending large amounts of money for a method consisting of "nice" chairs and pleasant music, she observed. The demonstration for the Soviets must hold the missing keys we'd needed to fully reconstruct Lozanov's method, she told us. From what we knew of music and music therapy, when we listened to the tapes we were able to recognize some of the pieces and figure out the reason why they were used. They had the slow tempo often used in music therapy to slow down body/mind rhythms.

Yoga emphasized rhythm as the road to supernormal mental ability. Dr. Bancroft's stopwatch led to a discovery. The material was read in a precise eight-second rhythm.

"The Russians got a mathematically precise presentation," she told us. "The Americans were shown chairs, background music, and material read without pacing." She deduced that precise, rhythmic pacing of material to very specific music must be one of the suppressed elements. It must help lead to super-memory. The other things they were doing must magnify the effect.

It occurred to us that the pattern Bancroft unearthed had a familiar ring—sixty beats with an eight- to ten-second activity cycle. In the fifties, two of America's most ingenious medical hypnotists researched this pattern to vastly accelerate learning and creativity by expanding a person's time perception. It worked, but subjects had to be in deep hypnosis. The Bulgarians seemed to be getting results with learners in conscious control.

Dr. Bancroft next made a series of visits to suggestology centers in the USSR and Hungary, conferred with experts and communist defectors involved with the system. She got tapes and videotapes of classes. All the varied snippets fitted into a clear-cut whole. Later our conclusions were confirmed by top sources.

Then something happened to further confuse Westerners. The Bulgarians added a *second* music or concert session. Now there was one used during teaching as well as the one to develop supermemory. This teaching concert featured completely different music by Romantic composers and a dramatic, emotional reading of texts over it. It's somewhat reminiscent of a radio commercial with voice over music. When Bulgarians were asked to demonstrate the concert session, they'd show the teaching concert and not the supermemory one (see Appendix).

Western Results

Dr. Bancroft combined our research materials with hers and published numerous academic articles. Finally, becoming deeply convinced of the potentials of the system, she brought out an explanatory pamphlet, *The Lozanov Language Class* (see Appendix), distributed by the Center for Applied Linguistics in Virginia, which revealed some of the long-suppressed, potent elements of supermemory. A friend of Bancroft, Dr. Allyn Prichard, then Director of Student Development for Reinhardt College, Waleska, Georgia, was among the first in 1975 to try this newly assembled supermemory method for remedial reading classes of retarded children and slow learners.

He and Jean Taylor at the Huntley Hills Elementary School in DeKalb County found that the initial class of ten made dramatic gains of almost a year's reading ability within a few weeks. Eighty percent of the next class of twenty children gained a year or more in reading ability in well under twelve weeks, a four-to-one speedup. The remainder made slightly less but nevertheless outstanding gains. "We could hardly help being encouraged," they said.

Prichard and Taylor discovered that the more relaxed and calm a child was during the concert session, the better the results. Many of their students were hyperactive and had trouble relaxing. "Mastery of some sort of relaxation technique may conceivably become a regular part of a child's educational experience," they report. They began to spend one to two weeks showing children how to relax and calm their minds. Three years later, results were continually improving and they were strongly optimistic. By 1978, they had gotten excellent results even with the most severely retarded. Rapid learning works in the American classroom, they say.

In 1972, Ray Benitez-Bordon of the University of Iowa and Dr. Donald Schuster, Professor of Psychology at Iowa State University, became interested in supermemory after reading *Psychic Discoveries.* Using an incomplete method, they began to try learning experiments.

After getting Dr. Bancroft's instructions, in the summer of 1975, Benitez-Bordon conducted two Spanish classes using the complete method. Students learned more than *a full year's Spanish in ten days* (four hours a day)—a seven-to-one speedup. The students were delighted with a method that took the drudgery out of language learning.

The Iowa professors broke down every element of the method as Dr. Bancroft had described it to see exactly what triggered supermemory. What did each of the variables do? Their tests showed that if students breathed rhythmically during a concert in which rhythmically paced text material was featured, their retention jumped seventy-eight percent compared to a jump of twenty-five percent if they did not. The addition of affirmations for pleasant, easy learning during the concert session pushed retention scores up still higher.

As mentioned before, "de-suggestion," or self-image therapy, is a much insisted upon part of Lozanov's teaching approach. In Hartford, Connecticut, the Higher Horizon One-Hundred project has explored self-image therapy for scholastic use. It was found not only to change the academic performance of the children but even to raise their measured IQ. In Iowa, tests showed that self-image therapy seemed to combine with supermemory synergistically, to produce even better learning than a supermemory session alone could.

After Benitez-Borden and Schuster, Iowan Charles Gritton at the Wilson Junior High School in Des Moines used superlearning to teach science to eighth graders in one-fifth the usual time. Enthusiasm for the method began to run high in the heartland.

At that point, Iowa researchers, teachers, and professors founded the Society for Suggestive, Accelerative Learning and Teaching, a mouthful that's known as S.A.L.T. The Society publishes a journal and a newsletter and runs a teacher-training program. It has also hosted three international conferences on rapid learning.

Just as Iowans had helped find the key to opening *outer* space with the discovery of the Van Allen radiation belts around the earth (Dr. James Van Allen and colleagues, University of Iowa), maybe Iowans, with their delving into the mind's capabilities, were heading toward being among the first to explore keys to *inner* space.

Early in 1976, Schuster convinced educators and state legislators to fund large-scale experiments. On a $100,000 grant, the achievement, adjustment, and creativity of 1,200 students in different public schools taught by twenty S.A.L.T.-trained teachers for one year, was compared with control groups. Schuster calls the preliminary findings "significant scientific documents."

Though some of the teachers never got their projects going, of those that did, many found their students' performance vastly improved. Junior high and high school students seemed to benefit more from rapid learning than did elementary students.

Charles Gritton was both science teacher and wrestling coach at the Woodrow Wilson Junior High, a school in a low-income neighborhood. You'd give a good lesson, Gritton says, and afterward you'd realize the kids didn't hear a damned word you said. You'd go home at the end of the day wanting to shoot yourself, he says, because you'd wasted your day there, their day, and all that energy.

The kids had their own worries to think about. "When a

police siren goes off down the street, there are a half-dozen kids in a class of fifty who look nervously around," says Dr. Schuster. "If there's a knock on the door and a policeman comes in that door, three kids go out the window. Every so often, kids don't show up in class: 'Where've you been?' 'Oh, I spent a couple of days in jail.' "

Pessimistically, Gritton had learned to live with limited results, only possible through heavy discipline. When Schuster and Benitez-Bordon told him about rapid learning, he was scornful. "Nobody can teach kids fifty or one hundred new science terms in a week, let alone a day, and make them like it."

Nevertheless he gave rapid learning a try. As his classes learned more easily, rapidly, and successfully, he began to get a kick out of teaching again. "Each group of students has achieved more because I have been more encouraged to try even more of the ideas."

In 1977, with a new group of classes, the mean percentages for the four classes were: 98.5 percent, 94.0 percent, 97.0 percent and 100.0 percent, with an overall mean percentage of 97.5 percent. "With those kinds of results, the students are highly motivated to work."

The kids, it seems, were elated, and proud of their new-found skills. For many, it was the best they had ever done in their lives. They had a new image of themselves and their capabilities. Gritton knew for sure there was something different about rapid learning when kids sent out in the hall for misbehaving didn't cut classes, but hung around his door trying not to miss anything.

"If S.A.L.T. helps but one, it would be worth it," says Gritton, "but when you have 115 students at a ninety-seven percent level in four days, teaching is a lot of fun!"

The kids' excitement was contagious. It changed Gritton from a pessimist to an optimist. The "illusion" that people are limited had been dispelled. He tried the same techniques on his wrestling team and coached them to the city championship.

Gritton prizes his daughter's compliment—"You're a much nicer person now."

Gritton added mind calming and environment records—soothing sounds from nature—to ease stress and anxiety. Kids come to him now and say, "I've got a headache," "I've got a pain," "can't we do mind calming?" It helps him too, he says. One girl told him the mind calming was helping her in family fights. When her mother hollered at her, she did a breathing exercise and felt very calm.

On a trip to Iowa in 1977, Dr. Lozanov dropped in on schools there and said he was deeply pleased with the work going on.

Dr. Owen Caskey of Texas Tech University told us their initial success with rapid learning of Spanish encouraged them to start all kinds of programs including a one-year head-start program for five-year-olds; an English program for Vietnamese; and a remedial reading program for military personnel.

There is military interest in rapid learning, not only for recruits who can't read but also for personnel who must learn the volume of technical data required to man modern military equipment. Somewhat to our surprise, from the time reports of the system appeared here, apart from teachers and private individuals, those most stirred by the possibilities of opening supermemory were the top brass in the military. Like their counterparts in the USSR, they seemed more immediately aware of what wide-scale rapid learning and supermemory could mean.

On the West Coast, Charles Schmid got hold of Dr. Bancroft's superlearning instructions. Schmid, fifty-one, was a former professor at New York University and the University of Texas at Austin. He dropped out of teaching, he says, because he was fed up with inefficient teaching methods. In California he studied the human potential movement. He had the idea of combining Lozanov's techniques with Gestalt and consciousness-raising methods. Trained in music, he expanded on Lozanov's music ideas. He prepared adult language programs incorporating all his new ideas. Schmid and Juanita Netoff-Usatch founded a center, Language in New Dimensions in San Francisco, which teaches French and Spanish with Schmid's Lozanov adaptation. Schmid claims he's had good results.

A director of the program, who had just sat in on courses, discovered one night in a Spanish restaurant that without realizing it, he'd talked to the waiter and ordered dinner in Spanish. Apparently he'd been painlessly absorbing the language.

Also in San Francisco is Ivan Barzakov, the Bulgarian who had worked in the Lozanov schools. Quite a bit has been said about yoga and emphasis on good physical and mental control in Bulgaria. Barzakov affirms its importance in superlearning. In Barzakov's case, such stamina led to an unenvisioned feat. As he tells it, while vacationing on a beach in Yugoslavia, Barzakov suddenly decided he would swim to freedom. "I put my passport and my father's picture in a plastic bag and tucked it in my bathing suit. Then I began to swim." He swam eight miles, just missing the searchlights of the Yugoslavian border patrol. Finally, he reached the shores of Italy, sent back for his baggage, and set out for America. At his Market Street headquarters he has now developed his own suggestopedia version—Barzak Education.

According to Dr. Bancroft, one of the best adaptations of the Lozanov method she has seen to date is being done at the Lycée Voltaire in Paris by Jean Cureau for the teaching of high school English. A well-known teacher in France, Cureau has put some of the learning systems described in Section II of this book (autogenics, sophrology, etc.) together with portions of the Bulgarian technique. The students are first trained in relaxation methods to heighten their ability to hear accurately, enhance concentration, and improve group rapport. They are given positive suggestions for better learning. Cureau then reads the English texts over baroque slow movements. Dr. Bancroft observed the classes. "The pupils can recite the new lines spontaneously after he has read them." Because of the concentration training, Cureau reports the students learn English with an excellent accent.

While political problems were circumvented abroad, others began at home. With her careful, intrepid, almost ceaseless work for five years, Dr. Bancroft was a main force in giving Westerners a way to develop their potentials of supermemory and rapid learning. She personally advised hundreds who'd written us asking about the promise of the Bulgarian system. Armed with her academic understanding and, fortunately, a bone-deep sense of humor, she struggled through the morass of communist politics in the summers, and year round she went to bat for the system with academics on an international scale. Finally, she had to take on a situation that could strain anyone's sense of the absurd. It involved her own government.

For one reason or another, new ways of increasing human capability tend to evoke a peculiar response from some of the sitting experts. They seize the new system to their bosoms, then crush it to death. For instance, when sleep-learning was introduced in America, experts rushed to test it. Many never bothered to find out *how.* They omitted the essential reverie-sleep phase timing of material, relaxation training, required repetitions. They blared courses throughout the night on loudspeakers while people slept, or tried to sleep, in dormitories. Then they tested the bleary students. They had learned nothing; the experts announced sleep-learning didn't work. Suggestopedia began to slough down the same road.

Various individuals and groups created their own programs which were only coincidentally related to suggestopedia, labeled them "Lozanov Method," and began marketing them. One could begin to imagine Kentucky Fried Learning Centers cropping up on every corner. Then the Canadian government "did its own thing" on a grand scale.

Hearing of suggestopedia through our reports in 1971, the Canadian government decided to try it for French bilingualism programs needed for their civil service. In 1972, the first Canadian team allowed into Bulgaria for training arrived in Sofia, "knowing practically nothing about suggestology," they wrote. Unfortunately, for political or other reasons, they returned the same way. Apparently, ignoring the "how-to" of successful Western adaptations, they manufactured their own unusual compound and called it suggestopedia.

Out went such supermemory elements as altered-state, correct music, right rhythmic breathing and pacing, to name a few. The teaching featured some instructors unskilled in language teaching, unstructured classes, and flawed programs. After several years, not one single case of supermemory. According to staff reports, on the French exams there were massive failures. Teachers quit and many students complained.

Undaunted, director Gabriel Racle traveled across the United States and from country to country, conference to conference, preaching this version of suggestopedia. From France to Mexico, Sweden to Senegal, he insisted that the others (like those getting a seven-to-one speedup) were on the "wrong" path. American and Canadian corporations and university educators believed that the government, after spending millions on suggestopedia, *must* know. They followed it down the same path to similar outcomes. Thinking they'd tried the real suggestopedia and it didn't work, they cast it aside. The government fiasco turned off many Americans to rapid learning.

After trying regular channels to no avail, Dr. Bancroft finally made public her protests in the *Montreal Gazette.* Outrageous bungling of suggestopedia by the Canadian government for years, she said, has prevented many Westerners from benefitting from its vast potential. "This is a program with such amazing possibilities that we can't afford to let unknowledgeable bureaucrats ruin it. Suggestopedia is the wave of the future, and we need it now. . . ."

That *now* is beginning to be realized. Effective ways to develop supermemory and thus learn at extraordinary speed are being adopted by businesses, teachers, and the public generally. A number of people have plunged into it on a do-it-yourself basis. For instance, in California students reported they'd leaped from C to A averages by using the method for homework, while a Japanese scientist wrote us, "Did English in seven days; French in fifteen."

The following chart gives an idea of where some of the recent projects have taken place. Numerous conferences on accelerated learning have also been held in California, Iowa, Washington, Ottawa; and Dr. Lozanov spoke at many of them.

Recent Rapid-Learning Projects

Colorado State University—(Dr. Kay Herr; German); Rutgers University, N.J.—(Gabe Minc; remedial reading); University of California, San Diego—(Dr. Elizabeth Philipov; Bulgarian); Pitzer College, Claremont—(Alan Harris; Hebrew); University of Illinois; University of Kansas; Texas Tech University—(Dr. Owen Caskey; Spanish and other subjects); St. Lawrence University in New York; University of Toronto—(Dr. Eleanor Irwin & Dr. Jane Bancroft; Greek); Institute of Management, Old Dominion University, Virginia—(Dr. H. Thorstad & Dr. W. Garry); Sandy Spring Friends School, Sandy Spring, Md.—(Mr. & Mrs. Peter Kline; interlocking curriculum); Language in New Dimensions, San Francisco—(Charles Schmid; French and Spanish); Institute for Executive Research, Glendale, California —(John Boyle); Lozanov Learning Institute, Silver Spring, Maryland—U.S. franchise—(Dr. Carl Schleicher; languages); Canadian Pacific—(French program); University of Iowa and Iowa State University—(Spanish); Brigham Young University, Provo, Utah; Catholic University, Washington, D.C.—(Catherine Leidecker); College Condorcet, Paris, France—(Micheline Flak); Lycée Voltaire, Paris, France—(Jean Cureau; English); University of Tübingen, Germany—(Dr. Elizabeth Philipov; Spanish); Ferdowsi University, Iran—(Douglas Shaffer; English); Uppsala, Sweden—(Christer Landahl).

The Bulgarian government awarded the commercial franchise for the method to a Washington, D.C., firm, Mankind Research, Unlimited, Inc. MRU president, Dr. Carl Schleicher, believes that in years to come, "a real revolution will take place in our teaching methods, which have for all intents and purposes remained unchanged since man began to communicate his first words."

Dr. Schleicher is one American with a good grounding in communist science and negotiations. He has brought many innovations from the Soviet-bloc countries to the West and worked indefatigably to have them adapted for our benefit here. The Lozanov Learning Institute that his firm began is in Silver Springs Maryland (see Appendix). Courses in languages and for learning instructors are being given. Further research is underway and courses in other subjects are in the works. Dr. Schleicher's firm also leases franchises of the Bulgarian system. A few have been sold and others are planned around the country. As you might expect, since the Bulgarian government made the trade agreement, Dr. Lozanov attempts to work with this group.

The first Western European suggestopedia center is the Ludwig Boltzmann Institut für Lernforschung, a school specializing in elementary education in Vienna.

In this book, adapting superlearning techniques for do-it-yourselfers, we have focused on the supermemory session, rather than on a whole teaching method which requires a manual of its own (see Appendix). As in sleep-learning, you can learn on your own with tapes. You can create your own programs to learn any information you desire. Using the relaxation techniques provided, you get into an altered state of slowed-down body/mind rhythms. Then you listen to the tape or a friend reading the material paced to the music.

At the moment, rapid-learning systems for factual material come in many forms. Although there is a great deal of contention as to which is the "true way," probably many of these systems work to one degree or another. For the superlearning do-it-yourself program in this book, we've taken from three sources. We've used the same background sources Lozanov drew from (such as Raja Yoga) and also others he does not mention. We've drawn from Lozanov's own highly creative work. Finally, we've tried to draw from the experience of those who've gotten rapid-learning results in North America. Where there are several ways of setting up superlearning elements, we have chosen the simplest one that works.

Supermemory techniques can help high school, college, and grammar school students learn the information they have to know, easily and effectively. In professional training, too, from law to engineering to medicine, superlearning can reduce the burden of memorization. It can help anyone learn factual information. On a broader perspective, if supermemory systems continue to prove themselves they could aid us in numerous ways. It could help many of the undereducated move ahead in a year or two instead of a half decade. It could overcome the "fact factory" approach to education, leaving more time to learn what to do with the facts.

It might be able to help turn around some of those increasing headlines: "National College Entrance Test Scores Decline to Lowest Level Ever"; "Simple Arithmetic Stumps Floridian High School Grads"; "46 Percent of Freshmen Flunk English at Three Canadian Universities."

Rapid learning might help with unemployment by making job retraining faster and something to look forward to. As some companies already realize, it could pay off handsomely in employee training. Older people could rapidly open up new interests, and the overspecialized might be able to balance lopsided learning. Women wanting to resume careers after child rearing could reequip themselves more rapidly.

Marilyn Ferguson, author of *The Brain Revolution* and founder of the *Brain/Mind Bulletin* says, "Claims for Suggestology or Suggestopedia may sound preposterous, but they are within the realm of the possible and even the probable in terms of research findings on the capabilities of the human brain." The fluent, liberating, creative aspects of altered states can be incorporated into consciousness, she says. This is "our open sesame to an infinitely richer life than we have believed possible."

Chapter 4
What Makes Superlearning Tick?

When many Westerners first heard about the supermemory system they were baffled as to how it worked. They tried playing music, sitting in comfortable chairs, and listening to language tapes—and nothing happened. Lightning learning was elusive. How do you learn so you retrieve what you perceive? people wondered.

The two basic secrets are relaxed state and synchronized rhythm. When you sit back and imbibe information you're in the middle of a smoothly-orchestrated whole. Yet Lozanov and others synthesized the elements from extremely diverse fields. It was this diversity that at first drove some specialists to near frenzy trying to figure out what makes superlearning tick. It was what began to fascinate nonspecialists. A look at the separate "active" components, their lineage, and other implications can give you some new thoughts about how you tick and how the world ticks—or maybe the word is *beat*.

Relaxed Concentration

Superlearning is a form of holistic education; it involves *both* body and mind working in harmony. It's based on the idea that the mind is able to learn faster and more easily when the body is running at a more efficient level.

For years, physiologists reported that if people relaxed muscular tension, they could better remember what they'd studied. If we could train our hearts to beat slowly while thinking, it would make mental work easier. Dr. Barbara Brown in *New Mind, New Body* says, "With a slower heartbeat, mind efficiency takes a great leap forward."

A slower heartbeat literally gives the heart a "vacation." Generally, our hearts beat at about seventy to eighty times a minute. Specialists believe that if we could get closer to the sixty-beats-a-minute range, we would be healthier and perform better mentally. Many biological bases for better learning are known, but not applied. (See p. 314.)

Dr. Lozanov discovered something else about the body/mind connection in his years of studying people with supernormal abilities, yogis with supermemory, and instant calculators. Instruments showed that at the moment these people performed astonishing mental feats, their bodies were in a state of rest, their brain waves were at a relaxed alpha rhythm (seven to fourteen cycles a second). They did not strain, will, or coerce the mind to function. It happened effortlessly. It actually seemed to happen *because* physical and mental effort weren't involved.

Here was a paradox, Lozanov thought. Relaxation mated with intense mental work. It's generally accepted that when a person does heavy mental work, pulse and blood pressure rise and brain waves speed up to the beta level (fourteen cycles a second and up).

Many well-known relaxation and meditation methods can break tension and bring the body to a relaxed state. Could there be a way to set up such a relaxed state in the body while at the *very same time* the brain was whizzing away at math or languages? If you could keep the body's motor idling instead of racing while the mind is "on," it should be possible for the mind to superperform.

After extensive experiments in his physiology labs, Lozanov concluded that physical relaxation was not enough. Probably if relaxation was *all* that was required, all those who have sat half-awake through early morning classes would have emerged wondrously brilliant. While profoundly relaxed, people can't concentrate intently; and without concentration, learning and memory are poor. But then, as soon as people concentrate intently, relaxation disappears and stress returns.

Drawing on yoga theories on music and research in psychoacoustics, Dr. Lozanov made an important observation. He found that a very *specific* form of music with a very *specific* rhythm can induce a relaxed state in the body—but, with one very major difference. The music-induced relaxation left the mind alert and able to concentrate.

Unlike other forms of meditation, nothing was required but playing the music. One didn't have to attend to the "meditation" and could occupy one's mind with the material presented. Physiologists found the rhythms of the body—heartbeat, brain waves, and so forth—tend to synchronize themselves to the beat of music. Lozanov used classical music with a very slow, stately, restful rhythm. The body rhythms of the students chimed in on this slow beat, relaxing to a more efficient and healthful rhythm.

During these concert sessions, people were monitored with physiological instruments. The pattern was extraordinary. It's the same pattern American researchers Wallace and Benson found comes from meditation. Heartbeats slowed by an average of at least five beats per minute. Blood pressure was down slightly. Brain waves showed beta waves decreased; brain waves slowed to the alpha rhythm. (Slow theta and delta waves tended to decrease, showing that this relaxed state was not like dozing; see chart.)

Physiological Changes During Supermemory Sessions Compared to TM

	Supermemory Concert of Slow Baroque Music (60 b.p.m.) During Intense Mental Activity (learning 100 foreign words)	Transcendental Meditation (Reciting a mantra)
Electroencephalogram (Alpha brain waves: 7 - 13 cycles per sec. Beta brain waves: over 13 cycles per sec. Theta brain waves: 4 - 7 cycles per sec.)	Alpha brain waves increase by an average of 6%. Beta brain waves decrease by an average of 6%. Theta waves unchanged.	Alpha brain waves increase. Some increase in Theta waves.
Pulse	Pulse slows by an average of 5 beats per minute.	Decreases significantly with a mean decrease of 5 beats per minute.
Blood Pressure	Blood pressure drops slightly (4 divisions of the mercury column on an average).	Tendency to decrease with intermediate fluctuations.
Body Motility	Sitting comfortably. Body relaxed.	Sitting comfortably. Body relaxed.
Awareness	Relaxed concentration	"Restful alertness"

Data drawn from *Suggestology*, by Dr. G. Lozanov, and *Consciousness East and West*, by K. Pelletier and C. Garfield.
TM is one of the meditation methods scientifically researched in the West which has been shown to relieve inner tensions, lower blood pressure, provide stress control, and improve physical and emotional health. Certain Baroque music appears to do the same.

But, there was that one all-important difference. At the very same time the people relaxed, they were also doing strenuous mental work. They had actually learned much more than would have been covered in a whole day of tough, fatiguing immersion language courses.

Lozanov had indeed found a way to let us have our cake and eat it too. We can be relaxed and mentally alert at the same time.

"Here was a paradox!" he says.

"Overwork (supermemory) → *rest."*

So, it seems we don't have to go to sleep, we don't have to be in a hypnotic trance to connect with added dimensions of ourselves and to learn and memorize way beyond normal. We can do it while we are awake and aware if we are sitting in a soundscape of the right music. This is something that other rapid-learning methods could not do.

This good feeling of relaxed alertness brought on by the music is one reason your mind begins to light up and click along with new power in superlearning. Your body is using its energies more efficiently. It also helps explain the seemingly strange phenomenon of students claiming relief from a variety of health problems while learning a language. Not surprisingly, health benefits are akin to those produced by many meditation and relaxation courses.

Lozanov is far from being the first medical doctor to have worked on relaxation techniques. He is also not the first doctor well grounded in hypnosis who determined to find a way for people to have some of the benefits of hypnosis without having to relinquish control of their own minds. The German M.D. Johannes H. Schultz embarked on the same quest. In the 1930's, he came out with Autogenic Training, a system for extraordinary self-control of body and mind widely used in Europe in medicine and now in sports (see Section II). Dr. Schultz found that genuine relaxation is a state of expanded consciousness, very different from the "tunnel vision" of hypnosis. From his own work, Lozanov is in strong agreement.

During the music sessions, people vary in levels of relaxation. That accounts for variation in amounts memorized, says Lozanov. Georgia researchers Prichard and Taylor found this to be true. The better the student's relaxation response, the better the results.

Originally, Lozanov's students in Bulgaria were given four days of preliminary relaxation training. In Moscow, students were trained to relax with autogenics (see page 163). Now, Lozanov feels relaxation training isn't a necessity—and maybe it isn't in slower-paced Bulgaria.

However, the majority of the most successful users of superlearning techniques in Europe, the USSR, and North America consider relaxation an essential.

American users of rapid learning found that in our hyper, hassled, and harassed environment, a week to ten days of relaxation training was needed before Americans could really relax and benefit from the music.

For most of us, relaxation is a skill, not an automatic response. Once learned, it's easy to do and a lifetime boon. But if you don't know how, just hearing the command "Relax!" won't make it happen. Therefore, we've included the full "how-to" of relaxation (see page 96).

The Beat of Memory

Yogi Ramacharaka distills the core of yoga principles in *The Science of Breath*. Rhythm, he says, "brings the whole system, including the brain, under perfect control and in perfect harmony and by this means the most perfect condition is obtained for unfoldment of . . . latent faculties."

Dr. Lozanov studied rhythm and learning. If material to be remembered was presented rapid-fire at one-second intervals, people learned only about twenty percent of it. At five-second intervals, they learned about thirty percent of it. When there was a ten-second interval between each item, the amount of material memorized was over forty percent.

This meant that if you were trying to memorize a list of unknown words, for instance, if you heard a new word about every ten seconds, you would remember more than if you heard the words at a faster pace.

A continuous, monotonous rhythm of somewhere around ten seconds seems to open up the mind's ability to remember. We know about heartbeats, but what's this—the beat of memory?

Years before, Soviet brain researchers and sleep-learning researchers threw some light on this curious mystery. After much investigation, they found that a pause between data-bits gave brain cells a chance to rest a moment so that they were better able to register the next item. Rapid-fire presentation of data seemed to blur registration in the brain. Soviet sleep-learning researchers also divided their material into fragments and paced it with pauses.

Timing is everything, the saying goes; and in superlearning, rhythm increasingly turned out to be a very "live" ingredient.

The Bulgarians began reciting the key items to be memorized every eight seconds. Why not ten? Perhaps because they also wanted to tie in with the beat of the music, which is not generally written in "five and ten" time.

American users of the system found heightened memory by emphasizing key items every eight seconds, and every twelve seconds.

Lozanov's system has some roots in ways to speed up learning and creativity through expanded time sense that were pioneered in America. In the 1950's, two M.D.s, Linn Cooper and the well-known hypnosis authority Milton Erickson, explored an identical rhythmic approach. They set a metronome at sixty beats a minute and used ten-second activity cycles. The beat apparently slowed body/mind rhythms. Listening to the metronome click, hypnotized subjects subjectively perceived the beats as slower than clock time. Time literally expanded for them. One woman, for instance, was able to design a dress in seconds. The hypnotist "tricked" her into this feat by telling her she had a whole hour at her disposal. And subjectively she actually felt as if she had that much time. In a sense, she was lifted out of time. This lifted her out of the suggestion that it takes so many minutes or hours to accomplish a project. Thus freed, she was able to perform with supernormal ability like the instant calculators. Lozanov's contribution is to use such rhythmic methods in the waking state.

Intonation

Rhythm helps you memorize, Lozanov found. But then another snag arose on the way to developing supermemory. The monotony of the rhythmic repetition made people tune it off. Repetition helped memory, but it also hampered it. Lozanov and his colleagues solved this problem by using three different intonations for the material being recited rhythmically:
1) normal (declarative)
2) soft whisper (quiet, ambiguous, misleading tone)
3) loud, commanding voice (with a domineering tone)
The intonation of the voice used for each phrase doesn't have any relation to the meaning of the words, and the "surprise" element of the odd combinations of tone and content helps break the monotony of the steady rhythm. Intonations can also have a psychotherapeutic effect.

Breathing to Learn

If you're panting to learn, one of the first things to do is to control your breathing. Rhythm seems to be at the heart of supermemory and so it seems is breathing. Iowa researchers took all the components apart and tested them separately. When people breathed in rhythm with rhythmically recited material, just these two things alone made learning suddenly shoot ahead by seventy-eight percent.

Doug Shaffer, the American teaching in Iran, found the same thing. Could it be that the rhythmic breathing leads to better brain oxidation, he speculates, and this leads to better learning. After all, the brain is said to need three times as much oxygen to function properly as the body does, especially while a person is working in a sitting position. We seldom give breathing much conscious attention, yet we breathe about five thousand gallons (thirty-five pounds) of air every day, about six times our food and drink consumption. Obviously, breath is life.

According to many cultures, you can breathe life—new, vigorous life—not just into your body but also into your talents and mental abilities. If instead of breathing haphazardly, you breathe to a regular beat, your mind sharpens automatically. If you know how to use it, this breathing beat can do something else for you. When between inhaling and exhaling, you go on holding for a few seconds, mental activity stabilizes and the mind can focus in on a single point or idea.

Yoga authority Mircea Eliade asserts that concentration is greatly promoted by rhythmic breathing and especially by holding the breath. Yogi Ramacharaka reveals in *The Science of Breath* that "by rhythmical breathing one may bring himself into harmonious vibration with nature, and aid in the unfoldment of his latent powers." How should you breathe to learn? Breathing is based on a slow human pulse. By harmonizing your breathing with your pulse, yogis and others say your whole body catches the vibration and harmonizes with the will. By getting yourself in synch, you have more power, mentally and otherwise. In superlearning, breathing is done in rhythm, approximately to a slow pulse beat. You just breathe along in time to the rhythmically recited material.

It may be new to American education, but the idea of increasing concentration by breathing in rhythm to chanted words is found in many great cultures—the Moslem tradition, to name just one. We probably have caught hold of the same basic idea, but on a space-age level. Modern information science has a law that says more information can be transferred over a smooth medium. Dr. Win Wenger wonders if this might be the secret of the synchronized rhythms of superlearning. Maybe the synchronized rhythms make the information transfer unusually smooth.

Dr. Hideo Seki, a Japanese expert in communication theory, and a superlearning do-it-yourselfer, told us he thinks the various synchronized components smooth out "psychological noise" currents in the brain, thus improving the signal to noise ratio.

Dr. Lozanov investigated breathing in a different way and found something that American researchers have uncovered too. In Bulgarian labs they found that, through particular breathing exercises, a person could control body functions and, at will, slow the pulse.

Psycho-physical expert Jack Schwarz has been studied extensively in U.S. physiology labs to probe the secret of his voluntary control over mind, body, and pain. He reveals that after particular breathing exercises instruments showed that brain waves and muscle activity in chest and abdomen *become synchronized*. "Head and body are aligned, harmonized," he states in his book, *Voluntary Controls*.

Perhaps we could add another kind of pollution to the current list—"rhythmic pollution." With all the hassle around us, it seems we get out-of-synch rhythms in mind and body that hamper learning and achievement. Breathing to a specific rhythmic pattern may be one of the easiest ways going to amplify internal awareness as well as to harmonize and relax the body. "We found that respiratory rate has a tremendous influence on states of consciousness," Schwarz reports.

Beyond the synchronizing effects of breathing, and the improved oxygen supply, there may be another side to breathing, too, that is very important to supermemory (see page 77).

Music-Induced Altered States of Consciousness

Not only breathing patterns can alter states of consciousness. Music and sound have also been found to change brain-wave activity. Tokyo researcher Dr. Norio Owaki did a ten-year study on the certain kinds of sound patterns that can induce alpha brain waves.

That certain sound patterns can affect consciousness is no news to students of music lore. They recall a particular story about Bach.

It was well past midnight and the Russian Envoy Count Kayserling tossed and turned in his sickbed. Another bout with miserable insomnia, he thought. He simply could not seem to sleep at night. Finally he told a servant, "Call for Goldberg." Johann Goldberg, a musician, was roused from his bed and brought to the count. "Ah, Goldberg, would you be so good as to play for me again please—one of *my* variations."

Goldberg went to the harpsichord and began to play a composition that had been specially written for Count Kayserling by Johann Sebastian Bach. The Count had told Bach about his terrible bouts with sleeplessness. "Could you possibly write some music that could help," he asked. "Something calm, yet bright."

In a short time, as Goldberg played this special music, the count found himself feeling rested and less tense. He asked for this same music to be played to him every time he felt sleepless. He had Goldberg installed in a nearby room ready to play this restorative music on request. In fact, Count Kayserling was so pleased with the curative effects of this music that he rewarded Bach with a very lavish gift of gold. The composition itself has come to be known as "The Goldberg Variations," in honor of the obliging harpsichordist.

In Iowa in 1977, Dr. Lozanov asked an audience of educators, "Do you think that the great composers, philosophers, and poets of the past knew about the yoga system? About relaxation? About different influences?"

He smiled and answered his own question. "Of course! Why not?"

Well, maybe not yoga exactly. In Lozanov's view, many great composers, writers, philosophers of the past were acquainted through Western esoteric traditions with the same ancient knowledge from which yoga also springs.

Lozanov studied in his lab the music Bach wrote for Count Kayserling, "The Goldberg Variations," and found that, in particular, the aria with which it starts and ends could induce a meditative state with many beneficial physical effects derived from its slowing down body processes.

Pieces by other composers of the sixteenth to eighteenth centuries, written in the same musical tradition, were found to have similar effects. Music history has it that Bach designed much of his music to appeal to the mentality. Lozanov and colleagues noted that with this music the body relaxed, the mind became alert.

The idea that music can affect your body and mind certainly isn't new. For centuries, people have been lullabying babies to sleep. For centuries, people sang sea chanties and harvesting songs to ease their labor. For centuries, from Asia to the Middle East to South America people have used music to carry them into unusual states of consciousness.

The key was to find just the right kind of music for just the right kind of effect.

Music by sixteenth- to eighteenth-century composers—Bach, Vivaldi, Telemann, Corelli, Handel—is often called Baroque music. In particular, the labs investigated the *slow* (or largo) movements of the Baroque concertos. (Each concerto has different segments to be played at different speeds.)

In the slow movements, we find again that familiar, and it seems, potent rhythm—sixty beats a minute. This Baroque music often has a very slow bass, beating like a slow human pulse. As you listen, your body listens too and tends to follow the beat.

Your body relaxes and your mind becomes alert in this most

simple of all forms of relaxation. You don't have to tell a muscle to relax, you don't have to concentrate or even say a mantra. All you have to do is be with the music. As Handel plays, the benefits of simple meditation begin to happen.

There are, of course, sixty seconds to a minute—and perhaps there's more to this than an arbitrary division of time. Soviet psychologist I.K. Platonov found that just a metronome beating at sixty affected people. The mind took hold more strongly than usual to what was said above the beat.

Bulgarian students were put through courses *without* any music, just rhythmically recited material. They learned but they also immediately complained of stress, tension, and fatigue.

So the overall effect of the music in superlearning is to give you a "sonic massage"—to eliminate the stress of hard mental work. The music helps fix the focus of attention inwardly instead of outwardly. The reverie state is highly orderly because of the highly structured nature of the music. Throughout the concert, the student is in complete control, superalert, lucid, and aware of everything going on—even to minute changes in the recited material.

The music you use in superlearning is extremely important. If it does not have the required pattern, the desired altered states of consciousness will not be induced and results will be poor. *It is not a personal choice and has nothing whatever to do with personal tastes in music.* It is specific music—sonic patterns—for a specific purpose (see page 111).

If you want to get results use only the type of music they have investigated so far, and don't substitute. At the institute, a series of slow movements (sixty beats a minute) *in ¼ time* from Baroque concertos are strung together to create about a half-hour concert. The final selection that ends the concert is usually a bright, faster movement to allow one to come out of the reverie state in a pleasant way. Such a group of selections would not be considered for a regular concert program by an orchestra, because there's little variation in pace.

Different beats do different things. American advertising companies did a lot of research on how music and rhythm influence people and found a seventy-two-beat-a-minute rhythm for voice, music, and drumbeat increases suggestibility. Wilson Key reveals in *Subliminal Seduction* that a commercial with a seventy-two-beat rhythm seemed to "suggest" people into having the very symptoms—throbbing, pounding headaches, for instance—that the product being advertised was supposed to cure.

Many Americans who first tried rapid learning slid right off the track with their music. They thought it was just background, akin to Muzak at the supermarket. They tried conglomerations of country-western music, folk music, pop classics, or the wrong parts of Baroque music. Consequently, results were poor. Only the very specific sound, rhythm, and harmonic patterns of this particular music induce relaxed alertness.

Music therapy, psycho-acoustic research, and industrial use of music—all these explore how music affects humans. Music to induce general relaxation is becoming available—for instance, Steven Halpern's *Spectrum Suite* (though this does not have the proper beat for learning). Like researchers at UCLA, Halpern, a psychologist and director of The Spectrum Research Institute, used Kirlian photography as one way to see the effects of music on the body. This photography shows a corona of energy around living things. We tried this too a few years ago. We took a Kirlian photo of Lynn's finger before and during the Third Brandenburg Concerto. In the "before" picture, the corona of light around the finger has a shaggy, diffuse look. While the music played, the corona became "classical" in structure, highly defined with fluted and beaded light.

Using music to induce altered states of consciousness has become one of the most significant music trends of the seventies, according to Robert Palmer in *The New York Times*. Discotheque bands, jazz musicians, electronic groups like Tangerine Dream "are beginning to explore the possibilities of rhythmic and modal repetition, which seek through absolute control of limited musical means to induce relaxation, contemplation, euphoria, and other psychological states, rather than merely to provide sound tracks for chemically induced ones."

The Shamans of Central Asia, the Jajouka musicians of northern Morocco, and certain Indian and Oriental musicians, all knew of musical methods of mobilizing altered states leading to such phenomena as trance, pain control, ability to walk on hot coals without damage. In the Third World, says Palmer, this kind of music was the oldest, nonchemical path to satori, or enlightenment.

Current lab research shows certain drumbeats act as a kind of pacemaker, regulating brain-wave rhythms and breathing, which leads to biochemical changes that produce altered states of consciousness. If you listen to a different drummer, you do see a different world.

The proposition that various kinds of music have vastly different effects, some helpful and harmonizing, others not, fits with yoga theories of music too. I.K. Taimni, in *The Science of Yoga*, says there is a fundamental relationship between vibration and consciousness existing on all octaves.

Because each level of consciousness has a specific vibration associated with it, according to yoga theory, particular states of consciousness can then be brought about by setting up sound vibrations tuned to the state of mind you want. This is the principle behind mantra meditation—meditating with sound— or toning. But music affecting the mind isn't a one-way street, says Taimni. When you change your state of mind, you are changing the vibrations being emitted, and these changed vibrations in turn can affect everything around us from plants to people.

Chapter 5
The
Not-Yet-Unraveled
Side

Apart from what is understood right now by our science, there is reason to think other elements are involved in vastly magnifying memory and learning. These may be root powers for they seem to hold clues about how to open super ability generally. For instance, there is something about how one breathes that Lozanov and colleagues do not mention. This something is at the very core of all traditional breathing exercises and of yoga itself. The main reason to breathe in rhythm, they say, is because it gives you more of a very special energy. This is where the catch comes in. Western science doesn't officially recognize such an energy. Yet, the energy idea is at the root of the systems from which much of superlearning has been drawn. Whether it's a metaphor or more, looking into the idea might tell us something.

An Energy of Genius?

Most Eastern philosophies hold that we live in a bright, vital sea of energy. Yogis call this prana. Oriental acupuncture recognizes this same energy and calls it Chi. This energy is in the atmosphere and also circulates along specific pathways in the body according to Chinese medicine. Just as we transform the food we eat to our own use, so do we transform prana to maintain and develop ourselves. Regulated breathing enables us to extract a greater supply of prana from the air. The body accumulates prana as a battery does electricity. This energy, yogis say, gives the body vitality and nourishes consciousness. Prana absorbed by the brain is responsible for unfolding mental abilities and psychic powers. Like oxygen, prana is said to keep us going whether or not we're aware of it. When we do become aware and start to learn to direct this energy, the fireworks begin.

Philosopher Gopi Krishna has inspired scientific centers in Europe and the United States to explore this energy and its ignited form, kundalini. This, he says, is the "secret" behind yoga and all other spiritual disciplines and esoteric psychologies. It is, he insists, the key to genius, artistic talents, scientific and intellectual creativity, psychic powers, and extreme longevity with good health.

This pranic stream is said to be affected by emotions, food, drink, sound, music. Is there really such an energy that can help make us smart, talented, and healthy?

A vital, all-pervasive energy, call it prana or what you will, has been discovered and rediscovered throughout Western history. It's gone under a horde of names from "odic force" to "X force," from "orgone energy" to "etheric force." Today, scientists in many countries are taking a new look at this concept that won't give up.

"The discovery of the energy associated with psychic events will be as important if not more important than the discovery of atomic energy," said Dr. L. L. Vasiliev, founder of Soviet parapsychology. The discovery of "another" energy became the number one goal of on-going Soviet psi research. In 1968, Soviet scientists announced that they had discovered a new energy system in the body. They showed lovely pictures of sparkling lights, miniature fireballs, and streams of energy moving through the body and flickering around it like the aurora borealis. They called it bio-plasma energy. Using high-frequency electrical photography (the Kirlian technique) they photographed this energy moving along the pathways described in Oriental acupuncture. It was a major breakthrough. Western scientists had always dismissed acupuncture because they couldn't find any energy, or any points, or pathways, in the body. Using Western methods, Soviet scientists proved, to their own satisfaction at least, that there is a kind of energy circulation in the body. It follows the paths noted by Chinese medicine for over four thousand years. The Soviets' newly christened bio-plasmic energy seemed to match the ancient Chinese Chi and the Indian prana. Soviets found this energy is heightened by breathing and is affected by many things—magnetism, sunspots, light, sound.

Internationally, scientists are making other discoveries about an "other" energy. Czech researchers label this "psychotronic" energy. They claim to have developed devices that store and use it. They say this energy is involved in healing, various supernormal abilities, and even rapport among people. In India, at the All-India Institute of Medical Sciences, researchers wanted to see whether or not the energy postulated by yoga could indeed heighten learning and perception. They tested people and animals. They even had rats doing yoga exercises—standing on their heads in glass cylinders! They concluded that yoga energy exercises did overcome stress and aid learning.

Korean scientists looking for proof of an unrecognized energy circulation in the body injected radioactive phosphorus into subjects. They traced it moving along the supposedly nonexistent pathways of acupuncture. A well-known Japanese scientist, Dr. Hiroshi Motoyama, tried a similar task. He put strips of liquid crystals (available here as a fever test) on subjects' arms. He applied heat to an acupuncture point and watched the energy pathways "light up" in the changing colors of the heat-sensitive liquid crystals.

Some outstanding American scientists, who were not trying to explore the ancient concepts of acupuncture and prana, have also moved to the idea of other energies associated with the body. Physiologist Dr. Barbara Brown, the biofeedback pioneer, found in her work that, just as yogis had claimed, people can learn to control involuntary body functions. But *how* does the mind act on, and control, the body, Dr. Brown wonders. "Is it possible that whatever the mechanism of biofeedback is, it is accompanied by an energy as yet undescribed?" she asks in *New Mind, New Body.* "It should not be unexpected that new and different forms of body energy will be discovered."

Dr. Harold Burr of Yale, many decades ago, found that all living things are surrounded by a web of energy—electrodynamic fields he could measure with a voltmeter. These "life fields," as he named them, are the link between mind, body, and cosmos, Burr believed. He and colleagues measured altered states of consciousness through these fields. In that direction, Dr. Burr discovered something highly important to understanding life in general, and now, to understanding superlearning in particular. He found that changes inside the body, changes in one's brain waves or heartbeat, were the *result* of changes in these energetic fields, not the other way around. These life fields, he felt, are the means by which mind affects the body.

Evidence is accumulating on many fronts that there is an energy exchange going on inside us and between us and the environment that has gone generally unrecognized in the West. So far, it shows a striking resemblance to that bright, fundamental energy always recognized in the East. Pandit Gopi Krishna speaks for many Eastern philosophies when he says this energy is at the basis of life; it is the nourishing force of genius and superb performance. You can "charge up" or heighten this energy through breathing, rhythm, and sound, all agree. Superlearning uses breathing, rhythm, and sound to spark supermemory and supernormal abilities. If you have genius longings, it might be very rewarding to research all the things that are supposed to enhance this "other" energy (pulsed magnetic fields, breathing, "live" food, sound, light) to see if and how they enhance learning.

As physicist F. Capra shows so lucidly in his *Tao of Physics*, modern physics and Eastern philosophy are beginning to meet in the middle. The ancient dictums of the East are becoming the propositions of physics in the West. Today, it isn't so strange to think of yoga as a science, something its practitioners always maintained.

Music as the Bridge to Awareness

Perhaps there is yet another story to be unearthed behind the reason for the particular *kind* of music used for superlearning sessions—the specific music by Baroque composers. The idea of music as the bridge to inner awareness goes way back to the hidden sources of music itself. It runs deep in the legends of Orpheus who used music as a means of "charming" living creatures.

As the reports poured out of Bulgaria about the effects of music, we began to wonder. A few minutes a day of this Baroque music, and listeners in Lozanov classes began to report not only expanded awareness and better memory but also a whole repertoire of health benefits. They felt refreshed, energized, centered. Tension and stress disappeared. Headaches and pains went. The impersonal physiological graphs printed out proof—lowered blood pressure, lowered muscle tension, slower pulse. Is it just the *beat* of this music that slows body/ mind rhythms to healthier levels, or is there something else about this particular music that makes it appear to be especially life-enhancing?

While this research on the benefits of Baroque music was going on in Bulgaria and the USSR, another kind of investigation into this same type of music and its effects was going on in other countries. Scientists around the world were uncovering the baffling effects of particular kinds of music on basic living cells—in plants.

This wave of discovery started after a California researcher, Dorothy Retallack, revealed years of work with plants. Plants grown in scientifically controlled chambers were given concerts of different kinds of music from rock to Baroque. Plants grown in the chambers given Baroque music by Bach and Indian music by Ravi Shankar rapidly grew lush and abundant with large roots. These plants leaned toward the music source "so as to almost embrace the speaker." Some leaned as much as sixty degrees. The plants in the chamber getting rock music shriveled and died.

What was going on? Researchers tried other kinds of music. To country-western music the plants showed no reaction. Ms. Retallack was personally partial to the music of Debussy. The plants didn't respond with better growth and they leaned away from the music by ten degrees. Jazz had a somewhat better effect. Plants leaned toward the speakers by about fifteen degrees and grew more abundant than in silent chambers.

Over the years, as the same experiments with plants were repeated in universities and research centers, the same fact kept emerging—plants responded and grew abundantly, rapidly, and more healthily when they were in a sonic environment of classical or Indian music compared with other kinds of music or silence.

If different kinds of music can have different effects on plants, what does it do to humans? Ms. Retallack asked. Possibly the Bulgarians could have told her.

What was the "secret ingredient" those early classical composers added to their music that seemed to make it so healthful for plants and people? Was it the instruments used? The combination of sounds? Or just what?

A little digging into the hidden sources of music shows that the art of music was once tied to medicine and to bringing about so-called "supernatural feats." Two books devoted to music are attributed to Hermes Trismegistus of Ancient Egypt. He set out the principles of a philosophy relating to music that was passed down for centuries through secret groups and through guilds of musicians, masons, and architects.

The gist of his philosophy was that there is a harmony and correspondence among all the different kinds of manifestations in the universe—the circling of the planets, the tides of the earth, the growth of vegetation, the lives of animals and people —all are related. *All-that-is* in the universe emanates from the same source, according to Hermetic philosophy, and therefore the same laws, principles, and characteristics apply to each unit —"As above, so below."

Ancient mathematicians looked out at the universe, noted the ratios of the different planetary cycles, counted the rhythmic periodicities in nature, calculated the ratios of the human body. They put together a "sacred geometry"—a set of mathematical ratios and proportions. They believed that these ratios, if used in the sound of music and the architecture of buildings, would resonate with the life forces of the universe and thus enhance life.

When you sound a note on one piano in a hall full of pianos, the same note will resonate on the other instruments, enhancing the power of your single note to fill the whole hall. In the same way, the ancients believed that playing certain harmonies and combinations of notes would resonate with other elements in the universe tuned to the same scale. Through this resonance, we could, at will, have our "single notes" increased in power. Thus we could harmonize and heal ourselves, and "tune in" to the energies of the planet to open our natural powers. Those energies of the universe included, too, the idea of prana, one all-pervasive energy.

Everything in our universe is in a state of vibration. Matter is made up of certain types of waves on pulsing vibration. There is a commonness between the vibrations in a musical note, in a color, in the bonds of a chemical, or the vibration of the electrons in an atom. Each vibrates at its specific frequency in a ratio. A below middle C vibrates at 213 cycles a second, relating to the color red-orange, and the metal copper. *B* below *C,* at 240 cycles a second, relates to yellow and zinc. Chemistry expert Dr. Donald Hatch Andrews puts it, ". . . we are finding that the universe is composed not of matter but of music."

He echoed the English writer Thomas Carlyle who said, "See deep enough and you/see musically; the heart of/nature being everywhere music/if you can only reach it."

The ancient schools of music believed that music was the bridge linking all things. Following the ideas of Pythagoras, they built a "sacred canon" of these specific harmonies, intervals, and proportions into their music—these would be the *linking* sounds. When people heard sounds made of specific ratios, the rhythms of their cells, bodies, and minds would be synchronized to the very same rhythms as the planets and plants, earth and sea. Disharmony and out-of-synch patterns in mind/body would be dissolved. These particular sounds and rhythms, they thought, would enhance life and make it healthier and more abundant. Music would be the bridge to the cosmos, opening body and mind to higher powers and amplifying awareness. Through music, microcosm and macrocosm could be connected.

Such ideas were handed down to the composers of Baroque music. Musicians in those eras were trained and made to use these particular numbers and patterns for harmony, counterpoint, rhythm, and tempo in their music. This "mathematical" Baroque music was supposed to affect us by aligning, harmonizing, and synchronizing our minds and bodies to more harmonious patterns. But is there more to it than that? So far, it seems, this particular kind of music *does* have a positive effect on plants and people. What does it do to matter itself?

Today, a new science, cymatics, developed by Dr. Hans Jenny, lets us actually see the effects of different sounds and music on various kinds of matter—metal filings, sand, liquids, and so forth. Certain sounds make metal filings take organic patterns like sea urchins or the spirals of jellyfish turrets. Mantras (meditation chants) show precise, balanced, geometric patterns.

The Delawarr Labs in England analyzed the wave fronts generated by various kinds of music as it played through a solenoid, a magnet. They got some surprising glimpses of this idea of underlying classic pattern. When the wave fronts from the final chord of Handel's *Messiah* were charted and overlaid, they formed a perfect five-pointed star.

Exactly *why* and *how* does this particular kind of Baroque music help open up supermemory in people, and enhance the health of humans and plants? Do "other" energies or magnetic fields play a role? Lozanov believes all elements of aesthetics are involved. As we explore supermemory, the riddle leads us further into the mysterious side of numbers and music.

As famed composer-conductor Alan Hovhaness puts it, "When music was melody and rhythm, when each melodic combination was a gift of the gods, each rhythmic combination a mantram to unlock a key of power in nature, then music was one of the mysteries of the elements, of the planetary systems, of the worlds visible and invisible."

Holography and Supermemory

How does supermemory work? Some of the things that spark the ability are known. Other possible elements deep below the surface are being explored. Enough is known to begin to open and use this potential. But how does supermemory work? Just as no one yet knows exactly how memory itself works, the whole story of supermemory remains an unknown. Recently the experts who try to unravel the mysteries of how you remember generally have turned to a new model of memory and brain—the holographic model.

The most common use of holography is 3-D photography. If you walked through the Holographic Museum in New York, you would see the image of a small ballerina standing there. You could walk around her, see her left side, her back with her hair in a chignon, her right side. Unlike a regular picture, the whole ballerina is there. She looks real, except that you can poke your finger right through her. There's nothing there except two wave fronts of light, crossing each other and at that point creating an image, a ballerina.

Holography is one more contemporary scientific development that seems to echo in modern form a time-honored idea —All in one: one in all. You can cut a holographic plate into tiny pieces. Each tiny bit contains the whole picture.

Stanford neuroscientist Dr. Karl Pribram has a decade of evidence that the brain's structure is holographic. Just as the hologram has information scattered throughout, the brain has each of its memories distributed throughout the system, each fragment encoded to produce the information of the whole.

Recently Dr. Pribram, with British physicist Dr. David Bohm, announced a new theory of how we and the universe work. As reported in *Brain/Mind Bulletin:* "Our brains mathematically construct 'concrete' reality by interpreting frequencies from another dimension, a realm of meaningful, patterned primary reality that transcends time and space. The brain is a hologram, interpreting a holographic universe."

Holography works in wholes, not in parts or step-by-step progressions. It involves frequency and phase relationships, just like the rhythmic synchronies of supermemory. At root, just exactly what is going on in holistic programs like superlearning that light up more of the mind's capacities will probably come into clearer focus as the experts fill in their holographic model of brain and memory.

Chapter 6
The Unobstructed Personality

The unobstructed personality—a personality sprung from old limitations, enjoying the free flow of its energies, a personality able to unfold more of itself in the everyday sun—this is the overall goal of superlearning. To achieve it, we have to let go of the suggestions that have trussed us into a limited image of ourselves. Dr. Lozanov believes history and society constantly pulse suggestions about our capabilities, and these suggestions radically underestimate what we can be. Belief in limits, he says, creates limited people. Or as a contemporary poster puts it—"You can fly, but that cocoon has to go!"

Many of the strands that bind us are unconscious suggestions. From the moment we're born we begin to pick up suggestions from those around us on how to act and what we should be like. If we are going to fly, we have to take the controls and become aware of the things that influence us, so we can take on what we like and unload the rest.

De-suggestion is what Lozanov calls the process of trying to overcome your preconceived ideas about the limitations of your personality and abilities. He has outlined three main psychological blocks people have about rapid learning and opening reserves of mind.

Psychological Blocks to Superlearning
and What to Do About Them

1. THE CRITICAL/LOGICAL BLOCK.

On the basis of critical reasoning, some people immediately are skeptical. "Superlearning must be a put-on. It must be nonsense. People are just taken in if they think there's anything to the idea of reserves of the mind." Or, "History shows people's abilities have never changed."

The second part of the logical barrier goes: "It might work for *other* people, but it would never work for *me*. I have never learned fast and easily in my life, so why should I now?" Or, "I already learn rapidly, so how much could I improve?"

Everyone has a learning "norm" suggested to him or her by society and by experience. Outstanding authorities today have changed their views about the learning norms of people. They have come to the view that we barely use even ten percent of our minds; ninety percent is waiting to be opened up.

Dr. Frederic Tilney, foremost French brain specialist, believes, "We will, by conscious command, evolve cerebral centers which will permit us to use powers that we now are not even capable of imagining."

Dr. Jerome Bruner, Harvard University: "We are only now on the threshold of knowing the range of educability of man—the perfectibility of man. We have never addressed ourselves to this problem before."

Jack Schwarz, psycho-physical expert: "We are hoarding potentials so great that they are just about unimaginable."

Many thousands of people have successfully demonstrated remarkable reserves of memory. Satisfying your critical judgment as to whether you can personally benefit from superlearning is best done by trying it yourself. Skeptical members of commissions in Bulgaria found suggestopedia worked for them. Try a sample session and give yourself before and after tests to see if you are beginning to learn more easily and successfully.

2. THE INTUITIVE/EMOTIONAL BLOCK.

From previous experiences, particularly repeated failures, a person may have emotionally accepted a low evaluation of his or her ability to learn and consequently lacks confidence. Through the years, comments by parents, siblings, teachers, friends, and various authorities can bind a person to the idea that he isn't bright enough to do well, or that his ability lies in only one area. In early childhood for instance, a parent may have said repeatedly, "You certainly are hopeless at arithmetic." This negative suggestion may have been accepted at face value by an uncritical child who then proves it true. Math will then always be a bugbear. Failing marks, poor showing in job tests, seeming inability to keep up intellectually with friends— a variety of things can reinforce a person's feeling of insecurity about being able to learn. And, of course, this emotionally charged belief further reduces chances of learning.

Sometimes lack of confidence comes from circumstances— "I've been away from school now for years. I'll never be able to go back to learning."

Even people who seem to learn with ease sometimes have certain subjects that cause them anxiety.

The superlearning system has built-in elements to help you combat worry, tension, and anxiety. Once tension is out of the way, learning becomes easier because it isn't being blocked. Success builds on success, and soon you begin to develop confidence in your abilities to learn. Superlearning systems also regularly use affirmation as part of their training. Self-implanted, positive affirmations, properly done, will also help dissolve blocks and lack of confidence (see page 102).

3. THE ETHICAL/MORAL BLOCK.

Many people are conditioned to feel that learning has to be hard work, drudgery, and a bore. "You don't get something for nothing," is the rationale. Many also believe that learning through suffering, deprivation, and hard knocks is the way to build character. They are convinced that learning without a lot of strenuous effort breeds a pattern of laziness.

In actual fact, with superlearning, far from putting in no effort, you are really being superdiligent. You are making the most economical use of your body's energy resources. The body has its daily fuel supply from nutrients consumed. If a lot of body energy is wasted on tension, strain, and boredom, there is less energy left for actual learning. In learning to play the piano or to dive, the unnecessary movements are gradually omitted. Playing or diving soon *appears* effortless because every movement is productive.

So the appearance of effortlessness in superlearning comes from all elements being productive, economical, and efficient. "The birth of knowledge should be painless," says Dr. Lozanov.

The effort involved is pleasant, and because it is efficient, you learn more than with the same amount of effort used in the old way.

According to those who have used the technique at the University of Iowa, the most successful way to overcome all three mental blocks is by flooding them—by starting right off at the first session with as many as one hundred new words or phrases so that immediate results can be seen.

"The de-suggestive barriers are simply flooded as the student finds out in the first session that he is learning much more than he ever has before in his life," say teachers Schuster, Gritton, and Benitez-Bordon. "Once this occurs, a snowball effect happens: At the first session the student will be learning more easily than before, but not close to perfection. During the second and ensuing sessions, the students on the average find that they can learn the material with close to 100-percent retention. This is the snowball effect in operation."

It's really learning to learn. The Slavic researchers found that students' ability to learn increased substantially by the last day of a course.

Conscious-Unconscious Link

Another psychological aspect of suggestopedia involves something particularly fascinating about superlearning systems. By harmonizing altered states of consciousness, rhythms of recitation, breathing, and music, we spiral into the reserves of the mind. Once this connection is made, awareness follows. The sphere of conscious perception grows larger. "Through expanded awareness we can control and select the perceptions we want," says Lozanov. "We become *self*-developed."

Suggestology strives to create a link between conscious and unconscious. Not surprisingly, this is also the basis of Raja Yoga, "the science of creating a union or link between the conscious and subconscious mind, thus producing a third state which becomes Superconscious." (See John Mumford's *Psychosomatic Yoga.*)

"When I'm giving a speech in an auditorium," says Lozanov, "I don't know how many lights are in the ceiling. But if you put me under hypnosis and ask, I do know. Because my focus is on something else, these peripheral things are beyond the threshold of conscious attention. Nevertheless, I am constantly picking up this information."

Superlearning makes use in a positive way of the peripheral information that we are all always receiving. It also works toward setting up two-way traffic on the conscious-unconscious connection so we can retrieve what we perceive.

In a class we pick up a great deal of nonverbal information from the teacher and the surroundings. For example, the textbook itself gives us unconscious suggestions. The teacher might say, "Learn one chapter in the French text by tomorrow." Students might grumble but most would do it. If she said, "I want you to learn seven chapters by tomorrow," they would rebel. The book with its chapters has suggested "reasonable limits" to them. Suggestology texts are reorganized to suggest expanded abilities. Other things in the environment and the teacher's behavior are orchestrated to create a positive atmosphere that enhances learning.

There is also the specific thing you want to learn itself. This, too, is tailored for both levels of the mind, for conscious and unconscious simultaneously. For instance, historical data would be organized for the conscious mind; rhythms and intonations are organized to gain the attention of the unconscious mind.

"By putting conscious and unconscious stimuli together, we stimulate the personality globally," says Lozanov, ". . . the whole personality holistically . . . right and left brain simultaneously."

At the 1977 Iowa conference, the topic of brainwashing came up. In Dr. Lozanov's opinion, suggestopedia is a way of counteracting brainwashing and various subliminal techniques used to influence us, in America particularly by advertisers. Speed-learning enlarges the sphere of awareness. "It puts subconscious perceptions into communication with the conscious mind," he says. People become more aware of the underlying influences feeding into them.

Bulgarian students tested after rapid-learning courses showed they'd become *less* suggestible. Intellectual activity grew and with each course they took, tests showed they became steadily less suggestible and less likely to be taken in by misleading statements.

When people wish to influence us subliminally, says Lozanov, they want to affect us *without* our knowledge, *without* our agreement, *without* our conscious consent to be influenced.

As Wilson Key points out in *Subliminal Seduction,* an exposé of how the media manipulate your mind for your money, "Anything consciously perceived can be evaluated, criticized, discussed, argued, and possibly rejected, whereas unconsciously perceived information meets no resistance or qualification by the intellect."

Key reveals some of the subliminal cues advertisers imbed in their ads to draw us unconsciously to products: skulls in ice cubes in liquor ads; obscene words in ads for children's toys; sex patterns in various art work; sub-audible commands in TV ads to "Buy, Buy." It would be interesting to see if, after trying superlearning, people here could spot the subliminal ad influences coming at them.

Lozanov also maintains that to try to use his system to pump information into people against their will would not work. Students are fully alert throughout the course; they notice even minute changes in course content and in the way the material is recited. If they didn't they couldn't learn languages. Unconscious perceptions are made conscious so that the critical intellect is constantly operating.

Of course, for do-it-yourselfers, there could be no possible problem, because you have total control over every item used.

Joy in Learning

"Life should be a ceaseless stream of happiness," Lozanov once said. "[Yet] the lives of many people are full of fears . . . fear creates tensions and poisons the climate of one's life." Lozanov also often remarks that "many of us are victims of methods of education." It was, after all, in the hope of alleviating didactogenic disease that Lozanov took the plunge into education.

Joy in learning is another basic tenet of the superlearning systems. Perhaps this sense of exhilaration is one more norm we've forgotten. Very small children have this joy naturally; if they didn't they'd never learn to walk, talk, or feed themselves. But then, they get caught up in what Alan Watts called "the conspiracy against knowing who you are." Or as Wordsworth put it in nineteenth-century terms, "Shades of the prison-house begin to close upon the growing boy . . ."

Superlearning systems aim at the painless birth of knowledge, free of tension, worry, and boredom. You're told that trying too hard will only hamper ability. Because superlearning is stress-free, learning is genuinely a pleasure, not a problem. "Students from our earlier classes come back to the institute regularly to tell us it was the happiest time of their lives," Lozanov says. Perhaps it could be a lifelong approach. Amidst the staid statistics in reports on suggestopedia from many countries, the words "joy" and "liberating" and "freeing from constraints" keep turning up.

Chapter 7
How to Do Superlearning

If you want to increase your potential quotient and feel good while doing it, there are some simple techniques that can help you on your way. They've worked for countless others, they will work for you. No matter what you want to learn—from guitar playing to real-estate law—you'll do better if you know how to relax and how to accentuate your positive abilities. All of the superlearning systems in this book—mental, physical, intuitive —use altered states of consciousness to ease stress and open awareness. As *Inner Tennis* author Timothy Gallwey points out, "Achievement is the inevitable and natural by-product of awareness."

The following mini-relaxation course will help you with any learning program. The exercises are of particular importance if you want to strengthen your memory and accelerate factual learning. Take some time, a week at least, to practice and to feel at home with these exercises before starting your memory program. It will pay off in learning dividends.

To get in shape for supermemory, the preliminary exercises to practice are:

1) Relaxation (Exercise A *or* B) with Affirmations
2) Mind Calming
3) Joy of Learning Recall
4) Breathing to a Beat

We have put together the following exercise sequence drawing on research by the most successful users of superlearning techniques in Europe and North America.

Relaxation Exercise (A)

Read through the instructions a few times and note major points. Then silently repeat the instructions to yourself as you do the exercise. If you wish, you can tape instructions and play them to yourself as you exercise or you can have someone read them to you. The "Art of Learning" exercises are available on a 20-minute cassette tape from Superlearning Inc. (p. 321). Practice regularly. It may take a week or so to really familiarize yourself with these techniques before you go on to using them with learning programs. Gradually, you will find that you can shift mental gears and reach a relaxed state without having to go through a step-by-step process.

The relaxation exercises not only help free the body of tension but they are also a first step in setting up a communications link with the subconscious mind. Once you've set up this awareness link, you can erase tension at will. And that's an asset in every area of life. As one man said when he finally unwound for the first time in years, "I feel like I've come home to myself." Though exercises may seem long in print, they only take a few minutes in practice.

This relaxation technique is designed to help erase muscular tension from the body. The tensing sequences should not be done as strenuously as physical exercises. Before starting, it's helpful to do some stretching and very gentle neck rolls to improve circulation to the head. Drop chin to the chest and roll head in a full circle to the right and to the left.

Find a place that will be free from interruptions. Get comfortable in a chair or, if you prefer, lie down on a couch or on the floor. Loosen any clothing that may be too tight. Make yourself very, very comfortable. Think of your bones and muscles and feel the weight of them on the floor. With your eyes closed, take a slow, deep breath. Exhale. As you exhale, feel tension beginning to float away and tell yourself to relax. Take a second very slow, deep breath, and on exhaling feel tension being carried away on the out-breath. Relax. Take a third slow, even, deep breath. Exhale. Imagine tension leaving your muscles. Tell yourself to relax.

Now, tense up your toes as tightly as possible. Curl your toes as tightly as possible. Hold that taut, tense feeling in the toes as you slowly count from 1 to 5. Now, relax your toes. Relax them completely and feel the difference.

Now tense up your toes, feet, and the muscles in the lower part of the legs. Make those muscles very, very tense, but keep the rest of the body relaxed. Hold that feeling of tension to the slow count of 5. Now relax. Enjoy that feeling of release from tension.

Now tense up the muscles in the upper part of the legs as well as the muscles in the toes, feet, and lower legs. Make those muscles as tense as possible. A little bit tenser. Feel that tension with your body and mind as you slowly count from 1 to 5. Now relax. Feel those muscles unwinding and letting go, unwinding and letting go. Now tell those muscles to relax still more.

Now tense up the buttocks. Hold that tension to the slow count of 5. Now relax.

Tense up the muscles in the lower back and abdomen. Note how it feels to have your body all wound up with tension. Tense those muscles even more tightly as you slowly count from 1 to 5. Relax, unwind, let go, and relax. Let the tension drain out of every muscle. Let go of all your weight. Tell your body to relax those muscles a little bit more. Note what this sensation of relaxation is like.

Now tense up the muscles in the upper part of the torso.

Hunch up both shoulders. Tense up the muscles in the chest and back. Make those muscles even tenser. Really feel that tension to the slow count of 5 . . . and relax. Exhale and feel all those muscles in your chest and back relaxing. Feel all those muscles relaxing, unwinding, letting go. Feel all the tightness and tension disappearing. Let those muscles relax a little bit more.

Now tense up your arms and clench both fists. Really feel that tension, as you slowly count from 1 to 5. Now relax. Let your arms flop to your sides. Enjoy the release from tension.

Next squinch up all the muscles of your face. Tense every muscle in the face that you can. Tense your jaws. Clench your teeth, tighten your scalp, squint your eyes. Hold it as you count from 1 to 5, then relax. Smooth out all the muscles of the forehead, relax your scalp, relax your eyes, relax your mouth, tongue, and throat. Remove all the strain and tension. Relax all your facial muscles. Really feel the difference.

Now tense up every muscle in the entire body. Start with your toes, work up to your legs, the abdomen and back, chest and shoulders, arms and fists, neck and face. Be as tense as you can. Clench every muscle in the entire body. Hold that tension as you slowly count from 1 to 5. Now relax. Let it go. Relax. Unwind. Let go. Feel the pleasant relaxing feeling spreading over your entire body—a comfortable, pleasant sensation of relaxation. Note how it feels to be completely relaxed. With your mind's eye, mentally scan your body from head to toe. If there is any muscle that is not relaxed, tense it, hold it, then relax it. Your body is now completely relaxed.

Let the pleasant sensation of relaxation flow through you from head to toes and back up again. Really enjoy it. Notice how complete relaxation feels. Waves of relaxation flow freely from head to toe and back up again. Enjoy this feeling. While you relax now, you can give yourself some of the learning and memory affirmations (see page 102).

Now tell yourself that after you count from 1 to 5, you are going to open your eyes. And when you do, you are going to feel alert, refreshed, energized, and free of tension . . . 1,2,3,4,5, open your eyes.

Each time you practice relaxing, it will be easier and faster for you. You will find that you will be able to shift very quickly into a relaxed state in which muscle tension drains away. The more you practice, the more easily you will relax. A few minutes of relaxation helps to relieve tension and fatigue and helps the mind stay alert, active, and better able to concentrate.

RELAXATION—CONDENSED VERSION

A condensed version of the preceding can be done by tensing up each of the muscle groups mentioned from toes to head, one by one, until the entire body from toe to head is tensed. Hold the tension for a couple of seconds, then let a wave of relaxation run down the body in reverse order from head to toe. Two or three cycles of this wave of tension and relaxation can be done to a slow count of 15.

Psychological Relaxation (B)

Many people find it's easier to relax through mental imagery rather than with physical tensing and relaxing, (progressive relaxation). In that case, this exercise can be used instead. Read it through for the gist, and then take yourself through it, or tape it.

Make yourself as comfortable as you can. Sit in a chair or lie down on a couch or the floor. Loosen any tight clothing. Make yourself very comfortable.

"I close my eyes and take several slow, deep, even breaths. As I breathe easily and deeply, I project myself to the seventh floor of a building. The walls are painted a vivid, warm red color. I walk down this red hallway to the end where I arrive at the top of an escalator marked "down." It is a very special silver-colored escalator. It is a smooth, noiseless, completely secure and dependable escalator. I step on and feel myself beginning to glide down. I have my hands on the rails and I am descending without any sound, very slowly . . . very safely . . . very securely. I am descending on a very relaxing journey to the main inner level, where I know I can make connections. I continue to ride down feeling myself unwinding and relaxing . . . unwinding and relaxing.

"I take a deep breath. As I exhale, I repeat "7" several times. I visualize this large number 7 standing out against the vivid red walls of the seventh floor. Red color seems to float past me as I continue my relaxing ride down. I have now reached the sixth floor. I get off the escalator and I see 6 printed on the bright orange walls of the sixth floor. Surrounded by this bright orange color I walk to the top of the next "down" escalator. I step on and again glide slowly downward.

"I take a deep breath and as I exhale, I repeat "6" several times and clearly see the pleasant orange walls all around. I feel myself unwinding and relaxing as I smoothly ride down to a still more restful and pleasant area. I have now reached the fifth floor. I see the fifth-floor sign and notice the walls are a very delightful golden-yellow color. I get off the escalator and walk through this corridor of yellow to the next "down" escalator. I take a deep breath and, while exhaling, I visualize the number 5. I mentally repeat "5" several times, while enjoying this beautiful, joyous golden-yellow color. I get on the next escalator and continue to float downward. I feel very comfortable, very easy as I let myself go and simply enjoy the colors. I see the fourth-floor sign and notice the walls are a restful, lush, grassy green. I get off the escalator on the fourth floor and walk through this clear emerald-green color to the next escalator.

"I take a deep breath and while exhaling I visualize the number 4. I mentally repeat "4" several times. I enjoy the clear, rich green all around me, as I step on the next escalator and glide calmly downward through the wonderful green to a still more pleasant and relaxing area. I reach the third-floor sign and see the walls of this floor are a beautiful blue color. I feel myself saturated with this peaceful, calm blue. I feel myself surrounded with blue. I pause for several moments on the third floor and I visualize a quiet scene from nature—a favorite place where I felt that I was the most relaxed . . . a blue lake or a calm blue ocean or fields or mountains spanned by a broad blue sky. I feel again the same sense of harmony, of deep relaxation I felt then. I enjoy the flowing blue color all around me and feel a very pleasant, very restful, very relaxing sensation.

"I take a deep breath and while exhaling I visualize the number 3. I mentally repeat "3" several times. I step on the next "down" escalator and begin once more to glide downward smoothly and easily to a still more pleasant, relaxing area of soft and restful color.

"I see the second-floor sign and I see that the walls on this floor are a rich, vibrant purple color. I get off the escalator. I take a deep breath and while exhaling I visualize the number 2. I mentally repeat "2" several times. I sense this rich purple all around me and I feel wonderfully comfortable and relaxed. I move through this purple, on to the next "down" escalator, descending through the deep purple to a still more pleasant and relaxing area of color. I see the sign "first floor" and notice that the main floor is a luminous ultraviolet color. The escalator glides softly downward and I get off on the first floor.

"I take a deep breath and while exhaling I visualize the number 1 and repeat "1" several times. I enjoy the luminous ultraviolet color all around me. I have now reached a very, very relaxed state. I feel very rested, healthy, and relaxed. I am now at my main inner level. At this level I can easily connect with other areas of awareness in my mind. I continue to rest and enjoy complete relaxation and to breathe deeply. For a minute or so I am completely relaxed." (Pause.)

(While you are relaxed, this is an ideal time to repeat some positive affirmations to yourself.)*

"To leave this main inner level, I count from 1 to 3. On the

*Autogenic training is probably the most thorough method for achieving relaxation. Once mastered it can allow you to relax whenever you want, wherever you are. If you're interested, see page 163.

count of 3, I open my eyes and feel alert, centered, refreshed, and free from all tensions."

Affirming Learning

When you reach a state of relaxation through either of the preceding methods, just before opening your eyes, try affirming your own abilities. Affirmations can be beneficial any time, but they will be most effective in this serene, relaxed state.

Choose a couple of the following phrases. You can also create some to fit your own circumstances. Try to make them short and rhythmic, use alliteration and rhyme if it appeals to you. Silently repeat your affirmations to yourself with meaning four or five times.

I can do it
Now I am achieving my goals
Learning is something I hugely enjoy
Learning and remembering are easy for me
My mind moves efficiently, effectively
I am supremely calm

Before an exam:

I recognize the right answers at the right time
I remember all I need to know
I am supremely calm and confident
My memory is alert, my mind is powerful

Visualizations for Mind Calming

The objective of this exercise is to gain practice in visualizing while at the same time soothing the mind. Calm and peaceful scenes from nature have been found especially helpful in erasing worries and distractions. You can imagine a walk in a park or a woods, sitting by a lake, a walk on a hill or mountain, a winter countryside, a beach in the summer, or any spot you know that has a particularly soothing quality for you. Some people also imagine works of art or a museum for this exercise. Here's a sample. Relax by your preferred method, then:

Visualize yourself on a beautiful beach.

Feel the warmth of the sun.

Walk along the beach and down to the edge of the water.

Feel the warm sand under your feet and the fine sand trickling between your toes as you walk.

Savor the blue of the sky and the blue of the water.

As you walk along the edge of the water feel the waves gently lapping around your ankles.

Feel a light breeze blowing and feel cares and worries gently drifting away.

In the distance, you can hear the seagulls calling to each other.

See the sparkling pattern of the sun on the water.

Enjoy this scene as much as possible. When you get ready to begin a superlearning session, take a few seconds and imagine yourself in this calm place in order to soothe the mind and release you from distracting worries, cares, and pressures.

Additional visualization exercises are in the Exercises (page 261).

Note: To avoid monotony, mind-calming exercises can be varied from day to day. Aside from additional mind-calming techniques in the Exercise Section, mind calming can also be done with records such as *The Environment* series or relaxation records such as *Spectrum Suite* (Halpern—Spectrum Research Institute, Palo Alto, CA.).

Joy of Learning Recall

In setting up links between conscious and unconscious, you have to help your mental messages get delivered to the inner mind so that your instructions are carried out. Just telling yourself "I learn easily. I remember perfectly," isn't enough to mobilize your memory to actually perform these things. In communicating with the inner mind, the "courier" that helps deliver the message is emotion.

Return to some time in your life when you really felt good about a learning success. Recall some experience when you got a kick out of learning or a moment when your memory really came through for you. It can be recent or a long time ago. It can be recalling that sense of triumph you had when you remembered a key word that solved a tough crossword puzzle, enjoyed learning something from a movie or a TV program, discovered something fascinating and exciting in a book, memorized a script; or it can be a childhood experience—the day you first rode a bike, or a time in school or college when you felt excited and pleased about something you learned, or achieved.

Recapture the feeling of that successful experience. Feel the details of that pleasant learning experience as completely as possible. Imagine yourself in that situation again. See exactly where you were. Were there other people there? How did your body feel? Take a look at how your head felt, how your hands felt, how your stomach felt. Recall your thoughts and attitudes. Savor the sense of eagerness and excitement you had about learning. Feel the pleasure of sensing your mind and memory functioning with ease. Hold onto that special feeling and let it flow through you when you relax during a superlearning session.

Breathing to a Beat

The objective of this exercise is to learn to breathe in rhythm, and through rhythmic breath control, to slow down body/mind rhythms.

Sit comfortably in a chair or lie down on a couch or bed. Put yourself into a very relaxed state. Make sure all parts of your body are relaxed. Close your eyes and take a very slow, deep breath through your nose. Inhale as much air as you can hold comfortably. Try to take in just a little bit more air. Now exhale slowly. Feel a deep sense of relaxation as you exhale. When you think all the air is out of your lungs, try to force out a little bit more. Practice taking these very deep breaths for a few moments. Inhale as much air as you possibly can. Distend your abdomen. Slowly exhale. Pull your abdomen in. Take another deep breath, as much air as possible. Hold it for a count of 3, and exhale very slowly. Relax. Try to inhale the air in a very even, continuous breath.

Now, try to make your breathing rhythmic. Inhale to a count of 4; hold to a count of 4; exhale to a count of 4; pause to a count of 4.

Inhale—2, 3, 4;
Hold—2, 3, 4;
Exhale—2, 3, 4;
Pause—2, 3, 4.

Repeat four cadences of this rhythmic pattern. Relax.
This time, try to slow down your cadenced breathing even more, by trying a count of 6.

Inhale—2, 3, 4, 5, 6;
Hold—2, 3, 4, 5, 6;
Exhale—2, 3, 4, 5, 6;
Pause—2, 3, 4, 5, 6.
Repeat four cadences.

Now try to slow down your cadenced breathing even more by using a count of 8.

Inhale—2, 3, 4, 5, 6, 7, 8;
Hold—2, 3, 4, 5, 6, 7, 8;
Exhale—2, 3, 4, 5, 6, 7, 8;
Pause—2, 3, 4, 5, 6, 7, 8.

Repeat four cadences of this rhythmic breathing pattern.

This breathing-control exercise can be done daily. It is said to help resynchronize out-of-synch body/mind processes and to slow down body/mind rhythms. It is also said to enhance the supply of prana, or life force, in the body.

Note: Several cadences of this breathing exercise should be done before a superlearning session to help slow down body/ mind rhythms to their most efficient levels.

Learning in a Supermemory Session

If you have done the preceding exercises, you now know how to bring yourself into the harmonized state of body and mind conducive to learning. There is only one other thing you need to know if you want to try memory expansion. Synchronizing breathing to the material spoken during a session helps develop memory control.

SYNCHRONIZING YOUR BREATHING

This is very easy to do. During the four seconds *when the material is being spoken, hold your breath.* During the four-second pause that follows, breathe out and in and be ready to hold your breath again when the next phrase is spoken. You don't have to think about it—just remember: always hold your breath when the material is spoken for a count of four.

spoken phrase—4 sec.	pause—4 sec.
la maison—house—la maison	——
hold breath 1, 2, 3, 4	exhale 1, 2 / inhale 1, 2

All the material spoken is precisely timed on an 8-second cycle so your breathing will naturally fall into a rhythmic pattern of:

hold 4; out 2; in 2.

(Before your first supermemory session, it's helpful to try a few practice run-throughs of this rhythmic breathing pattern. Hold your breath for a count of four; exhale for a count of two; inhale for a count of two, and so on.)

THE MEMORY SESSION

Before beginning the supermemory session, it is important to go over the material you wish to learn and review it as vividly as possible. You can even try going over it as a game, play, or dialogue. For the session itself, you need only a tape recorder (either cassette or reel-to-reel), and/or someone to read your material aloud to you.

Supermemory sessions are in two parts. First you silently read along with the material recited to you. In the second part you close your eyes and listen to the same material recited again, this time with music behind it. (For how to script or pretape material that you want to learn, see Chapter 8.)

Before beginning part one, do your relaxation exercises. Take five minutes or so. Affirm your power to learn. For a moment see yourself in some favorite outdoor spot, begin to feel welling up in you that light, satisfying feeling that comes when you learn something successfully. Take a few deep breaths. Then begin part one. Turn on your supermemory tape or have someone read your material to you.

PART ONE—WITHOUT MUSIC

There are only two things you have to do. Silently read the material as a voice recites it rhythmically. Second, try to breathe in rhythm on the eight-beat cycle. As you'll hear, the teaching voice pauses for four seconds, then recites the information during the next four seconds, then pauses four seconds and so on. Breathe out and in during the silence. *Hold your breath for the four seconds when material is being delivered.* That's all you have to do.

Let's say it takes fifteen minutes to run through the material once. In fifteen minutes you can imbibe as much as eighty to one hundred new bits of information. Most people begin with forty to fifty new things.

PART TWO—WITH MUSIC

Immediately after running through the material once, put down your paper, dim the lights, lean back, and close your eyes. Listen to the same material recited again, but this time *with music.* Pay attention to what is being said. Breathe along with the recitation—breathing out and in during the silences, easily *holding your breath as the information is delivered.* As you begin to feel comfortable with the technique, try visualizing the material to further hook your memory. But don't strain and don't try too hard. Just *listen* to the words and *breathe*, and review images of the material.

AFTERWARD

Most people give themselves a short quiz after the session. Think of this as a feedback device, helping you keep on course. Any items missed can be added to your next program. It's important to try to *use* the new material you've learned within the next few days, to really make it yours. Remember superlearning has a snowballing effect. Don't give up before trying the system for several days at least. The process of learning to learn, like any skill, tends to improve and become easier and faster. You should be able to learn more in the seventh session, for instance, than you did in the first. And too, as people from Sofia to San Francisco found out, you often don't realize you are learning.

Once you've learned to learn, you will probably find that you don't need to listen to a lesson for more than a few repetitions.

Unlike other forms of learning, the superlearning process is beneficial all by itself. You get health benefits and tension relief just by relaxing and listening to the music program.

Some people who have done these supermemory sessions over a period of months or a year or so have found themselves developing semi-photographic-memory ability, so that they only have to glance at a page of a book in order to learn it.

Chapter 8
Preparing Your Own Program

Just as you can prepare your own program of material for sleep-learning, you can do the same for a supermemory session. You simply tape yourself reading the material aloud over the music at the required slow-paced intervals. Just as you play your sleep tape later, when you are relaxing into the "reverie" phase of sleep, you play your supermemory tape to yourself later, when you are in a "reverie" state of mental relaxation. (Of course, reading the material aloud to the tape recorder is not the supermemory session.)

As an alternative to taping, you can work with a friend or relative. After you do the mental relaxation techniques to get into an altered state (slowed down mind/body rhythms) and you're breathing rhythmically, you can have a friend read the material aloud over the music at the required slow-paced intervals.

All you have to do to prepare your own supermemory program is: record a few minutes of the specified music; tape yourself reading aloud at the required slow-paced intervals over the music.

The material you choose to memorize can be any type of factual data.

The first step is to record some of the music. Some people find listening to a tape of this music is such a restful and centering experience that they like to listen to it just on its own. "It's as comforting as curling up in front of a crackling fire on a winter evening," one person told us.

How to Make a Music Tape

If you're learning on your own, you have to put together fifteen to twenty minutes of the right kind of "music to remember by."

Once you have a tape you'll be able to use it over and over again as you learn different material. To make your own tape, choose from the music selections listed, or similar ones.

Each selection has a slow, restful tempo of about sixty beats to the minute and is generally in ¼ or ¾ time. These selections are usually brief, averaging about two to four minutes, so you may need as many as six or seven of them. The same short selection can also be taped more than once. For some variety in your concert tape, choose selections featuring different instruments (violin, harpsichord, flute, mandolin, guitar) and different keys, major and minor. This slow, stately music is used in superlearning to maintain a state of relaxed concentration. For the last two minutes of the tape, add a couple of minutes of faster, peppier music—allegro movements—to aid the transition back from the relaxed state. You may want to make several music tapes for use on different days. Tape at *low volume* so the music won't overpower the text you'll be reading over it.

To aid in pacing your four-second time frames you can tap with a wooden stick every four seconds while recording.

(To make the music part easy, a special music tape is available from Superlearning Corp., Suite 500, 450 Seventh Avenue, New York, N.Y. 10123. See page 321 for details.)

MUSIC LIST

Bach, J.S.
—Largo from Concerto in G Minor for Flute and Strings, BWV 1056 (2:53)
Bach and Telemann Flute Concertos
Jean-Pierre Rampal, Saar Radio Chamber Orchestra, Odyssey—Columbia Records.
—Aria (or Sarabande) to *The Goldberg Variations,* BWV 988
Millicent Silver, harpsichord, Saga Records.
—Largo from Harpsichord Concerto in F Minor, BWV 1056 (2:40)
Greatest Hits of 1720
Judith Norell, harpsichord, Philharmonia Virtuosi of New York, Columbia Records.
—Largo from Solo Harpsichord Concerto in G Minor, BWV 975
6 Concerti after Vivaldi
Janos Sebestyen, harpsichord, Turnabout, Vox Records.
—Largo from Solo Harpsichord Concerto in C Major, BWV 976
6 Concerti after Vivaldi
Janos Sebestyen, harpsichord, Turnabout, Vox Records.
—Largo from Solo Harpsichord Concerto in F Major, BWV 978

Corelli, A.
—Sarabanda (largo) from Concerto no. 7 in D Minor
Corelli: 12 Concerti Grossi op. 5
(violin, cello, and harpsichord)
Gli Accademici di Milano, Vox Records.

—Preludio (largo) and Sarabanda (largo) from Concerto no. 8 in E Minor
Corelli: 12 Concerti Grossi op. 5
Gli Accademici di Milano, Vox Records.
—Preludio (largo) from Concerto no. 9 in A Major
—Sarabanda (largo) from Concerto no. 10 in F Major
both from *Corelli: 12 Concerti Grossi op. 5*
Vox Records.
From Corelli's *Twelve Concerti Grossi, Opus 6,* any of the largo movements can be used.

Handel, G.F.
—Largo from Concerto no. 1 in F (brass)
from *Music for the Royal Fireworks*
London Symphony Orchestra, Angel Records.
—Largo from Concerto no. 3 in D (brass)
from *Music for the Royal Fireworks*
London Symphony Orchestra, Angel Records.
—Largo from Concerto no. 1 in B-flat Major op. 3
(woodwinds and strings)
Handel: Concerti Grossi op. 3
Mainz Chamber Orchestra, Turnabout, Vox Records.
From Handel's *Twelve Concerti Grossi, Opus 6,* any of the largo movements can be used.

Telemann, G.
—Largo from Double Fantasia in G Major for Harpsichord
Telemann: 6 Fantasias for Harpsichord
Leonard Hokanson, harpsichord, World Series: Philips.
—Largo from Concerto in G Major for Viola and String Orchestra
from *Telemann*
Wurttemberg Chamber Orchestra, Turnabout, Vox Records.

Vivaldi, A.
—Largo from "Winter"
from *The Four Seasons*

Lola Bobesco, violin, The Heidelberg Chamber Orchestra, Peerless Records.
—Largo from Concerto in D Major for Guitar and Strings from *Baroque Guitar Concerti*
Konrad Ragossnig, guitar; and the Southwest German Chamber Orchestra, Turnabout, Vox Records.
—Largo from Concerto in C Major for Mandolin, Strings and Harpsichord, P. 134 (1:55)
—Largo from Concerto in D Minor for Viola D'Amore, Strings and Harpsichord, P. 288 (2:15)
—Largo from Concerto in F Major for Viola D'Amore, Two Oboes, Bassoon, Two Horns and Figured Bass, P. 286 (4:27) from *Vivaldi: Three Concertos for Viola D'Amore, Two Concertos for Mandolin*
The New York Sinfonietta, Odyssey Records.
—Largo from Flute Concerto No. 4 in G Major
Vivaldi: 6 Flute Concerti Opus 10
Jean-Pierre Rampal, flute, Louis de Froment Chamber Ensemble, Turnabout, Vox Records.

Tips on the Music

People have asked a great many questions about the music, so we will try to give extra details. Do the music selections have to be played by specific performers or orchestras such as those given in the list? Generally, no. The music performance can be by any good orchestra. Most music libraries and music stores have the Schwann Catalog which lists under the composer's name the various musical compositions written, the different orchestras or performers that have recorded them, and on which label. Concertos by various Baroque composers can be used.

In choosing a recording of a slow movement, simply check that the tempo is about 60 beats a minute. When a composer writes a piece of music, he indicates the speed at which he wants each of the different movements or segments to be played. These indications of tempo are generally always given in Italian. (You will often see them on the different movements of a concerto.) For instance, allegro indicates a tempo of around 120 to 168 beats to the minute, andante around 76 to 108, adagio from around 66 to 76, larghetto 60 to 66, and largo, 40 to 60 beats to the minute. Some performers and conductors may set a tempo somewhat faster or slower than what the composer indicated. To check out the tempo of a recording to be sure it's at around sixty beats a minute you can check it with a metronome or against a clock with a second hand.

If you play a musical instrument yourself such as the piano, organ, or classical guitar, you can record some of the appropriate selections yourself at the desired sixty beats a minute tempo.

Can the music be substituted? No. Don't substitute the *type* of music. The choice of the music has nothing to do with personal tastes in music. It is not background music like Muzak. This particular Baroque music is like a mantra and is used to evoke a specific psycho-physical state of relaxed concentration.

East-German researchers of suggestopedia at Karl Marx University in Leipzig (who have reported extraordinary success with the method) observed that slow movements from Baroque instrumental music featuring *string* instruments gave the very best results. Vocal music or chants were ruled out because the lyrics compete with the text to be learned. Music with a slow, constant, monotonous rhythm, a non-distracting melodic structure (not the hum-along kind), and harmonic patterns based on specific ratios, has so far given the best results.

Much more physiological research is needed in America to check out additional music that would be suitable, including the music from Asia, the Orient, India, and the Middle East. (The Indian vilambita, for instance, has the required rhythm of sixty beats a minute.) The psycho-physical effects of different rhythms, time signatures, and harmonic structures determine the usefulness of a composition for relaxed concentration. For the time being, it's better to stick to the music that's been tested so far.

In Bulgaria, special music has been composed to meet these requirements, specifically designed to enhance learning with this system. This could be done in the West too.

In general, in choosing music to use for superlearning, look for adagio, larghetto, or largo movements from concertos by Baroque composers and check for a rhythm of sixty beats a minute. Other compositions, that is, suites or variations, may also have the same rhythm. The time signature should be ¼ (four beats to the bar) to fit the cadenced breathing and recitation pattern. Providing you always use a timer to pace reading aloud, ¾ time can also be used.

(Most commonly, music uses two, three, or four beats to the bar. The time signature is written like a fraction—that is, ¾, ¼, or ²⁄₂. The top number gives the number of beats to the bar. The bottom number tells the duration of the sound of the note. ¼ would mean four beats made up of four quarter notes. ¾ means three beats of three quarter notes. ²⁄₂ means two beats of two half notes.)

Should you have any questions about various selections or about identifying the right part on a record, consult a music librarian or music teacher. (Some people have inadvertently taped fast movements from concertos and found themselves panting along at triple speed.)

What Kind of Things to Use Supermemory For

You can tackle the factual body of any subject. Superlearning is particularly helpful with the basics. Furthermore, it will help you learn such studies as anatomy, geography, history, or biology, in which you need to remember unfamiliar words and names. Of course, it is ready-made for languages.

Superlearning can help you with more than academic

facts. Think about your work or hobbies. You can memorize price lists, radar manuals, stock ticker symbols, technical terms, business phone numbers. If you're a bird-watcher, you can memorize descriptions of various birds. If you're a sport, memorize the odds for different moves in specific gambling situations.

You can remember what vitamins do what and where they're found. Or memorize speeches and Bible verses. Or you could try astrological or astronomical tables. If sports or trivia collecting is your interest, you've got your work cut out for you. You might start on the *Guinness Book of World Records*—and make a record of your own.

READING ALOUD

Superlearning uses an eight-second cycle for pacing out spoken data at slow intervals.

Think of the eight-second cycle as two bars of four beats or two frames of four seconds each. Each beat is one second.

$$1 \quad 2 \quad 3 \quad 4 \quad | \quad 1 \quad 2 \quad 3 \quad 4$$

You recite the bits of information within this eight-second cycle. *You do not have to recite in time to the beats* of music or metronome. You simply have to pace what you want to say into a certain space of time.

For example, to make it easy, let's say you are going to do the multiplication tables. Use a clock or preferably a metronome or other sort of time clicker. The beats are one per second. During the first four beats of the cycle you remain silent. During the next four beats you say the data.

We've found that a "timer tape" is a big help when pacing material. Simply record a tape of timed clicks—one click every four seconds. Play the timer tape so you know when to read aloud and when to be silent.

1	2	3	4	1	2	3	4
	silence				$2 \times 2 = 4$		
	silence				$2 \times 3 = 6$		
	silence				$2 \times 4 = 8$		
	silence				$2 \times 5 = 10$		

Or, for French vocabulary, for instance:

1	2	3	4	1	2	3	4
	silence				rabbit, *le lapin*		
	silence				bed, *le lit*		
	silence				book, *le livre*		

Again, you do *not* recite in time to the beats, you simply try to fit what you have to say into a time frame of four seconds. If you have only a couple of words to say, you can speak slowly. When there's more material, you speak more quickly. You'll find that without sounding like Donald Duck, you can get quite a bit of information into four seconds. You can think of this as being like cheerleading—Two, four, six, eight—then say what you have to say. Or you could think of it as speaking on an answer-phone. When the click sounds beginning the second frame of the cycle, you speak.

That simple old way of counting seconds, "One potato, two potatoes, three potatoes, four potatoes," gives an idea of how many words fit into four seconds. If you speak rapidly, more words can fit in. (See the language manual page for an example.)

INTONATION

The Bulgarians found that to keep the mind interested it helps to vary the tone of your voice as you go through cycle after cycle of information. They use three tones of voice: normal speaking voice, soft whispering voice, loud commanding voice. These three repeat over and over.

1 2 3 4	1 2 3 4	Voice Tone
silence	$2 \times 6 = 12$	normal
silence	$2 \times 7 = 14$	soft
silence	$2 \times 8 = 16$	loud
silence	$2 \times 9 = 18$	normal

Or for French vocabulary:

silence	to plot, *machiner*	normal
silence	a store, *un magasin*	soft
silence	to eat, *manger*	loud

If you use intonation, check your material off ahead of time in sets of three so you can easily go through the normal, soft, loud tones as you recite. (Don't try to make your tone fit with the sense, it's not supposed to.) Some people have done superlearning successfully without intonation. It seems to be an optional component. But remember, the more components you use, the greater the learning.

This is the basic superlearning cycle. It takes a little practice to recite easily to the eight-beat cycle. But here again, you'll soon find your sense of timing becomes fairly automatic. You'll be reciting easily to the clicking of the timer. In superlearning courses, when they've become accustomed to the method, people usually learn between 50 to 150 new bits of information per session. At that rate, one could learn the basic multiplication tables in a session or two.

You can learn factual material at any level of difficulty and you can learn any spoken language with this method. For example, you might want to learn the periodic table of the elements. You could block it out for superlearning by giving the atomic number, the name, the symbol.

1 2 3 4	1 2 3 4	Voice Tone
silence	one...hydrogen...H	normal
silence	two...helium...HE	soft
silence	three...lithium...LI	loud
silence	four...berylium...BE	normal
silence	five...boron...B	soft
silence	six...carbon...C	loud

Perhaps you're a movie buff and you'd like to remember Oscar winners. For the Best Actor you could block it out this way: year, actor, movie he played in.

1 2 3 4	1 2 3 4	Voice Tone
silence	70...John Wayne...*True Grit*	normal
silence	71...George C. Scott...*Patton*	soft
silence	72...Gene Hackman...*French Connection*	loud
silence	73...Marlon Brando...*Godfather*	normal
silence	74...Jack Lemmon...*Save the Tiger*	soft
silence	75...Art Carney...*Harry and Tonto*	loud

LONGER MATERIAL

In Bulgaria, when longer material is being learned, they often use the last two beats of the first frame. The key material to be learned is kept in the second frame. You might want to use this for learning foreign phrases. The English would be said fairly quickly during the third and fourth beat of the first frame.

1	2	3	4	1	2	3	4	Voice Tone
silence		I'm sorry I'm late		Je regrette d'être en retard				normal
silence		ninety-eight		Quatre-vingt-dix-huit				soft
silence		I'm hungry already!		J'ai déjà faim!				loud

If you're interested in art history, you might want to remember sculptors and their principal works. Say the name of the artist, the name of the work, plus a short description.

1	2	3	4	1	2	3	4	Voice Tone
silence		Lorenzo Ghiberti		Bronze doors, baptistery at Florence				normal
silence		Michelangelo		David, standing nude poised for action				soft
silence		Benvenuto Cellini		Perseus, holding Medusa's severed head				loud

Bulgarian researchers found that, in studying languages, vocabulary material presented in short sentences was learned much easier than in long chunks. But, for learning rules, principles in math, long definitions, or propositions, it is better *not* to cut the thought or concept into short fragments. People memorized long definitions more easily when the complete thought was put into a very long sentence and simply read over the music taking as many beats as needed.

THE TWELVE-BEAT CYCLE

In America a twelve-beat cycle has also been used with success. This is simply three frames of four seconds each. Eventually, you might want to experiment with it. To teach spelling and vocabulary you could block it out like this.

1 2 3 4	1 2 3 4	1 2 3 4
dyslexia	d-y-s-l-e-x-i-a (spell out the word)	impaired ability to read or write
fulsome	f-u-l-s-o-m-e	excessive, insincere
taxonomy	t-a-x-o-n-o-m-y	the science of classification

Or, a lot of us would like to be able to read foreign menus. You might block out the general food category, the name, and a short description. For example, a Chinese dish

1 2 3 4	1 2 3 4	1 2 3 4
chicken and vegetables	Moo Goo Guy Kew	Chicken balls fried in batter

However, if you give it some thought, you'll find you can fit most of the things you want to learn into the eight cycle. (Note: If using the twelve-beat cycle, the breathing pattern is: inhale 4 counts; hold 4 counts; exhale 4 counts.)

WHEN YOU KNOW HOW TO READ ALOUD

Once you know how to recite to the eight-beat cycle, reading aloud is simple. Use a clock or start the metronome clicking and read through your cycles of information. Use intonation if at all possible. Do ten to fifteen minutes worth of material.

Stop, then do the same thing again, only this time have your slow Baroque music playing at *low* volume. Keeping to your eight-second cycle, just read over the music. If possible, try to begin the first beat of your cycle with the first beat of the music —or with an accented musical beat. Don't worry about it too much. Be sure you are clearly audible over the music.

If you're learning alone, tape your information on a thirty-minute cassette. Recite the material through once, then recite it again with music. Store your tape until you're ready to get into a "reverie-like" mentally relaxed state to listen to it.

Alternatively, instead of reading the data aloud a second time with the music, when you're ready to listen to it, just use two tape recorders. Play the music tape on one and the data tape on the other. There's no need to synchronize data and music beats precisely. (The music will change tempo from time to time.)

If you're learning with another person and it's your turn to read aloud just go through the material: (a) recitation, and (b) recitation with music.

The twelve-beat cycle is done in the same way, recite once without and once with music.

ORGANIZING COURSE MATERIAL

Here's how a sequence of several phrases would be paced on the eight-second cycle. This is from an English-language course manual for Bulgarians.

A. 2 seconds	B. 2 seconds	C. 4 seconds	
Pause	Bulgarian translation	English phrase	Intonation
	"	"There is a gramophone with records."	normal, businesslike tone

"	"There are no chairs in the classroom, are there? "	whisper, conspiratorial tone
"	"No, there are only armchairs here."	loud, commanding tone
"	"Are there any desks?"	normal
"	"No, there is a square table."	whisper
"	"There's a blackboard on the wall."	loud

(Note: In the original procedure in Bulgaria, only the material to be learned was intoned, and not its translation.)

On average, a maximum of nine short words fit the four-second time frame. You can split your material into fragments of nine words or fewer. People find vocabulary lists really lend themselves to the superlearning setup.

On the eight-second cycle, you can cover seven and a half data units (phrases or words) per minute. One hundred words take around thirteen minutes. A session lasting twenty minutes is generally recommended.

A twenty-minute music tape (the length most widely used) might work out like this:
four minutes of introductory music
thirteen minutes (one hundred cycles of eight seconds)
three minutes of fast music to end the concert session

Fifty vocabulary words can be covered in around six and one half minutes. Eighty words take about ten minutes.

Tourists' foreign-language phrase books have material organized into brief phrases and can easily be adapted for superlearning. Other course materials that are readily adaptable are those prepared for another rapid-learning system, sleep-learning. (Sleep-Learning Research Association, Olympia, Washington.)

Room to Explore

As you begin to explore superlearning, many fascinating things come to light about the way all the different elements work together to produce supermemory and enhanced mental abilities. As you discover what each of the different variables can do for you, you can tune them to your individual requirements for better performance, rather than slavishly repeating a whole ritual.

You may find, for instance, that a specific element, such as doing breathing exercises beforehand, greatly improves your performance; or that more attention to relaxation gives you even better results; or that affirmations for better learning can do a lot for you. Playing the music again during the quiz may aid recall.

Iowa researchers Schuster and Benitez-Bordon have tried to examine the different components separately to see what they do for immediate and long-term memory. They found that affirmations for better learning gave a sixty percent boost to performance. Synchronizing breathing to slow-paced data read over the music gave a seventy-eight percent immediate improvement. Groups given all the elements in one smoothly orchestrated whole got a 141 percent improvement. The elements all interact cumulatively, they report.

Doug Shaffer found in his explorations that the synchronized breathing seemed absolutely key to getting the very best results. At the same time, Georgia researchers noticed that many young children didn't quite catch onto the breathing pattern, but that a good relaxation response could make up for it.

The more of the elements you are able to use, the better the results.

Much more research is needed to explore the psycho-physical effects of various components of the system—various kinds of music; different rhythmic cycles for verbal repetition and breathing; different music time signatures; the relation of rhythmic breathing to memory, brain oxidation, and learning; and so forth.

Few in the West have explored the outer limits of the system's potential for supermemory—the possibilities for very large programs in one day. Could the system even work on a dual-channel basis, for instance, doing two languages at once?

In education so far in the United States rapid learning has been used mainly in urgent areas—to help people reach basic standards.

Work needs to be done to see what the full potential of the method is. Gifted children are often neglected in our system. Sometimes, on their own, they stumble onto ways to concentrate or develop photographic memory, but these "learning to learn" techniques are not generally orchestrated to the maximum potential. In some Bulgarian school experiments, rather than have students far ahead in regular subject courses, education is broadened so that they cover a greater number of different subjects—extra languages, various fields—a more Renaissance approach to balanced knowledge, not overspecialization.

Obviously, suggestopedia is basically an audio system and so is not suitable for people with hearing impairment. But now, in Bulgaria, a visual system has been added. For instance, a specially composed opera for rapid learning based on a Grimm fairy tale is broadcast on TV and has arithmetic material connected to the plot pulsing visually in one corner of the screen.

As more people explore rapid learning, many more things will be revealed that can enhance our natural learning powers.

Chapter 9
Coaching Children

A few supermemory sessions may be an easy way to help a child memorize homework and improve grades. Whether or not you want to try supermemory sessions, you can do your child a favor by teaching her or him the basic superlearning techniques: how to relax body and mind and do positive affirmations; how to visualize and to reexperience the feeling of successful learning. These abilities will last a lifetime and help give your child a chance to do his or her best in any learning situation.

Educators with the Georgia State Department of Education who got excellent results using rapid-learning methods for remedial reading, now say that probably everyone could learn faster if given relaxation training. "Mastery of some sort of relaxation technique may conceivably become a regular part of a child's educational experience . . ." they assert.

Sometimes a child does poorly because of anxiety over tests. Anxiety and trying to *will* remembering end up by completely blocking memory during the exam. Learning how to learn can help ease this problem too.

Supermemory has to do with factual learning, and there is,

of course, a great deal more to education than becoming a storehouse of facts. However, if a child can grasp the basics quickly and surely and gain increasing confidence in his ability to learn, then more and better quality time can be devoted to learning how to reason, analyze, experiment, synthesize, and create.

If you are going to try supermemory sessions, probably your goal as homework coach is to give faltering memories a boost with spelling, arithmetic, foreign vocabulary, and other school courses, rather than trying to teach a subject from scratch. For parents or teachers interested in the classroom teaching procedures that go with the supermemory session, see the Appendix.

American users of supermemory systems find children seem to learn much faster and make the greatest gains if they are well trained in relaxation, breathing, and visualization. The preliminary exercises to get one in shape to be a superlearner and, if desired, to do supermemory are in Chapter Seven. Exercises specially organized and worded for children are in Chapter 19. If you are working with young learners: for relaxation see page 291; for affirmations, page 102; for visualization and mind calming, page 294; for joy of learning, page 104. One of the authors, Nancy, who has had experience with these exercises for children, found that most children genuinely enjoy them. The only learning exercise that sometimes is difficult for young children is breathing rhythmically. Special instruction is given on page 293. If you are going to do supermemory sessions, if at all possible try to teach your child to breathe properly.

To teach general learning exercises, have children sit in an easy chair, or lie on a bed, couch, or floor. You can guide them through the exercise as they relax. Or, you can tape the programs and have children play them. Do these preliminary learning exercises with your child for a week beforehand. Wait until you feel your child is achieving a good relaxation response and can do the breathing pattern for rapid learning before trying memory reinforcement.

Catching Interest

To catch a child's interest in this idea of learning in a new way, it's important to create a positive, expectant atmosphere, and one that is different from their usual classroom or homework setup. Set the stage for something different.

Fill them in on some background and procedures of superlearning. You might explain that you've been looking into research on a new breakthrough in education that makes it possible to speed up learning and make it easier, better, and more fun. This research shows that people's learning ability is much higher than was thought possible before. You just have to know how to do it. Because it lets you use more of the mind, this superlearning method gives better results for the same amount of effort.

You might say, "These are new space-age techniques, and you can make use of them right now." Tell him or her how good it feels to learn relaxation, how interesting it is to see mental movies and learn visualization. This is the sort of mind/body training the Olympic athletes and even cosmonauts do (see Chapter 10). Space-age learning gets rid of boredom. You can get a kick out of learning, because you'll see how good you really are. All kinds of students have tried this. And they got a surprise. They found it was easy to learn no matter how they'd been doing before. Even those who didn't catch onto it the first or second try were successful the next time around, and results tended gradually to get better and better. Even if you think you've already been trying as hard as you can, don't worry. Many scientists say we usually only use about ten percent of our brain power. These new methods can help you plug in to the parts you don't usually use. You'll find you have a lot more learning equipment than you thought.

If your student has any questions or qualms, check the basic psychological blocks to improved learning on page 88. The point of the introduction is (a) to de-suggest the idea of limited learning abilities; (b) to encourage the student; (c) to raise his or her expectation level.

Homework Coaching

Before beginning the supermemory session itself, try to go over the homework material as vividly as possible. Try to make a game of it. There are various learning picture books and games available in toy departments, or you can have children try to invent a game that would make the material more fun. Bingo games or battleship games can be used for learning colors or numbers in foreign vocabularies. They can be adapted for spelling words too. You can make up a set of cards, or use playing cards for an arithmetic game. You deal out the number cards and try to match numbers with the right answers.

Another technique for coaching that people have found really works is to have the children pretend they're doing a TV commercial for the homework material and try to visualize it or act it out.

Another technique that is often used in a Lozanov-type teaching situation is role playing . . . acting the part of a person involved in whatever the subject is: being a geologist exploring for minerals; an airplane pilot calculating a navigational plan; a tourist in a foreign country ordering dinner.

If you're going over vocabulary words, you and the child can try to think up some vivid images that could be associated with each word—some vivid pictures that would make them easy to remember. An easy way to do a list of words is to pronounce a word, spell it, try to build an image or idea around it, and use it in a sentence (see the Exercises for more tips, p. 266).

After reviewing homework material, begin the supermemory session. Follow the instructions on how to organize and recite material given in Chapter Eight. During the relaxation preliminaries, give the children lots of affirmations for easy learning. Then begin reading the material aloud at slow-paced intervals. Recite the information once without music as your student follows along silently reading the data to herself. Next, read the same material again over the music. This time your student leans back, closes her eyes, and absorbs information.

During both run-throughs, students should try to breathe properly, that is, hold their breath while you're speaking and breathe during the pauses. If you are working with words from a list of spelling demons, you would set it up like this:

1 2 3 4	1 2 3 4	Voice Tone
silence	a-c-c̆-e-p-t accept	normal
silence	d-e-s-s-e-r-t dessert	soft
silence	e-l-i-g-i-b-l-e eligible	loud
silence	f-i-e-r-y fiery	normal
silence	l-i-b-r-a-r-y library	soft
silence	r-e-c-e-i-v-e receive	loud

Spell the word, pronounce the word, pause; spell the word, pronounce the word, pause; and so on. Fifty words will take about thirteen minutes to read through *twice,* once without the music and once with.

Lists of things to be learned such as spelling, arithmetic, vocabulary, scientific names, and so forth are very easy to teach. But you can reinforce any factual information, including complex subjects, as long as you break the material into short phrases. For instance, your child may be learning about different countries of the world. Say the country is Nigeria. You could break up information like this:

1 2 3 4	1 2 3 4	Voice Tone
silence	Nigeria, west coast of Africa	normal
silence	Nigeria, African republic	soft
silence	Population, seventy-five million	loud
silence	Capital, Lagos	normal
silence	English, official language	soft
silence	Major export, oil	loud

After a session, have the children do a quiz and check their own results. The quizzes are just feedback to see how they're doing. As they begin to see improvement each day, the quizzes become something to look forward to. Some children found it helped recall to have the music played during the quiz.

A Sample Coaching Session

Iowa teacher Charles Gritton tutored two eighth graders, a boy and a girl, who, their teachers and parents agreed, were students with learning disabilities. Unable to do fractions or percentages, unable to spell, they didn't care about school anymore. Working in their own living room, Gritton spent some time teaching them relaxation and talking about the new learning system. He asked them to take a pretest in spelling and arithmetic. They tried the spelling. Both refused to try the math.

Gritton began with a rapid-learning session of fifty spelling words from their toughest list. The two scored their own papers. They began to look surprised. On the pretest they'd gotten scores of thirty and twenty. Now each had ninety percent right. Pretty soon, as the tutoring went on, the "disabled" children were telling Gritton, "It's fun to learn, it's easy. There's nothing to it." They found it was very easy to recall the material if the music was played during the quiz.

He reviewed the math that they'd previously refused even to try. They took off, Gritton says. Their acceptance of themselves was very high, and they were so excited and pleased about learning. They could work all the problems and had no difficulties.

The next day they did another fifty difficult spelling words. The girl got 100 percent on the quiz. The boy was stunned to discover he'd gotten almost everything correct. His self-image as a person unable to spell was so fixed in his mind that he insisted on erasing correct words and making them wrong.

On another day, they did another fifty spelling words and more math rules. "It's very simple," the kids said and asked Gritton to go on with ratios and more difficult things. They remembered math rules, he reports, with "amazing ease." After four days their attitudes about themselves had completely reversed. Gritton was surprised too. This was one of his first trials of the system. The approach, he says, "worked beyond any expectation I had had."

The tutoring scores for the two students looked like this: *Spelling:* pretest 30 percent and 20 percent. First session: 90 percent and 90 percent. Second session: 100 percent and 60 percent (with the boy erasing correct answers). Third session: 100 percent and 60 percent (with erasures). *Math:* pretest 0 and 0. First session: 90 percent and 90 percent. Second session: 100 percent and 90 percent. Third session: 80 percent and 90 percent.

Recap for Supermemory Session

· Ahead of time, make sure the child knows how to relax and do the other learning exercises.

· Go over homework as vividly as possible.

· Have the child relax, affirm his ability to learn and reexperience for a moment the good feeling that comes with successful learning.

· Read the material through at the proper pace while the child follows it, reading silently to himself.

· Read through the same material again, this time over the music while the child, eyes closed and relaxed, simply listens.

· Give a quiz and let the child score results.

Afterword 1979
Other Innovators, Similar Systems

Superlearning techniques are flourishing in many countries. If you look to the roots of this new flowering, you will usually find they do not lead back to Bulgaria or the Communist bloc. The more you look into the situation, the more uncanny it begins to seem—uncanny except that we all know about the idea whose time has come.

In the last few decades, people in various countries, completely independently, and without any knowledge of one another's work, were suddenly inspired to explore the very same roots—ancient techniques from India and the Orient said to enhance mental and physical abilities—and after years of research, developed new learning techniques based on the very same principles.

One of the outstanding superlearning systems developed in a Western country is called sophrology. Sophrology learning and memory courses have been used in Spanish schools and colleges for many years.

L. Alfonso Caycedo, a medical doctor, Colombian by birth, created Sophrology and launched it while a professor on the faculty of medicine at the University of Madrid. As a young doctor specializing in neuropsychiatry, Caycedo had become fascinated with hypnosis. This led him to investigate techniques new and old that permit a person to modify states of consciousness and thus act on body or mind. Like Lozanov, he became deeply interested in Raja Yoga, the science of concentration, and went to India to study some of the famous Raja yogis. He also went to Japan to investigate Zen. In Tibet, the Dalai Lama authorized him to live in a lamasery to study certain Buddhist techniques. He returned to Spain after his two-year journey with the idea that the West was still at the neolithic stage in its knowledge of human consciousness.

He decided to throw out all the old terms. People had preconceived ideas about them. He would start with a new "ology" derived from Greek: sophrology from *sos,* harmony; and *phren,* consciousness or mind—the study of the harmony of consciousness.

Like Lozanov, Dr. Caycedo and a team of physiology experts did lab studies of all the Eastern exercises said to arouse "different" states of consciousness. He and his researchers demystified and modernized these methods. They soaked loose the active essence from centuries of archaic traditions. They also examined Western approaches to mind/body. Then they selected those techniques they considered the best, methods that help a sick person heal himself physically and mentally, methods that help a healthy person improve his or her mental and physical performance.

The Centre of Sophrology was founded in Barcelona, Spain, in 1960. Initially, Dr. Caycedo used sophrology medically (as Lozanov used suggestology) in many areas, including gastroenterology, psychiatry, and obstetrics. Sophrology is really a way of teaching, he says. "We teach people how to breathe properly, how to anesthetize themselves, and how to relax. We reinforce in a person his capacity to take charge, and thus his capacity for hope."

From medicine, sophrology moved to sports and to education, because, like Lozanov, Caycedo observed that people developed hypermnesia, or supermemory, through certain Raja Yoga methods.

In 1970, the first international conference on sophrology took place in Barcelona and was attended by 1,400 specialists from forty-two countries. The second world conference took place in 1975, with 1,500 delegates from fifty-five countries. Conferences have also been held in France.

Seemingly, without knowledge of each other's work, Lozanov and Caycedo followed parallel paths at about the same time in the exploration and development of yoga-derived systems with similar names. Sophrology has moved toward medicine, sports, and education; suggestology has moved toward medicine and education. Both doctors worked in countries governed by dictatorships.

When we contacted Dr. Caycedo, we discovered the "Coincidence Bureau" seemed to be working overtime. Dr. L. A. Caycedo's first name is *Lozano*.

An intense, compact, prematurely-balding man of 47, obliged to wear dark glasses constantly because of poor eyesight, Caycedo is noted for his dedication to medicine and nonstop hard work. Eighteen years of research into supermemory and heightened concentration through Raja Yoga and Zen led Caycedo to develop both a Sophrology Memory System and a Sophrology Learning System—with sets of techniques designed for both normal and "problem" children (those with learning disabilities and coordination difficulties).

Dr. Caycedo told us that for many years some thirty to forty teachers in Spain in centers in Madrid, Barcelona, Valencia, Gijon, and Malaga have regularly been using the Sophrology learning package. Students practice specific exercises for fifteen minutes every morning before daily classes so that these "learning-to-learn" techniques can be used during the day for every subject. Teachers report excellent results.

Caycedo has been honored in various South American countries where sophrology is used for regular learning as well as for retraining of juvenile delinquents.

In France, too, sophrology is spreading, with teachers at the Lycée de Calais, Lycée Voltaire, and the Paris School of Journalism reporting good results for classes in English and stenography.

For retarded and learning-disabled children, results have been amazing. In Madrid, pediatrician Dr. Mariano Espinosa has used Caycedo's sophrology training system on problem children from all over Spain and North and South America. Experts were astonished by what they saw at his institute. Retarded youngsters with severe motor incoordination were performing sophrology physical exercises with extraordinary skill; moreover, after several months of training body/mind as one, their I.Q.s had soared. Dr. Espinosa was awarded the international gold medal in pediatrics in 1974 for his achievements with sophrology.

The sophrology system as applied to sports training, described in the next chapter, has started a revolution in European athletics.

Just like Lozanov's suggestology, Caycedo's sophrology brings not only learning, but therapeutic spin-off, benefits: improved self-confidence, improved creativity, improved emotional development and self-expression, and freedom from limited ideas about capabilities.

Looking in on a sophrology learning class, you see students doing visualization and relaxation exercises. Then while students are in a meditative state (called sophroliminal) and breathing in a rhythmic pattern, the teacher reads the text rhythmically in specific intonations.

The basic principle in both systems is identical: to create a link between the conscious and unconscious mind. This communications link leads to voluntary control of body and memory. It helps develop heightened concentration and alleviate stress. Both systems utilize an altered state of consciousness to set up this mind/body link—a state of relaxed concentration. Lozanov calls it a "pseudo-passive" state. Caycedo calls it a "sophronique" state. The superior learning state is character-ized not only by slowed-down body/mind rhythms, but by *synchronized* body/mind rhythms.

Lozanov's system accomplishes this by using music with a slow beat to slow and synchronize body/mind rhythms, and by having course materials read rhythmically over the music to stimulate both left brain and right brain simultaneously.

Caycedo's system uses visualization exercises to develop a relaxed state with slowed-down body/mind rhythms. He achieves synchronization of body/mind rhythms by specific rhythmic breathing exercises. Caycedo's system also uses sound, but instead of an orchestra—the human voice. Left brain and right brain are stimulated globally by having the course material read almost in a singing way with special rhythm and intonation. This technique he calls "terpnos logos," and it goes back to the ancient Greeks. Plato described it as a special tone of voice—a soft, soothing, monotonous, melodious tone somewhat like an incantation. This, he said, acts on mind/body to produce a state of calmness, tranquility, and supreme concentration. Many mothers instinctively use this soothing tone of voice when comforting a child. Physiological research, such as that of Russian physiologist K. Platonov, bears out the contention that a specific pitch and tone of voice can have a definite positive effect on the body. Sophrology teachers are given some voice coaching along the lines of an actor's or singer's.

Caycedo's overall learning system uses his own "dynamic relaxation method" and a wide variety of physical and mental exercises drawn from Raja Yoga and Zen to aid relaxation, reduce stress, and improve visualization and concentration. Initially, Lozanov, too, used relaxation exercises.

Finally, both doctors insist that the learning environment, both physical and social, be positive, and that there should be good rapport in the "alliance," as Caycedo calls it, between teacher and student.

Sophrology Memory System

Caycedo's sophrology memory system is a four-day course. The techniques are practiced afterward by students at home and gradually lead to hypermemory. Results showed students made good learning gains because of improved ability to recall material.

"Long years of investigation have shown me that people have, in the form of positive memories, an emotional reserve of extraordinary value, not only for the development of memory, but for the entire personality," Caycedo says.

Patients came to him still suffering from the trauma of the Spanish Civil War, he says, and through his memory therapy he was able to completely restore their mental health.

Caycedo's memory training system is derived from Japanese Zen, which he considers "a perfection of Raja Yoga," and from his own "dynamic relaxation" technique.

At the very root of his memory training system is an expansion of the Joy of Learning Recall in Chapter 7. "Divide your life into three sections, and pick a positive recollection from each timespan," he asks students. Once you've selected these positive memories, you're asked to put each one through five stages:

1) evocation (evoke the positive recollection from the past)

2) fixation (concentrate on this positive sensation)

3) association (associate colors, objects, and persons with this positive sensation)

4) repetition (repeat the positive sensation so it is impressed on the mind)

5) presentation (amplify this positive sensation in a written or oral form)

Dr. Caycedo believes that the physical and psychological are inseparably linked and that the body is the ideal instrument for developing or training the memory. He insists on:

a) rhythmic abdominal respiration;

b) coordination of the breathing with the thoughts, recollections, or material to be memorized;

c) exercises to improve circulation and oxygen supply to the head;

d) three specific postures from Japanese Zen designed to enhance relaxation and concentration.

A specific posture is used for the various functions of memory, and as his physiological research has shown, can assist people in reaching altered levels of consciousness.

Initially, Lozanov's system also used postures, especially the Savasana Yoga relaxation posture, and the institute had special reclining chairs as an aid.

Dr. Jane Bancroft investigated the Spanish schools using sophrology learning and memory programs and confirms the good results. She photographed sophrology students in convent schools; she experienced the four-day memory course firsthand at a session on the Costa Brava. She reports that, after the course, students could spontaneously absorb and recall quantities of data from the blackboard, concentration and memory improved, and stress was eased.

"Caycedo's and Lozanov's systems are practically mirror images of one another," she says. While each doctor approached the Eastern disciplines from a different philosophical viewpoint (Caycedo, from Latin Catholicism and European phenomenology; Lozanov, from Marxism and Soviet psychotherapy), both explored Eastern techniques physiologically to find the active ingredients. "Both doctors have traveled the royal road of yoga and both have been greatly influenced by the traditions of the East," says Dr. Bancroft. "Behind different names and different terms, one finds the same (or similar ideas) in sophrology and suggestology and in the pedagogical applications of these systems."

Caycedo was surprised at the many similarities when Dr. Bancroft pointed them out to him in Barcelona in 1979. "I've never been in touch with Dr. Lozanov," he said. "My name Lozano comes from my mother's maiden name. Perhaps we are even distantly related," he added, smiling.

Spanish and Bulgarian students aren't the only Europeans who have come to realize that learning doesn't have to mean sitting up straight and pounding the books. In West Germany some years ago, another man set forth independently on a familiar path. Professor Friedrich Doucet began to cull superlearning techniques from ancient Eastern sources. First he looked into the possibilities of improving education by training students in autogenics (a famous German relaxation program) so they could develop voluntary control of body and memory and thus increase learning. At his Munich institute, Avalon, this psychologist, therapist, and author went on to explore not only the exercises of the East but also the music of the East. His research draws on the ancient knowledge embodied in music, focusing on the effect of various harmonics on body and mind.

Doucet combined his findings on the inner workings of music with autogenics to create a new teaching method. His system was demonstrated on German TV and appears similar to Lozanov's. Relaxed students listen to language texts read over carefully selected Eastern music. Apparently the method does indeed enhance learning, and Deutsche Grammophon is said to be negotiating for the recording rights to Professor Doucet's "Autogenic Pedagogy."

Meanwhile, in France, a medical doctor has carved a new field of scientific inquiry through research on the effects of sound on people. Dr. Alfred Tomatis, Director of the Association Internationale d'Audio Psycho-Phonologie, is internationally recognized for his pioneering efforts to help dyslexic children with sound therapy. He uses Baroque music because, he says, it is rich in higher frequencies. Not long ago, Dr. Tomatis' Baroque music method was adapted for language training. It improved learning.

Across the border in Switzerland, a teacher, Jacques de Coulon, came out of left field onto the superlearning path. Instead of sifting through the hoary canons of the East, de Coulon began his archaeological hunt for the keys to superpotential by digging through the records of another ancient culture, Egypt. From this, he pieced together exercises for inner/outer concentration, breathing patterns, and best body postures for concentration. As you can guess, de Coulon then devised a teaching method based on these techniques. He found, in particular, that if students breathed in rhythm with a recitation of math or reading texts, a great improvement in learning takes place.

These Europeans and others not mentioned have devised entire teaching systems. A great many more people here and abroad are melding new elements into classroom programs to create a more holistic education. To cite just a single example, in California, Marjorie King of Sacramento Union High School and JoAnne Kamiya of the Langley-Porter Neuropsychiatric Institute have helped bring biofeedback into the public schools. Instead of doing relaxation exercises, children work out on these "biological jungle gyms," as one scientist terms the machines, to learn to reduce stress. Biofeedback is yet another way of setting up a link between conscious and unconscious and getting voluntary control of body/mind. Children are learning to improve attention and creativity and to overcome learning blocks. The most important benefit noted is a greatly improved self-image, which in turn greatly improves a child's ability to learn.

Head-Space Race?

Psychology Today, in discussing the implications of the communist world's advances in learning via suggestology, raises the question, Are we in a head-space race for the superpowers of the mind among the superpowers? It would seem that the political cold war has added education to sports as another area of competition between East and West, complete with secrets and cover-ups.

Insider reports from suggestopedia centers in East Germany and the USSR reveal surprising current results. The Soviets are using relaxation training and the original Bulgarian program. Bulgarian educator Aleko Novakov developed courses for them. A special report on Soviet learning achievements prepared by Rupprecht S. Baur and P. G. Rühl of the University of Hamburg indicates hard-to-believe Soviet results based on their ten-year head start on us. For instance, centers such as the University of Tbilisi in Soviet Georgia charted stress-free accelerated learning with language test scores near the 100 percent level.

The Soviets have built their systems from the original Bulgarian methods. The original Bulgarian methods? In the last few years the Bulgarians have been exporting a "new" version of suggestopedia. This version seems to have veered away from synchronizing mind/body and instead concentrates on what might be called charismatic teaching. Compared to the documented techniques published in Lozanov's own book, the new version as of late 1979 includes the following changes: 1. Omission of the altered state of relaxed concentration. "Relaxation for students is embodied in the person of the teacher," Lozanov now says. 2. Omission of intonations. 3. Omission of rhythm. 4. Omission of breathing exercises. 5. Omission of slow music. "Substitute Beethoven, Wagner, Chopin," is the current word.

What's left? Basically a highly dramatic, very demanding, complex presentation over music by the teacher, plus emphasis on the psychological atmosphere in the class—student role playing, suggestive decor. To this point, no one has published any scientific data to show whether this method brings the extraordinary results of the original. There's no documented proof that the new Bulgarian version speeds learning or expands memory. The elements of both approaches are readily testable and don't have to be a matter of opinion. For instance, Jean Cureau in Paris ran comparison tests on the "new" music list. When he substituted Wagner for slow Baroque, results were disastrous. The University of Toronto also found results nose-dived when fast music was substituted for slow Baroque. Why these seeming drastic changes were instituted in Bulgaria is an open question, one that probably has a number of answers, some of which may or may not have to do with underlying political reasons.

The Canadian government teachers were given this package. As mentioned, their multimillion-dollar civil service program terminated after "massive failures." Upon completing a contract with the Max Boltzmann Institute in Austria, the Bulgarian government dispatched Dr. Lozanov and Evelina Gateva to Vienna with the new methods. Dr. Franz Beer, Director of the Institute, reports the Italian language program failed. It was, he says, extremely expensive, and somehow it was not possible to have Austrian teachers properly trained. The Austrians did better with a Bulgarian program geared to children. There were initial problems: printed course material was unsuitable; video tapes contained communist propaganda; and the Bulgarians, probably not realizing the irony, sent the Viennese waltz music. However, the Viennese teachers took the program in hand, added visualization and relaxation exercises similar to those used in Iowa, and results improved. On the plus side, many of these teachers were pleased with the holistic, psychological approach taught by Lozanov.

Anyone who's ever gone to school would welcome more creative, dramatic, humane teaching. But as far as the U.S. is concerned, the new Bulgarian-style teaching can hardly be considered an innovation. Some of the ideas have been around since the days of John Dewey, our most famous educator, whose influence spread out into the schools in the early decades of the century. More currently, competent holistic teacher training is being given at such places as the Institute for Wholistic Education in Massachusetts. And, the highly dramatized approach to foreign language training has been well developed in such systems as the successful Dartmouth Intensive Language Model already used in fifty-eight U.S. schools (a thousand-word vocabulary in fourteen days). In line with this, when Lozanov and Gateva presented their program at international professional conferences in Sweden and Switzerland, many educators felt the "new" Bulgarian way seemed "quite old-fashioned." On the other hand, people who took courses at the Lozanov Learning Institute in the U.S. generally seemed pleased with the experience and felt they'd learned well. This corporation is interested in development and research and hopes to have scientific data on their methods available soon.

In Paris, both approaches are being taught. Fanny Saferis, known as an outstanding teacher, bought the rights to the new Bulgarian system and has indeed gotten good results in conversational English training. For comparison, at the Lycée Voltaire, Jean Cureau has been teaching English with eclectic superlearning methods for several years and getting spectacular results—about a ten-to-one speedup in learning in a positive, stress-free atmosphere. He believes the slow Baroque music, relaxation, and soothing intonations from sophrology are most important.

The superlearning package in this book, of course, is not the Bulgarian one, but has components drawn from original sources in Raja Yoga and from the successful research of pioneers in various countries, including Bulgaria. Some duplicate "failsafe" elements are included because not everyone responds in the same way to the same stimulus.

Machinations in Bulgaria, squabbles over teaching models, don't have much meaning for most of our lives. The real news has to do with something that does—that timewave that seems to be bringing techniques to carry us into the unused reserves of ourselves. More and more people are putting these techniques to work; more and more people are experiencing expanded achievement. Dr. Bancroft has brought the benefits of her long years of research to her students. In 1978, she and Dr. Eleanor Irwin of the University of Toronto got "vastly improved results" with students studying Greek, simply by playing tapes of the course read in rhythmic patterns over slow Baroque music. Currently, Dr. Bancroft is using taped superlearning for her university French course. Accelerating achievement is showing clearly on the regular university exams. Fringe benefits from the taped relaxation programs she uses are showing up, too. Enthusiastic students claim they've overcome stress-related health problems; many say they've gained in self-confidence and come to an enlarged idea of just how much they can really do.

In using the taped courses, Bancroft follows the early Bulgarian pattern. Suggestology Institute graduates told us that, originally, classes listened to supermemory material on two tape recorders: one for the music, the other for course material. This ensured identical presentation for all classes and eased the burden on teachers.

Elsewhere in Canada, in early 1979, a major corporation, Canadian Pacific, revealed that, using a program put together on the advice of Dr. Bancroft and Charles Schmid, their employees had more than doubled their speed in learning French. The courses continue.

In Iowa, the professional accelerated learning society S.A.L.T. is expanding, publishing reports from teachers across the country who are trying the new techniques in their classrooms. The system has moved far beyond language training. For instance, a course in Naval Weapons Systems, noted for being truly dull, was learned at double speed by students using accelerated learning in 1977 at Iowa State University. Instructor E. E. Peterson reports midshipmen had "learned the art of learning" from the experience.

As news spreads it seems to be nudging that once famous American ingenuity and pioneering spirit. Business trainers, motivation consultants, therapists of all sorts, teachers at every level, and students are grabbing hold of superlearning techniques. On their own, they are probing, experimenting, adapting them for their particular purposes. Through Superlearning Inc. alone we have received hundreds of letters indicating happy results. To cite just one documented case, there is the ongoing experiment of Dr. Donald Vannan of Bloomsburg State College in Pennsylvania.

Dr. Vannan teaches a course in Elementary Science Methods. Would accelerated learning techniques work as well in the sciences as they reportedly did in languages? he wondered. To find out, Vannan taught his course in the regular way for three different semesters in 1975. This would be his control group. In 1976, he trained his students in relaxation methods. Then, in- stead of the usual lecture, after a question session he had his relaxed students read along silently while listening to the material recited with intonations on tape. After another question session, he told his students to lean back, close their eyes, and listen to the same taped recitation with music behind it.

Tests in this course are quite straightforward; most questions are factual and scored by computer. In 1975, Vannan taught 220 students, 11 percent of whom received an A grade. In 1976 he taught approximately the same number with accelerated techniques. Seventy-eight percent scored an A. Vannan had found a new teaching method. In 1977, out of three semesters' worth of students, 84.6 percent got an A, and in 1978, 82.9 percent. Obviously, Vannan's students learned the facts and remembered the facts. And they did it without stress. (For Dr. Vannan's publications, see Sources, Section 1.)

Ingenuity, that's one of the better qualities superlearning can empower. For all the seemingly spectacular results, we are in truth just beginning to edge into the vast unused reserves of the human being. We've just passed the starting line. The father of Humanistic psychology, Abram Maslow, once remarked, "When the only tool you have is a hammer, every problem begins to look like a nail." We've hammered out ten percent of our talents. Now we have a few new tools. These could be used to help us build even better ones—at an accelerating rate, of course.

SECTION II
SUPER-
PERFORMANCE

Chapter 10
Super-
performance
in Sports

The scene is Lausanne, Switzerland, the office of a dental surgeon. A young woman is sitting in one of the rooms watching a light show of colors dance on a wall. She grimaces, then stretches her arms out in front of her, rolling her head in every direction. Then she leans back and relaxes. She imagines feeling her arm is very heavy. She feels a fresh breeze on her forehead. When she feels completely relaxed, the melodious voice of the doctor comes from a small TV screen in the room, and she repeats affirmation formulas after him:

"Dynamic relaxation improves my skiing form. I am more aggressive. I have confidence in my abilities as a skier. I concentrate from the start. I am completely free of fear of the crowd, the TV cameras, the chronometer, or of an accident."

This woman is a European skier, in training for an important event. Now she imagines in complete detail an upcoming competition. She feels the skis on her feet, feels her body lean into a curve, sees the snow-covered course ahead of her. She must perform every maneuver perfectly in her imagination. If she falls or makes a mistake, she must go back to the top of the slope and do the stretch over again perfectly.

In another room a young man is stretched out on a couch, relaxing. From the cut of his hair and his clothes, he looks successful, and he is—at twenty-five, the director of a European marketing association. The doctor's voice comes over the TV screen and the young executive repeats after him: "I have confidence in myself. The others do not frighten me. I *like* to speak in public. I speak perfectly, and my listeners are pleased and satisfied."

The young man is working out at the doctor's office because he's unnerved about making a presentation to businessmen much older than he. Although he's in perfect health, he suffers from severe stage fright, sometimes becoming so anxious he stutters. After several sessions he should be able to bid good-bye to stage fright without a stammer.

These people are practicing a type of modified autogenics training that has turned many thousands of Europeans into better athletes, better public speakers, better performing artists—in fact, better performers in virtually any area. This is the office of Dr. Raymond Abrezol, an outgoing forty-eight-year-old dental surgeon with a longtime love of sports. The doctor and the sportsman got together in Abrezol. Why not approach the athlete as a whole person? Why not make sports training holistic? Dr. Abrezol is in large part responsible for a major trend in European sports: coaching both mind and body. Through his office have passed a host of people who became celebrated champions and stars, as well as scores of people in everyday fields, who discovered that superperformance abilities could light up their lives too.

Autogenics training was developed in the 1930s by the German psychiatrist Johannes H. Schultz and has been widely used in European clinics for a range of stress diseases. Autogenics teaches conscious control of various so-called involuntary body functions like heartbeat and metabolism. Visualization and affirmations are also a part of the training.

Abrezol's sports program is based on a modified version of autogenics and yoga called *sophrology,* created and developed by Dr. Alfonso Caycedo in Spain. Sophrology is a fairly common term in Europe, but almost entirely unknown in America.

In the early 1960's when Dr. Abrezol began experimenting with sophrology, he worked with amateur tennis players and skiers. He taught them how to learn to eliminate upsetting mental conditions that harmed their performance: nervousness before or during an event, lack of concentration, lack of combativeness, lack of confidence, fatigue, fear of errors, and fear of defeat. In 1967, when Peter Baumgartner, of the national Swiss ski team, heard about the remarkable results Abrezol was getting with this mind/body training program for sports, he asked him to work with the Swiss team. At the time, the Swiss teams were not exactly dominating the Olympics.

Four skiers were coached with sophrology—Madeleine Guyot, Fernande Bochatay, Willy Fabre, Jean-Daniel Daetwyler—and something new began to unfold in international competitions. Of the four, three won medals at the 1968 Winter Olympics in Grenoble. Rumors whirled in sports circles. What had the Swiss discovered—a new megavitamin, a new physical treatment? Or could working out mentally actually pay off in superperformance? The Swiss team stuck with sophrology. Four years later, at the 1972 Winter Olympics in Sapporo, Japan, there were three new Swiss medalists—Marie-Therese Nadig, Roland Collumbin, and Bernard Russi.

Abrezol believes his mental programs liberate competitors from unconscious fear that could cost them several hundredths of a second—and a prestigious medal.

It worked not only for skiers. Modified autogenics training helped Fritz Charlet, a boxer on the verge of abandoning his career. After going into training mentally, he became a European featherweight champion.

Across Europe, there are many, many athletes and sophrology coaches involved in mind training for better performance: jumpers, skaters, fighters, yachting teams, air acrobatic teams, football players. As soon as a sportsman works seriously at his exercises, says Dr. Abrezol, his progress accelerates and his performance improves. Basic to the mental practice is visualization, running through the entire performance sequence in vivid detail. "The imagination is more powerful than the will," says Abrezol. Trying to "will away" nervousness only adds one more stress to the tension you already have.

In France, when doctors tested and evaluated the effect of sophrology training on their athletes, Doctors H. Boon, Y. Davron, and J.-C. Macquet reported: physically mind training improved precision of movement, economized energy expenditure, controlled posture. Psychologically, mind training improved concentration and attention and enhanced perception. It improved rapport with teammates and coaches. It eliminated fear, stress, nerves, worries about mistakes, and so forth. After competitions, medical tests showed speeded-up recuperation—and this permitted athletes to run repeated trials. In cases of pains or muscle contractions caused by exertion, sophrology techniques brought relief. Pain control can, of course, be of great benefit to anyone, not just athletes (see Chapter 12).

Dr. Abrezol points out that mental programs like sophrology can also help various physical ills: vascular and respiratory problems, skin troubles, insomnia, headaches, and can even help control cholesterol level. Lab research shows that with autogenic-like methods people do learn to control muscle potential, blood flow, skin temperature, brain waves, and metabolism. That is why, in Europe and the USSR, modified autogenics is one of the most popular forms of medical therapy, often favored over drugs. It is also favored over drugs for those healthy people who suffer wobbly legs, shaky hands, froggy voices when a roomful of eyes turn on them.

Even celebrated performers can develop "network nerves" when asked to appear on national talk shows, says Dr. William Kroger, who treats such celebrities. It's a jump up from stage fright and comes from realizing that literally millions are watching you. Symptoms are "panic, stomach distress, flushed skin, tightness of the larynx, poor circulation, fast pulse, even vomiting—all coupled with a strong desire to flee."

Autogenics would allow such performers to "get their acts together" and let talent, mind, *and* body work for them. People who have learned through autogenics to communicate with the body say it's as if the body had always been on automatic pilot and suddenly you discover you can take over the controls.

The German M.D. Hannes Lindemann found he could take over the controls well enough to sail his canoe across the Atlantic. "A special grace," he calls it. "But also an obligation." To fulfill that obligation, he teaches classes in autogenics. "As a remedy it is offered as the *ideal* method," the doctor says, "to increasing one's capacities and health . . ." By health, Lindemann means more than that middling state of there being nothing terribly wrong, which many of us take for health. He also means the ability to have healthy, undamaging relationships with others and with society. "We are so immature and undeveloped psychosocially that it should be our duty to engage in autogenic training." It helps athletes perform, he says, and it can equally promote the performance of businesspeople, professionals, and laborers.

Some German business organizations like the chamber of commerce have run autogenic programs. Businesspeople who've taken up the exercises regularly report significantly improved creativity and production, less absenteeism, fewer accidents, better health, and better interpersonal relationships.

These are some of the benefits claimed for autogenic training. They are also claimed for sophrology. Many basic techniques are the same—relaxation and control of the body, the use of affirmations and visualizations

However, Dr. Caycedo's sophrology developed further methods including a special "dynamic relaxation." Dr. Abrezol's contribution was to develop sophrology's use in sports.

Seeing Success

Long before Western Europe caught on to the idea, the Soviets had researched and discovered brawn-plus-brain was a winning combination in sports.

It is mind-development programs that have helped Soviet athletes become superperformers and capture most of the gold medals in the Olympics, say Western experts. Dr. Richard Suinn, head of the Department of Psychology at Colorado State University, remarks, "Their [Soviet] athletes make a career out of competition, and they place a great deal of importance on the mind determining athletic success." Thanks to these techniques, Russians captured first place in the 1976 Montreal Olympics and the East Germans second. Russia won forty-seven gold medals, and the small country of East Germany forty.

Professor Suinn, who developed a mind-training program for the 1976 U.S. Olympic ski team, says the United States, and most other countries, are just beginning to look into the possibilities of mind power in sports.

One American who has apparently looked to the possibilities is Charles Tickner, the person who upset the Soviet defending champion to take the gold medal in world figure skating in March 1978. Reporters had heard he used a mental program. Tickner, a sophomore at the University of Nevada, explained that every morning he puts himself into a relaxed state. "I just repeat a few confidence-building words for a few minutes."

The mentalist Kreskin, aside from demonstrating mental techniques on his TV show, is also involved with psychology research programs at Seton Hall College in New Jersey. He had access to Soviet reports on mind training and made a detailed study of athletic programs. He believes that the Russians have experimented with mind power in athletics from the 1940's onward. "It has meant their gradual superiority over the past years in the summer and winter Olympic Games and other world sporting events," he says. The East Germans, according to Kreskin, have also instituted these programs in their nationwide sports complexes.

In the 1976 Summer Olympics, there was one long minute that strained the collective muscle of the millions watching. Vasily Alexeyev bent to lift a weight heavier than any human had ever hoisted before. Tensions released in a great flood of applause as Alexeyev stood there triumphant, arms upstretched, the crushing weight high above his head. Vasily Alexeyev is practiced in mind training. In the area of suggestion, an interesting thing happened en route to the gold medal. In weight lifting, 500 pounds had long been an impenetrable barrier no human could cross, just as the four-minute mile had once deflected all comers. Alexeyev and others lifted bars just below this cut-off point. In one event, his trainers told him he would lift his world record: 499.9 pounds. He did. They weighed the bar and showed him it actually was 501½ pounds. A few years later at the Olympics, Alexeyev hoisted 564 pounds.

Among the secrets of the Soviet training, according to Kreskin, is learning to mentally erase past mistakes and fear of failure and learning to picture mentally the successful outcome of an activity. You don't tell your mind what you want. You tell it that *what you want* you already have. It's an adult "tell and show." As with sophrology, athletes are coached in concentration, so they can tune out the noise and confusion of the crowds watching them and focus solely on success.

Many Soviet sports scientists now believe the average athlete doesn't realize half his or her potential performance if brain power isn't used. According to psychotherapists Dr. V. Rozhnov and Dr. A. Alexyev of the Advanced Medical Training Institute, Russians are working on extended ways to give athletes the power of brain over brawn. When you teach the brain to "command" the body, then *all* the body's organs are mobilized to work together in the most effective way. Rozhnov and Alexyev, both authorities on holistic sports education, maintain that training the emotions is also involved. The goal is to mobilize all the forces of the individual, so the power of the body can fully express itself.

Some Soviet boxers, they say, do a ten-minute mind program before going into the ring so that they have no tensions and their nerves are ready for very rapid reactions. Young Soviet divers, who become nervous or even panicky before a diving competition, now are using mind calming to restore confidence and visualization to prompt the body to make the best possible dive.

Three-way training is used on a big scale today in Russia according to Rozhnov and Alexyev. It involves athlete, coach, and mind trainer. The same approach is also widely used in the performing arts—in ballet and music, for instance. Even Soviet cosmonauts are trained in mind/body techniques. Like sophrology, the Soviet programs are modified autogenics. Methods have been streamlined for simple step-by-step practice that takes just a few minutes each day. No special equipment is needed. No strenuous physical exercises. No particular effort. No special belief in it. *Practice* and *imagination* are the two keys. Gradually, through practice, you set up communication links with the unconscious to tap the reserves of the mind. Gradually, conscious control of so-called involuntary functions develops. Gradually, relaxation of stress becomes automatic.

Once the body is under autogenic control, affirmations for better performance are particularly potent. In the relaxed autogenic state, competitors run through vivid mental movies. Experience shows this mental practice can be as effective as physical practice. Professor Suinn in Colorado has Olympic skiers practice imagining their ski runs, mentally correcting errors they have made in physical practice. Mental reruns, he finds, have a positive effect on subsequent performance. Some thirty or forty years of research by Soviets and Europeans reveals mental practice can help in every performance area from playing a concerto to archery or tennis.

Mental movies as the key to superperformance are no news to American champions like Jack Nicklaus. He claims that his success is entirely owed to practicing concentration and visualization. Nicklaus makes the arresting assertion that his golf game is only ten percent involved with the actual swing. Hitting specific shots, says Nicklaus, is fifty percent mental picture and forty percent setup. His technique? First, he tunes out the world, gets into a state of concentration; then, he does a mental movie of the entire shot in his head, sharp, and in focus, with plenty of zooms in and out. "I never hit a shot even in practice without this color movie," he says. In his book, *Golf My Way,* Nicklaus reveals, "First I 'see' the ball where I want it to finish, nice and white and sitting up high on the bright green grass. Then the scene quickly changes and I 'see' the ball going there: its path, trajectory, and shape, even its behavior on landing. Then there's a sort of fade-out, and the next scene shows me making the kind of swing that will turn the previous images into reality."

Tony Jacklin, winner of both the U.S. Open and British Open feels that when he is able to develop "a cocoon of concentration" during a golf game, it allows him to tune in and know what to do and how to do it.

Body builder and weight lifter Arnold Schwarzenegger, five-time Mr. Universe, four-time Mr. Olympia, and the star of the movie *Pumping Iron,* maintains that in weight lifting it's all "Mind over matter." "As long as the mind can envision the fact that you can do something, you can.... I visualized myself being there already—having achieved the goal already." Working out, he says, is the physical follow-through, a reminder of the vision you're focusing on.

Creative Performance

Not just athletes work on following through on a vision. The trained ability to picture vividly is also one of the circuits of creative genius and performance. A visualization that was to radically affect all of us lit up one February afternoon at dusk as a tall, dark-haired scientist strolled through a Prague park with his assistant. He began to recite a poem of Goethe's about the sunset. Suddenly, he stood stock still staring at the sun.

"Don't you see it?" he asked his bewildered companion. "It's right here in front of me. Look, it runs perfectly smoothly."

He picked up a stick and began tracing circles of a diagram in the dirt. The man was Nikola Tesla; what he drew in the dirt was the long-sought alternating current system of power generation. This was the discovery that allowed him to harness Niagara Falls and give us the age of electricity.

In our century, Tesla is one of the greatest examples of an all-around unobstructed personality. The range of his powers didn't file easily into the usual cubbyholes, which is perhaps why, until recently, he has been one of our most neglected geniuses.

Tesla trained his visualization faculties to such a degree that he could mentally construct an invention in detail. Then, as if equipment and lab were actually before him, he could turn on his imagined device and predict exactly how it would perform when constructed. Tesla felt the trial-and-error approach that men like Edison used was wasteful and time-consuming.

Tesla could do instant math like an electronic calculator, he rapidly learned twelve languages, he had photographic memory. His associates reported he could remember every detail of more than five thousand experiments conducted over fifty years. And his employees insisted he had "supernatural" powers and could read their minds. Tesla himself recorded he was telepathic and on occasion received long-distance mental images from his mother. Tesla credited his mother with developing his talents. When he was a child in Yugoslavia, she purposefully and consistently trained him in visualization with a variety of games she concocted. They also played ESP games.

Tesla produced prodigiously. His seven hundred inventions include high-frequency voltage, neon and fluorescent lighting, the tesla coil, the oscillator (the heart of our TV and radio broadcasting), our basic electric motors, remote-control devices, and other extraordinary developments that have been shrouded in neglect if not secrecy—a planetary power system for cheap energy, a defense power beam, wireless energy beams to power planes, and even an interplanetary communication system.

Tesla's powers of visualization were so sure his highly skilled machinists said that if he were inventing a new turbine, a solar engine, or some type of electrical equipment, he would produce every single measurement from his mind, including dimensions down to ten-thousandths of an inch.

Though he was an inventor of a different sort, Thomas Wolfe, like Tesla, was also able to see things as precisely in his mind as he did with his eyes. In his memoirs, Wolfe spoke of this picturing ability that was so useful in his writing.

"I would be sitting, for example, on the terrace of a café . . . and suddenly I would remember the iron railing that goes along the boardwalk at Atlantic City. I could see it instantly just the way it was, the heavy iron pipe; the raw, galvanized look; the way the joints were fitted together. It was all so vivid and concrete that I could feel my hand upon it and know the exact dimensions, its size and weight and shape."

It seems that those who excel with the mind and those who excel with the body draw from some of the same sources, such as working from a finely tuned mental picture—though probably neither group is aware of the similarity. As George Leonard remarks, "Athletes and intellectuals often live in different worlds, to the detriment of both." In *The Ultimate Athlete*, Leonard points out that the combined, global, mind/body approach to sports is an integral part of Oriental acrobatics, aikido, kung fu, and other martial arts. He believes the split between mind and body in Western athletics must be repaired. When wholeness is regained, he feels sports can be a path to personal enlightenment—the process of playing the game, the process of motion, the process of experiencing our bodies linked to the forces of the universe, would be emphasized as much as winning is at the present time. With this approach instead of either ignoring or overemphasizing the physical, one experiences and glorifies the spirit through the body.

Perspectives are finally beginning to shift and enlarge in

American sports. There's a trend to lifelong sports; there's a focus on process instead of competition and above all on the mind/body link as a way to greater enjoyment and transcendent performance. Books like *The Zen of Running* by Fred Rohe, *Inner Tennis* by Tim Gallwey, *The Innerspaces of Running* by Mike Spino, *Inner Skiing* by Gallwey and Kriegel, and *The Centered Skier* by Denise McCluggage explore this approach. There are new-style workshops for golfers, tennis players, skiers, that emphasize relaxation, balancing, centering, visualization, and sensing inner energy flow.

We've begun to learn from the East. It would seem we could also learn from the West. Mind-training programs have been the key to enhanced health and superperformance for hundreds of thousands of Soviets and Europeans. Without drugs and without costly biofeedback equipment, people are learning to control their own physiology. Aside from athletics and the performing arts, modified autogenics training is widely used to heal the body, and also the mind, in Europe, being second only to conventional psychotherapy. By the mid 1970's, there were more than 2,500 scientific publications on autogenic training and its myriad benefits, yet only a handful of them were in English.

We were able to obtain and translate one of the typical Soviet mind-training programs, few if any of which have ever been available in America. It comprises most of the following chapter and, as we have found ourselves, it is a satisfying way to learn basic autogenic relaxation and control.

Chapter 11
A Soviet Program for Peak Performance

Learning the basic mind/body program is easy and takes very little time from your day. Anyone except very small children can do it. Research and experience show it is simply a matter of practice. Do the exercises in seven- to ten-minute sessions (some people have done as little as two minutes) and sooner or later the desired effect will appear. Eventually, the response becomes almost automatic, when stress appears so will release, moving the whole body/mind back into harmony.

In 1971, a Soviet doctor, A. G. Odessky, put out an everyday guide for Russians of all kinds who wanted to master autogenic techniques that helped their dancers and athletes soar to success. Autogenics gives that extra measure, Odessky points out, that allows you to come through with your best, to succeed in any sport, "skydiving, swimming, or volleyball." Among the sports, Odessky includes that Russian favorite—chess. But this is far from being for athletes only, he says. "It is important for anybody, and especially for teachers, actors, dancers, military people, cosmonauts, and"—Dr. Odessky, a medical man himself crowns the list—"even for physicians."

"The word *auto-genous* is from the Greek *Auto* (self) and

Genous (giving birth, being born, productive). All of these meanings apply to our training program. It is an active method conducted by the person himself or herself." The Russian program, like sophrology, is based on Dr. Johannes Schultz's original discovery published in 1932. Odessky continues, "Our training develops people's ability to control consciously their various physiological processes, for example, to control digestion, breathing, blood circulation, metabolism, and also to control emotions, moods, and to sharpen attention."

Soviets have researched yogis extensively and realize many can also control inner states. There is much that is useful in yoga, Odessky says, but there are also problems. For Soviets there is the problem of "mysticism and idealism" and for almost everybody there is the problem of "doing tough physical exercises, spending a prolonged amount of time, living a life of deprivation." Modified autogenics makes it possible for the vast and busy majority of us to assume control of our inner states. "Sometimes," Odessky remarks, "we call it psychological gymnastics through which a person can attain a complete control of his psyche."

In the USSR, autogenics plays a dominant role in psychotherapy. Odessky considers it a remedy for phobias, neuroses, obsessions, bed wetting, stuttering, involuntary tics, chronic alcoholism, and—apart from illness—a great help in painless childbirth. Western experts would add that it is a real help in sexual problems including impotence and frigidity and also in weight control. And there is help with extreme mental problems, too. Dr. Paul Grim, one of the relatively few American psychologists who regularly uses autogenics training in his practice and who is familiar with the worldwide research, remarks, "Suicidal patients report the training gives them something tangible to use in combating despair. A year's follow-up on a group of these patients demonstrated that not one had relapsed into depression."

Grim would back up European and Soviet contentions that autogenics heals organic disease as well. In Russia, among such treated, Odessky cites spastic colon, heart trouble, bronchial asthma, ulcers, gall bladder disorders. But perhaps the finest contribution of autogenics in the long run will prove to be its ability to prevent disease and promote worthwhile longevity.

Dr. Schultz began life as the typical frail child plagued with sickness and prohibitions. He once remarked that his father, a theologian, worked to save souls, while he wanted to save bodies. He may have wound up doing both. Schultz himself lived and worked until he was eighty-six.

If autogenics is beginning to have the ring of a panacea, Odessky is quick to point out there is nothing supernatural about the program. Many years of research attest to these effects; scientists have elaborated, at least in part, how they occur. (For more documentation, consult a medical library. See also Appendix.) Simple as it sounds, a major element in the ability of autogenics to heal even severe disorders is relaxation. Apparently, when the tensions that skew us are released, body and mind move toward normalization, all healing being at base self-healing.

Do straight medical autogenics in coordination with an expert, Dr. Odessky advises. But that still leaves so many other things anyone can do. To name just one, he goes on, we can rid ourselves of all those unhelpful emotions and sensations that tend to go with us as we head into any big moment—"exams, public appearances, competitions, surgery, important business and personal meetings."

Autogenics or psychological gymnastics, as Odessky puts it, has two levels of training. Many of the accomplishments mentioned can be done with the base training alone. If you exercise daily or do sports or practice music regularly, you'll find it especially easy to incorporate these few minutes of training as a daily routine. The second-level exercises involve techniques you're already familiar with—visualization and self-tailored suggestion.

When you've mastered the course you should be able to bring about the relaxed, attentive autogenic state in thirty seconds to a minute, anywhere, under any circumstances. To learn, however, choose a comfortable place, secure from disturbance. "Autogenic exercises are good at any time," Odessky explains, "but they will be best if you wait at least an hour and a half after meals." (The French doctors Boon, Davron, and Macquet report no bad effects have ever been found from autogenic exercise.)

Autogenics can be useful in almost infinite ways—increasing your capability and enjoyment of anything from sport to business to extrasensory adventuring. But there's something more. A great deal of the enjoyment is in the getting there. You feel better, happier doing the exercises. There is a surprising feeling of release from feeling heavy and warm. The following instructions are based on Dr. Odessky's program.

Position

Assume one of the following positions, whichever is most suitable under the circumstances.

1. THE COACHMAN: Think of an old-fashioned coachman relaxing during a long journey. Sit on a chair or stool. Let your head hang slightly forward, forearms and hands rest loosely on your thighs, your legs are positioned comfortably, feet pointed slightly outward. Your eyes are closed.

2. THE EASY CHAIR: Ease comfortably into a lounge chair, your head resting against the back. Arms and hands are on the chair arms or resting on your thighs, legs and feet comfortably positioned with feet turned slightly outward. Your eyes are closed.

3. RECLINING: Lie down on your back, your head slightly pillowed. Your arms, a little bent at the elbows, rest palms down beside your body; your legs are relaxed and not touching each other; feet point slightly to the side. (If your feet are pointing straight up, you're not relaxed.) Your eyes are closed.

Warm-up

The warm-up, like everything in autogenics, is simple. It involves putting on your own "relaxation mask" and a cycle of breathing.

Imagine you are putting on a relaxation mask. This wonderful mask smooths out frowns and tension wrinkles. All the muscles in your face relax, let go. Your eyelids close and rest gently, with eyes aimed at the tip of your nose. Your jaw hangs loosely, your mouth slightly open. Your tongue touches the gumline of your upper teeth (silently pronounce *d* or *t*).

Now start a gentle cycle of deep breathing without straining yourself. This is "belly breathing." As the air flows in, feel your abdomen fill with it and puff up. As you breathe out, feel it sink in. Breathe slowly. Exhale twice as long as you inhale. With each breath the duration increases. For instance, *inhale,* two, three; *exhale* two, three, four, five, six. *Inhale* two, three, four; *exhale* two, three, four, five, six, seven, eight. Begin with one beat in, then go up the scale to six or so—don't strain.

Then reverse the cycle. Breathe in six and out twelve beats; breathe in five and out ten beats, and so on down to the count of one.

Spend two to three minutes on this warm-up. Then move right into the exercises.

First Exercise—Heaviness

You are learning to arouse a delicious feeling of heaviness in your body. Begin with your right arm (if left-handed, start with that arm). Silently, meaningfully repeat the formula.

My right arm is getting limp and heavy	6–8 times
My right arm is getting heavier and heavier	6–8 times
My right arm is completely heavy	6–8 times
I feel supremely calm	1 time

Then open your eyes and throw away that heaviness. Bend your arm back and forth a couple of times, take a few deep breaths. Check your position and your relaxation mask, then begin the cycle again. Including the warm-up, spend about seven to ten minutes at this two or three times a day.

Repeat the formula verbatim. Speak to yourself in an appropriate tone and imagine your arm getting heavier and heavier. Keep to the exercise, but don't try too hard, don't make this a matter of will. As someone has said, just abandon yourself to the words and to the feeling of heaviness. If you do have trouble imagining heaviness, between sessions hold something heavy, feel that heaviness and say aloud, my arm is getting heavier and heavier. The effect is cumulative; persistence pays. If you do the exercise regularly, heaviness will appear.

Do the heaviness exercise with your right arm for three days. After that, continue with the exact same formula with the following substitutions, that is, instead of "right arm" for the next three days you'll be saying "left arm."

My left arm is getting limp and heavy, etc.	3 days
Both my arms are getting limp and heavy	3 days
My right leg is getting limp and heavy	3 days
My left leg is getting limp and heavy	3 days
Both my legs are getting limp and heavy	3 days
My arms and legs are getting limp and heavy	3 days

The heaviness exercise takes twenty-one days. If a genuine feeling of heaviness appears early, you may go on to Exercise Two. Generally, it's best to build a sure foundation and take the full time. It may help to check off steps as you go to keep your place. Regular practice brings quickest results. Some people have exercised only once a day and gained control, though it usually takes longer. If you keep at it, eventually the desired effect will appear.

Second Exercise—Warmth

You are learning to arouse a feeling of warmth in yourself at your desire. Begin with your warm-up for about two minutes. In the autogenics program, you always recapitulate the previous exercise as you move ahead. Do one cycle of the last formula for heaviness in arms and legs, which should take about forty-five seconds to a minute. Heaviness established, begin the exercise for warmth, which follows the same general formula:

My right arm is getting limp and warm	6–8 times
My right arm is getting warmer and warmer	6–8 times
My right arm is completely warm	6–8 times
I feel supremely calm	1 time

As you repeat the formula for warmth, use your imagination.

Following the pattern, do right arm three days, left arm three days, both arms, right leg, left leg, both legs, both arms and legs for three days. Then do the final formula summing up the first two exercises. You no longer have to do the "heavy" cycle before this.

My arms and legs are getting limp and heavy and warm	6–8 times
My arms and legs are getting heavier and warmer	6–8 times
My arms and legs are completely heavy and warm	6–8 times
I feel supremely calm	1 time

Between cycles of the warmth formula, open your eyes, move and throw off some heaviness and warmth. Then repeat. As you mentally say the formula, use your imagination to recapture a time when your arm was warm. If you wish, visualize your arm immersed in a tub of warm water or remember the feeling of the seashore sun beating down, warming your arm. If necessary, to get the feeling, between sessions, put your arm in hot water, saying aloud, my arm is getting warmer and warmer. You can also imagine sending inner warmth to your limbs. Only begin the warmth formula for a limb if it feels heavy. If not, say the appropriate words until heaviness appears.

Third Exercise—A Calm Heart

You are learning to have a calm, steady heartbeat. Warm-up. Repeat in short form the heavy/warm formula, reciting each phrase three or four times. In the beginning at least, do this exercise lying on your back. Mentally feel for your heartbeat. Sense it in your chest, throat, or wherever. (If you're subject to headaches don't feel for it in your head.) You may prefer to rest your right hand on the pulse point of your left wrist or even on your chest. Usually, in a relaxed state, you can feel the beat. Repeat them silently:

My chest feels warm and pleasant	6–8 times
My heartbeat is calm and steady	6–8 times
I feel supremely calm	6–8 times

Do this exercise two or three times a day for seven to ten minutes for two weeks. A very, very few people find this exercise either eludes them or puts them off. If this happens after some trying, go on to the next.

Fourth Exercise—Breathing

You are learning to have better control over the rhythm of your breathing. Do the warm-up. Repeat in short form the following:

My arms and legs are getting limp and heavy and warm	1–2 times

My arms and legs are getting heavier and warmer	1–2 times
My arms and legs are completely heavy and warm	1–2 times
My heartbeat is calm and steady	1–2 times
I feel supremely calm	1 time
My breathing is supremely calm	6–8 times
I feel supremely calm	1 time

Do this exercise to gain control over your breathing for fourteen days, seven to ten minutes, two or three times a day. It is considered successfully mastered when you are able to breathe calmly and rhythmically at your own command after light physical activity or some sort of nervous stimulation. Instead of saying the usual, "I feel supremely calm," at the end of this exercise, Dr. Schultz preferred, "It breathes me."

Fifth Exercise—Stomach

You are learning to arouse a pleasant feeling of warmth in your solar plexus (the stomach above the waist, below the ribs). Do the warm-up. Repeat in short form the heavy/warm formula, the heart and breathing formula. Then:

My stomach is getting soft and warm	6–8 times
I feel supremely calm	1 time

If you wish, you can rest your right palm on your solar plexus during the exercise. Gradually you will experience a clear feeling of warmth. Instead of the above formula some people prefer to say, "My solar plexus radiates warmth." If you find this easier to imagine and visualize, use it. Do this for seven to ten minutes, two or three times a day for two weeks. The exercise is considered mastered when you feel a definite warmth.

Sixth Exercise—Cool Forehead

You are learning to experience a feeling of coolness on your forehead. Warm-up. As usual repeat in short form the formula for heaviness, warmth, heart, breathing, and stomach. Then:

My forehead is cool	6–8 times
I feel supremely calm	1 time

Imagine a fresh breeze cooling your forehead and temples. If necessary to catch the feeling, between sessions, stand in front of an air conditioner or fan, saying aloud, my forehead is cool. When you repeatedly experience a definite coolness the exercise is considered completed. Do this two or three times a day for seven to ten minutes for fourteen days.

Don't leap out of a session. Open your eyes and begin to move gradually. Stretch, flex your joints, throw off heaviness, and get active.

Recap

Repeat all formulas verbatim, but *not* automatically. Say them carefully with intention and emotion so that each sinks down into your consciousness. Combine the suggestions with imagination. The heavy/warm formulas often produce a deeply pleasant drowsy state, which shows they are well mastered. However, you do not want to go to sleep. If you do, learn from the experience. Perhaps you should exercise sitting up. Perhaps you've let your mind and/or imagination wander off. The aim of autogenics is relaxed awareness, and your consciousness should become more acute as tensions release. Imagine yourself retaining a center of awareness during sessions. If sleeping is a real problem, suggest to yourself, "My body may sleep, but my consciousness remains alert and aware."

You have already been saying what is in effect your final formula.

My arms and legs are heavy and warm
My heartbeat and breathing are calm and steady
My stomach is soft and warm, my forehead is cool
I feel supremely calm

Eventually most people using only one or two repeats can achieve the pleasant, self-possessed autogenic state. This state will strengthen as you regularly use the technique whenever you need to relax and be at your best. The maintenance dosage is practice twice a day for five minutes. When the skill is well mastered, people often find they can simply say: "Arms and legs heavy, warm; heart and breathing calm, steady; stomach warm, forehead cool, calm" and switch into the autogenic state.

Dr. Odessky brings his program to an end at this point. After a brief mention of second-level autogenics (see p. 176) he moves on to other Soviet therapeutic gambits like music therapy.

With these six simple exercises, you have mastered basic autogenics. If you're like most people, you've long since begun feeling its effects. Dr. Lindemann found in his classes that it was commonplace for people to experience relief of various complaints well before the end of the program. He cites as a typical case an official in his fifties who, by the time he'd gotten to the third exercise, found he could stop taking drugs for migraine, something he'd been unable to do since childhood. As body/mind come into closer communion, not just old physical tensions but psychological cramps and crystalizations seem to dissolve as well. As Odessky, Lindemann, and others attest, people typically feel a gain in self-confidence, a decrease in fears and worries. You have the means to bring yourself into equilibrium whenever the need arises.

Now that you have the skill, you no longer need to spend much time on training formulas when you practice. You can make the most of what are called "resolution formulas." Autogenic ability is like good fertile earth. It potentizes any seed you may want to plant. Resolution formulas are tailor-made affirmations to help strengthen yourself in one department or another. The simplicity of the practice belies its strength. This is the kind of exercise that can turn a sweaty-palmed stutterer into an eloquent speaker, or help guide a Lindemann across the Atlantic.

Self-Tailored Formulas

Obviously, each of us has different circumstances to deal with, different aspects of our personalities or different skills we wish to improve. With self-made formulas, you are taking conscious control of the suggestions that shape your behavior. You are shifting focus and energy away from patterns that have built up unthinkingly over the years. Here are some general suggestions to help you create your own formulas.

In the relaxed autogenic state, repeat your custom-made formulas for about three or four minutes twice a day. At first, at least, stick to only one subject at a time. Wait until you begin to feel the desired effect taking hold before moving on to other things. For instance, if you get inner tremors anticipating playing the piano in front of people, you might say, "I enjoy playing the piano in public. I feel pleasure sharing my talent with others . . ." Or if playing baseball is your love, "I am confident as I step up to bat." Or, "I throw fluidly, powerfully." Try to wholeheartedly mean what you say during the time you are reciting your formulas. Suspend disbelief, act as if what you're saying is actually true.

Suggestions can be short and specific: "My eye is on the ball." "Chin tucked as I dive." Or they can be more general nourishment for the whole person: "I forgive myself for all mistakes in the past. I am free. I am at peace with myself and the world." A combination of both is good, and as you end the session, affirm you are taking these qualities into the world with you now.

Keep your phrases short. Rhythm and alliteration help the ideas root in the mind. So can rhyme. Don't worry about literary merit, phrases can be horrific as long as they stick. An example of this is a popular old self-help phrase that is hard to shake once heard: "The locusts of lack have eaten their last."

Phrase your formulas with care. The deep mind is a literalist. Instead of saying, "I will train with enthusiasm and joy," say "I train enthusiastically and joyously." Cast sentences in the present, for the future is always something coming, never arrived. Most importantly, construct your phrases positively. Avoid saying, "I do not lose my concentration . . . I do not forget my speech . . ." Say, "My concentration is complete and steady. I easily remember my speech." Those small negatives *don't, won't, not* can get overwhelmed. To avoid the negative, some people prefer to label things "immaterial." For instance, "Smoking immaterial. I breathe fresh and free. I am satisfied."

To recap, say your formulas with attention and meaning. Keep them short. Secure your desires in the "now" in a positive structure. And speak kindly to yourself.

If you run a hectic schedule or have many responsibilities, an autogenics break can do you more good than a coffee break. In four or five minutes you can do it anywhere, in the office, in a cab or plane. Take a minute to get into a wholly relaxed autogenic state. Then use a formula such as: "I am fresh and alert and in good humor. I let go of tensions." If needed, say, "Tensions and anger dissolve."

With resolutions, think of performance in its widest sense. Build yourself up, appreciate yourself before exams, job interviews, or any personal confrontation. With a little creativity, you can create phrases to enhance sexual performance and rapport, a common use of autogenic resolutions in Europe. Many have also used autogenics to help overcome compulsive smoking or drinking. It's a novel aid in dieting because it depends not on willpower, but on imagination. Consider using it whenever you feel at a disadvantage—if you're in a minority of some kind, if you're undergoing job retraining, if you're a woman reentering the work world—whatever, autogenic resolutions properly used can help equalize matters.

Second-Level Autogenics

Second-level autogenics trains and sharpens the imagination making it an extremely powerful tool. It can improve performance of any kind and improve relationships and personality. Again, six exercises are involved. You gain the ability to clearly imagine color, to imagine objects, to mentally experience abstract notions like courage or compassion, to improve self-image, to contemplate relationships with others, and finally, to receive answers from extended resources of consciousness. The last-mentioned can be a great help in personal and professional problem solving. It involves reaching into the knowledge of subconscious and supraconscious for answers. Some think of it as communicating with the superego. Many call it going to the higher self, to the wise old woman or wise old man for guidance. Dr. H. Hengstmann, a German physician, calls second-level autogenics the "purest form of psychological communication, in depth a person [can have] with himself and others."

Exercises to strengthen each of these six autogenic skills are in the exercise section (see page 271).

Athletes and other performers, as we've seen, use mental movies to enhance their prowess. Obviously, if you are going to be a mental movie maker, it helps to have good powers of visualization and imagination. If you don't, exercises from second-level autogenics and mental yoga can give them to you.

Mental Movies

A star basketball player pulls up lame. For the next couple of days when the rest of the team practices, he joins in, carefully going through the various plays and shots—in his mind. This way of keeping faculties sharp has been working for European athletes. Even in top shape, many find that working out in mind movies does more for performance than spending that much additional time in actual practice. You can run through any activity this way, public performance or private, learning to drive on a superhighway or getting the hang of a new dance step.

After a few minutes of autogenic relaxation begin your mental movie. Take it step by step, moving through a wholly superb performance. See yourself moving with perfect, serene technique. (Of course, beforehand know what correct technique is. Don't insert wrong information.) If you're a bowler, for example, see yourself holding the ball, taking your steps to the line, releasing the ball, following through smoothly—watch the ball rolling down the alley, hitting the head pin at just the right angle for a strike. Work on various shots. If it's a business meeting, focus in on yourself entering the conference room. See yourself giving a presentation that's well received.

As a movie maker, use your assets. Zoom in and out at important spots as Jack Nicklaus does in his golf visualizations. Look from various angles. Put your movie into slow motion; this is particularly good with an activity requiring split-second timing like high diving or gymnastics. If you make a mistake, go back and shoot that section again, get it right. After watching yourself perform with finesse, get back inside yourself in the movie. Feel the golf club or bowling ball in your hand. Go through your paces sensing your oneness with this activity. If you're giving a talk, see your audience, watch their faces alert with understanding. Feel the rapport growing. Enjoy yourself.

For Sports in Particular

Regular autogenic practice will improve mental and physical poise, coordination, and muscle movement generally. There are certain specific autogenic techniques that large numbers of athletes agree have helped boost performance. For instance, one can use affirmations to keep motivation high, to sustain the zest for training and daily practice. Obviously, they can also be used to help ease any number of anxieties or psychological blocks—fear of failure or injury, nervousness, lack of concentration, anger at teammates, a decline in performance whenever an opponent gets ahead. For the latter you might affirm, "Opponents immaterial. Calm and confident, I play well." Sophrology coaches often link such affirmations with rhythmic breathing. A short resolution is repeated with each exhalation. Just as steady autogenic practice reduces sports injuries because one is not so likely to go into action with nervously tensed muscles, many athletes extol the recuperative powers of the system. After a game or workout, as soon as possible shift into the autogenic state to rebalance and rest body and mind.

To train athletes, sophrology practitioners use autogenics plus a wide range of exercises drawn from sources like Zen and yoga. Many of these are similar to exercises in other parts of this book. Sophrology tries to tailor a program for each individual; however, one can get some general idea of the sort of techniques that might be helpful. For instance, sophrology coaches often suggest progressive relaxation as a basic exercise (see Chapter 7). Athletes are told to focus awareness on the contraction and decontraction of each set of body muscles and to attempt to gain a strong picture of their entire body pattern. To further strengthen awareness of the whole body, its energy fields, and the expansion and contraction of these fields, sophrologists use an exercise like the one we've called Energy Field Awareness in Chapter 17.

A trapshooter who regularly practiced progressive relaxation under sophrology reported that during competition, time seemed to expand. Though he had only eight-tenths of a second to sight his target, his growing ability to concentrate mind and body made it seem to him that he had plenty of time to aim and fire. For another technique that supposedly can lead to this ability to experience actual play in slow motion, see the Color

Motion Exercise in Chapter 17. Sophrologists also pay great attention to breathing exercises to suit specific situations (see Chapters 7 and 17).

On the psychological side for sports, sophrologists use the many exercises that develop concentration, enhance perception, and increase rapport (see Chapter 18). For a person who has had a losing streak, they might prescribe an exercise like Improving Your Self-Image to transform images of failure into those of success. To prepare for future events, sophrologists use the mental movies method. In their mind's eye, athletes picture in detail the coming competition, they imagine their own highly successful performance, they try to be as aware as possible of the physical and mental sensations that accompany this picturing of success. Finally, they are instructed to reproduce this feeling when they enter the actual event. See Joy of Learning Recall in Chapter 7 which can also be used as joy of winning or joy of best performance.

Autogenics once mastered is a means and a vehicle. Simple yet high-powered, it can carry you in greater style through any activity you choose. Whether you're learning to have a heavier arm or are involved with a full sensorama movie, don't try too hard. If you have a steel will, set it aside to use elsewhere. As Mack the Knife sings, "It's useless, it's useless, trying ain't enough." And as the grandfather of all modern suggestive systems, Emile Coué, wrote, "When the imagination and the will are in conflict, the imagination invariably gains the day. . . . In the conflict between the will and the imagination, the force of the imagination is in direct ratio to the square of the will."

A person with stage fright or one who fears losing a sports match has a mental image of failure. The more the will tries to struggle with this image, the more energy the image gains. "The fatal attraction of the bunker for the nervous golfer is due to the same cause," says Coué. "With his mind's eye, he sees his ball alighting in the most unfavorable spot. He may use any club he likes, he may make a long drive or a short; as long as the thought of the bunker dominates his mind, the ball will inevitably find its way towards it. The more he calls on his will to help him, the worse his plight is likely to be."

Our imaginations can work for us or against us. Using the techniques of sophrology and autogenics we can take that transforming power in hand to realize more of ourselves. It's a creative act.

Some few people have learned to use human potential so well that they seem an evolutionary leap ahead of the rest of us. One of them is a man who can accomplish the extraordinary in many areas, but he shows what an unobstructed personality can do most clearly, in terms of his own flesh and blood. He's a man at the center in more ways than one.

Chapter 12
Pain Control

A tall, sinewy man with a silver Vandyke beard seems like a still point at the hub of a circle of men watching him with almost crackling intensity. A rather bemused look in his eyes, the tall man gazes at a five-inch-long needle being pushed through his arm and out the other side. When it is extracted, no blood shows and no puncture marks are visible. Then one of the circling men, slowly, deliberately presses the red, smoking end of a cigarette into the tall man's flesh. He doesn't cry out, he doesn't even flinch. It's as though it wasn't happening. No blister will appear to prove it did. Jack Schwarz isn't being tortured, though he discovered the strength of his ability to control pain and heal his body at will in Nazi torture cells while fighting with the Dutch underground.

With the charisma of an actor or a superb teacher, Schwarz looks as if he could be cast as the magician in an Ingmar Bergman film. But in real life, he's far too outgoing, jovial, and empathetic to remind you of the saturnine magician.

Today, Jack Schwarz is a leader in efforts to bring new methods of pain control, healing, and health maintenance into widespread practice in medicine, and into public use.

A great many scientists and many renowned institutes have tested Schwarz, including the Langley Porter Neuropsychiatric Institute of the University of California Medical School, the Max Planck Institute in Munich, and, particularly, the Menninger Foundation in Topeka, Kansas. There, some years ago, Dr. Elmer Green and his wife, Alyce Green, began putting the claims of generations of yogis to the test with impartial equipment. The Greens broke from the mulish Western tradition of insisting that anyone who claimed to control "involuntary" body processes was clearly a faker, not worth investigating. The Greens found Schwarz and others were indeed self-possessed. "Jack Schwarz has, in the realm of voluntary controls, one of the greatest talents in the country and probably in the world," Dr. Green reports. Schwarz and a few of the others the Greens examined are able to do such things as direct their circulation, alter heartbeats, raise and lower temperature in various parts of the body, block pain, control bleeding, and drastically speed healing. One man, Swami Rama, was even able at the Greens' request to create a small growth on his hand. He was also able to make it dissolve again.

In his continuous striving to open the reserves of the mind, Jack Schwarz has claimed for his own a number of other abilities. For one, he has learned to see and interpret the shifting bioenergies surrounding a person's body—the aura. Doctors at Menninger and elsewhere find his diagnoses from studying this aura agree with those made by conventional tests and even pick up items that have been overlooked. For five years, Jack Schwarz has been teaching doctors to develop pain control and other reserve abilities. He is a consultant to the Menninger Foundation and heads the Aletheia Foundation in Grants Pass, Oregon. For a long time, he envisioned an educational and therapeutic complex where work could progress toward realizing full human potential—"spiritual, psychological, and physical health." His organization now has 118 acres of woodland, and the idea is moving off the drawing boards. A holistic outpatient clinic opened in late 1978 where Schwarz works daily with health professionals.

As Schwarz moves more deeply into the teaching of professionals, there is another man putting body and limbs on the line in an attempt to show us something. If you have to be a world-record holder to get attention for what you believe in, then Vernon E. Craig decided he'd be one. A slightly chunky man of average height, Craig's appearance tempts one to reach back to childhood stories and call him the jolly Swiss cheesemaker. He is an Ohio cheesemaker by profession. In his spare time, Craig metamorphoses into *Komar,* complete with turban, bare chest, and pantaloons. With a slightly abstracted air, Komar saunters barefoot across yards of glowing coals. He holds the Guinness World Record: a twenty-five-feet walk through coals burning at 1,494 degrees Fahrenheit.

Craig began turning into Komar—climbing ladders of swords, having strong men ring down a sledgehammer to crack concrete slabs on his chest—when he first put the act together for charity, to help the retarded. Shortly he began thinking, we are all retarded—we develop so little of our natural ability. "I'm just an ordinary man. What I can do, you can learn to do," Komar emphasizes. As a boy, he found a yoga text and decided to see if he could learn, as yogis claimed, to control pain.

"I'm just an ordinary man," he repeats to the audience as he stretches out on a bed of six-inch nails. Another slab of nails is lowered, points down onto his torso, making Komar the filling in a nail sandwich. Six of the heaviest people in the audience are going to sit on top of the sandwich. Komar cajoles, "Don't be pussycats, sit down, all together." They do and the Ohio cheesemaker smiles. When he's released, no blood, wounds, or bruises appear. For this, he holds another Guinness World Record: 1,642½ pounds pressing down on his double bed of nails.

For Komar, the entertaining theatrics exist for a reason beyond show-business hype. "My main interest, of course, is the whole field of mental control, of developing our potential," Craig says. "Because it's dramatic, I use the pain demonstration. It gives them a hint of what an ordinary person can learn to do. It might start people thinking."

Increasingly, he is catching people's attention. He speaks now at professional conclaves of doctors and scientists. He, too, has laboratory certification. Dr. C. Norman Shealy, director of the Pain Rehabilitation Center in La Crosse, Wisconsin, tested him with various methods used to measure a person's tolerance to pain. Calm and smiling, Komar kept going off the top of the scale. Whether they froze him, stuck him, or used rising electric shocks, Shealy and other doctors couldn't seem to hurt Vernon Craig. Craig's basic aim is to keep other people from hurting, too. To help, he's publishing the pain-control program he followed (see Bibliography, Section II, Steiger).

Physiologists have, of course, checked to see that both Schwarz and Komar have normal sensitivity to pain when they are not in an altered state that activates mind reserves. How does a Jack Schwarz or a Vernon Craig instantly switch off pain? They have learned how to control body processes and finally how to take themselves off to somewhere else. Schwarz says, "I get out of myself and imagine I'm standing next to my body. I don't stick a needle into *my* arm," he says. "I stick a needle into *an* arm." This is reminiscent of a remark once made by Nijinsky. Someone once said to the great ballet star, "It's a pity you can't see yourself dance." "Oh, but I do," he replied. "I'm outside myself, watching and directing."

"The abilities that I demonstrate in experiments are within everyone's reach," Schwarz says, explaining they spring from harmonious interaction of body and mind. To achieve such harmony "you need to develop a non-attached point of view, an awareness of the purpose of life, and a flow of energy or consciousness that is not hindered by fear or repressed emotions."

Schwarz teaches that you develop this through creative, active meditation—not a closed system, but a collection of techniques and tools to harmonize body/mind. Many such tools are outlined in this book but at the center of Schwarz's teaching is a subject that in direct terms we've only touched upon. Indirectly, some people will see it throughout the book as the underlying agent of super abilities. That subject is energy: bioenergy, subtle energy, prana, kundalini, the energy that rises to form the backbone and crown of Eastern philosophy and yogic science.

Schwarz teaches how to exercise this energy, whether you consider it "real" or "imaginary," to harmonize and strengthen the power centers of the body. This is the energy Pandit Gopi Krishna calls "the energy of genius." Even in the West, there is increasing reason to think that it is part of the subtle means, part of the transducing power that allows us out-of-the-ordinary accomplishments, from black-belt karate to supermemory. Schwarz tells how to exercise this energy in his book, *Voluntary Controls.*

Once when we were with Jack Schwarz on the west coast, a couple of people sidled up to let us in on a secret: "Jack isn't really human you know." There were rumors he just might be from Pluto. It stood to reason if he could do those things . . . After some consideration, we have to say that Jack Schwarz and Vernon Craig are human. If you think about it, you might say they are even more human than the rest of us, for they are displaying more of the abilities inherent in our kind.

Anyone who uses the methods of superlearning and superperformance outlined in this book will soon discover that among the spin-off benefits are better health and control over various symptoms. You can learn to extend these techniques to help you control pain—at the dentist, or for strains and cramps from overexertion in sports or dance. As mentioned in Chapter 2, one of the first ways Dr. Lozanov used suggestology was for pain control, even as anesthesia for major surgery. One of the major applications of sophrology, too, is in painless childbirth.

Neurologist, neurosurgeon, C. Norman Shealy is an unusual man himself, another spearhead in the move toward holistic medicine. Shealy is the sort of person who one day decides, "There has to be a better way," and sets out to find it. It occurred to him that continuously drugging those in chronic pain and chemically tranquilizing people who are upset is not really a healing way. From experience, he knew that surgery and, in his field, the dangerous tests that often accompany it, are not always the answer either.

Today Dr. Shealy and his medical associates have assembled a battery of nontoxic treatments to release people from the solitary confinement of long-term chronic pain (see Bibliography). From on-the-spot experience, Dr. Shealy has also developed a rounded program to help anyone find new dimensions of well-being. At the heart of it is "biogenics," a greatly expanded program of autogenics that Shealy calls a "holistic approach to life and health which you may constantly appreciate anew and expand as you practice." As the doctor says, "You create your own reality." He hopes for the day when autogenic principles will be taught in the country's schools.

Autogenics, self-control, is basic in many pain reduction and self-healing programs. Drawing on yoga and other traditions, Jack Schwarz and Vernon Craig taught themselves. They are spectacular proof that these are learnable abilities.

Once you have mastered basic autogenics, and know how to visualize and imagine clearly, you have the techniques you need to begin to learn pain control and self-healing. Day-by-day programs like Schwarz's, Craig's, and Shealy's are books in themselves. Here, we can only give a few exercises to get you started. (Of course, if you don't know why you have a certain pain, always check with your medical advisor.)

Breathing Away Pain

Modern pain-control methods have been fed by various streams of yogic experience. Around the turn of the century, the accomplished, scholarly Yogi Ramacharaka published a lucid text to make some of these traditional exercises available to the "eminently practical Western mind."

One of these is based on "rhythmic breathing." Rhythm in this instance varies with the individual. It reinforces the rhythm of one's own body and is based on the heartbeat.

In a relaxed state, feel your pulse. Count aloud long enough to really get the sense of the rhythm so you can breathe to that count without concentrating on it. Most beginners find it comfortable to breathe in to a count of six pulse beats. Hold the breath for three, breathe out six, pause for three, and start again. Eventually, you'll find it easy to breathe to a longer count. (Always breathe through the nose unless otherwise instructed.)

For pain control, sit up straight or lie down on your back. Do rhythmic breathing to your pulse long enough to get well into the swing of it. As you do it, conjure the thought that you are breathing in prana: absolute energy, the active principle of life —bright, vital force. Inhale prana. As you exhale, mentally send the prana to the painful part to reestablish proper circulation and nerve currents. Then inhale prana again, this time with the thought of using this energy to drive out pain. Exhale thinking the prana is now driving the pain from you. Alternate these two ideas—strengthen the body's healing forces; drive out the pain. Do this seven times, then rest. On the way to the rest, Ramacharaka suggests a yogic cleansing breath: take a full deep breath filling the abdomen, lower and upper lungs. Hold it a few seconds. Pucker up as if you were going to whistle, only keep your cheeks flat. Expel the air in short, forceful bursts through your mouth. If needed, repeat cycles of seven. Will or trying to force the issue won't help, Ramacharaka says, calm command and a good mental picture will do the trick.

Light

This is another time-tested yoga technique, used to control pain, to relax tensions, or recharge parts of the body. You are going to take pure, energizing light from a great battery in your solar plexus (the stomach above the waist a little below the ribs) and transfer it to wherever you throb or ache, for instance, to your head.

Imagine the mighty solar-fueled energy of life itself. Sit up straight or lie on your back. Knuckles facing each other, fingers bent, place your hands and fingertips lightly on your solar plexus. Begin to breathe deeply, smoothly, slowly. Imagine you are breathing in white light, bright and vital as the core of the sun. Imagine this light energy flowing into your abdomen, then your chest, as your lungs expand. Then exhale.

Once you have the rhythm, as you inhale, imagine that great light flowing down through your solar plexus and into your fingertips charging your hands. Hold your breath and slowly move your fingertips to your forehead. Then slowly exhale, visualizing the light energy flowing from your fingers in through the middle of your forehead until your whole head is flooded with light. When you've exhaled completely, pause as you move your hands back down to your solar plexus, then begin the cycle again.

Jack Schwarz recommends that you visualize this light not only filling your head, but also flowing out through your forehead as if you were wearing a miner's hat with a headlight.

Do this exercise twenty-one times. Repeat after a rest if necessary. Constant, vivid visualization of the white light is important. Try imagining bright sun on pure white snow. Yogis say it takes awhile to develop this energy-charging ability. As this technique is also used to relax tensions, it might be a good idea to try it once a day for a time, before you get a specific pain.

The "Numbing Touch" for Pain Control

Here's a pain-control technique that one of the authors found can be a boon in all sorts of situations. As a student of voluntary control, she, like hundreds of others, practiced and quickly learned to do this simple method for pain relief. Later, she was able to demonstrate this form of voluntary control for doctors and see it register on monitoring instruments. She found it was a great benefit on many occasions, such as minor hand surgery or the removal of stitches. Many people find it's a helpful ploy, too, after trips to the dentist when the anesthetic wears off. It can be helpful also for aches and strains that come from overexertion in sports; in fact, for any sort of ache or pain that can be eased by an anesthetic effect.

If you've tried the basic mind-training exercises (Chapter 11) and learned to make your arms and legs heavy on command, you should be able to master this step easily. It involves learning to change the temperature of your hands.

Use your preferred method of relaxation to get into a comfortable, relaxed state, breathing easily and deeply. Now tell yourself, your right hand is becoming heavy, *cold,* and numb.

Imagine plunging your right hand into an ice bucket. Feel it getting bluer, and colder. Feel it getting numb. Visualize your hand as being freezing cold.

Say to yourself, "My right hand is becoming heavy, cold, and numb." Practice for several minutes.

When you sense that your right hand is cold and numb, touch the top of your left hand with the first two fingers of your numb right hand. Say: "The spot I'm touching with my right hand is also becoming cold and numb." Test for numbness by pressing your nails into the numb spot. Practice until you can develop coldness and numbness at will on your left hand.

Finally, tell yourself that any area of your body you touch with your numb, cold right hand will also become anesthetized, cold, and completely numb, as if you'd had a shot of novocaine. For instance, after a trip to the dentist, you can turn your right hand cold and numb and give the "numbing touch" to your sore gums to ease discomfort.

With practice, you should be able to bring on coldness and numbness when necessary in a very short time. Of course, any pain-control technique should be learned and practiced *ahead of time,* rather than waiting until you are already racked with pain.

Other Ache Removers

1. Headaches have been found to respond to a slightly different approach. Biofeedback researchers discovered that for headaches, voluntary control of temperature in the hands should be turned to *warm* rather than cold. Use the same method as above, but instead, visualize and feel *both* hands and arms becoming heavy and *warm.* Say to yourself: "Forehead cool: hands and arms warm."

If necessary, picture yourself sitting with an ice pack on your head and your hands in a bucket of hot water.

When programming, always focus on restoring health—not on the problem. Say, "My head is clear. I feel refreshed and alert."

2. Another helpful technique for tension and aches involves a different kind of visualization. Get into a relaxed state. Mentally picture a large colored ball in front of you. The ball should be any color that appeals to you at that particular moment—your personal color. Hold the ball in your hands. Visualize it getting smaller and smaller. Then throw it away.

(The key to this exercise is that your unconscious mind will select the right color for you relating to the particular form of stress that's generating your aches, whether they're from mental strain, anger, emotional tension, or whatever.)

3. Another method of removing aches involves thinking about an ache as a short circuit in an electrical device. Energy has to get flowing again. Picture your legs and feet as grounding wires for an electrical device. Now, put one hand on your solar plexus (palm flat), and put the other hand on the back of the neck (palm flat). Have the little finger touching the top, Atlas vertebra, and the remaining four fingers on the vertebrae below. Hold your hands this way for three minutes.

Now reverse hands and repeat for three minutes.

Visualize energy flowing through you and going out your forehead.

You may notice with this technique that the fingers on your

neck begin to feel hot while the hand on your solar plexus feels less warm, and you may feel a slight churning sensation.

As you breathe slowly, steadily, and evenly, picture energy flowing through and out, through and out, through and out, removing any short circuits and letting the pain flow out.

Autogenic Relief

If you do find yourself unpracticed and in pain, try riding with it. Don't hunch against the pain, let it go. Try to relax and concentrate on your even, steady breathing. Try breathing the pain away. This is picking up discord on its own note and slowly resolving it to harmony.

Dr. Elmer Green, speaking of self-healing done in a deeply relaxed state says, "Creativity in terms of physiological processes means physical healing, physical regeneration. Creativity in emotional terms consists, then, of establishing, or creating, attitude changes through the practice of healthy emotions—emotions whose neural correlates are those that establish harmony in the visceral brain . . ." A creative act, that's what self-healing is. With the holistic approach you can begin to realize your creative power is there. Too often in the past, we've used it unconsciously, negatively, to create disease.

In autogenic practice, the general rule of thumb reads: When the pain is exterior—skin, teeth, head, toes—send coolness. For deep-seated inner-organ pain, send warmth. But always determine professionally why you hurt. With "biogenics" Dr. Shealy finds patients in chronic pain lose unpleasant sensations during very deep relaxation. With practice they can bring some of this well-being back into active life.

You can control pain in another way with autogenics by using the full force of the regime to maintain and enhance health, to work out small problems before they magnify. If problems have developed, autogenics—whose major use still is medical—is an effective adjunct therapy. There are, for instance, resolution formulas for specific ailments. Dr. Shealy includes some in his book, *90 Days to Self-Health,* as does Dr. Lindemann in his, *Relieve Tension the Autogenic Way.* As a general example, the formula for rheumatism-arthritis might include: phrases to release anger in particular, and tensions generally; affirmations of peace, of joint flexibility and comfort; affirmations that an elbow or knee is free of pain; and the sending of warmth to the afflicted joint.

Pain voices dis-ease, disharmony. At the Pain Rehabilitation Center, Shealy has added on to first- and second-level autogenics to create a program designed to bring patients back into physical, mental, emotional, and spiritual harmony. He says he can give examples of almost any illness being cleared by biogenics and also of almost any illness being badly aggravated by negative emotions. If emotions can cause disease, Shealy concludes, "By controlling emotional excess mentally, one can learn to control most symptoms and most disease process." It's a big statement for a doctor. Yet many doctors today are beginning to take a holistic view and are realizing as never before how the mind can heal and harm. They are keeping an eye on the work of such doctors as Carl Simonton of Austin who is training cancer patients in specific meditative and visualization techniques. When these holistic techniques are used, some patients diagnosed as "terminal" shift to nonterminal.

Wilhelm Von Humboldt, a scholar-diplomat and one of the founders of the University of Berlin, supposedly said that he believed the day would arrive when it would be shameful to be sick, for sickness would be seen as coming from perverse ideas. None of us need to feel embarrassed yet. Not only were we never taught to be well in this sense, in many cases our surroundings in effect taught us to be sick. That is why Dr. Shealy, Dr. Lindemann, and other knowledgeable doctors think that teaching autogenic training techniques in the early school years would be one of the most valuable forms of education—something to last us a healthy lifetime. "If autogenic training were to be taught in school, the world could heal itself," Dr. Lindemann says. We won't come to disease-free nirvana, "but I believe that autogenic training could prevent more sickness and disturbed behavior than can doctors who will continue to be more interested, and perhaps justifiably, in cure than in prevention," he concludes.

The autogenic doctors are giving us an unstated challenge along with their techniques. They want to put the responsibility for well-being back in our own hands and minds. They're challenging us to realize another potential—health.

SECTION III
SUPER-RAPPORT

Chapter 13
Future Abilities

Changes are upon us, "more far-reaching than those which emerged from the Copernican, Darwinian, and Freudian revolutions," says Dr. Willis Harmon, former director of the U.S. Educational Policy Research Center. A major change in the way we view ourselves and the world is under way, he says, that will increasingly affect education, business, and life generally. According to Harmon, there are several harbingers of this profound change. One is our ripening ability to control inner states. This includes the ability to learn how to learn as a skill in itself.

As we've seen, this learning turns into superlearning when the whole person is evoked. Part of that whole are right-brain abilities as they are popularly termed—intuition, creativity, imagination, spiritual insight. In this area, too, are some "other" abilities that have recently regained admission to polite intellectual circles. For instance, Dr. Harmon, now Director for the Study of Social Policy at Stanford Research Institute, sees something else helping to shape our future: parapsychology. He has looked into contemporary research. He remarks, ". . . probably we will eventually discover that all persons have the full range of psychic phenomena as potentialities, all unconsciously understood . . ."

These are the "other" abilities that are beginning to stir, ready, it seems, to be consciously owned and used. If you're interested in intuition, creativity, or so-called ESP, the relaxation and visualization techniques you've picked up in this book are tested equipment to get a head start on learning these future abilities.

Even if it's ESP you are after, you probably won't be the first on your block. Those familiar with the psi field, including Harmon, will tell you that mainstream people with such abilities have been revealing themselves in unprecedented droves during the past decade. Some are engineers and farmers, some are teachers, physicists, and doctors. Some haven't decided what they're going to do because they're only eight. And some are presidents of corporations.

For instance, among businessmen who have said publicly that ESP played a role in their success are Alexander M. Poniatoff, founder and chairman of the board emeritus of the Ampex Corporation; William W. Keeler, chairman of the board emeritus of Phillips Petroleum; and John L. Tishman, board member and executive vice-president of Tishman Realty & Construction Company.

In 1969, the American Association for the Advancement of Science recognized parapsychology as a specific field of scientific inquiry. Today, well over a hundred colleges give courses in the parasciences. And for a while now, it has seemed as though the back-page ads of occult magazines have moved up front into news stories—"Psychic Bends the Unbendable at Naval Lab," "Government Funds Think Tank Telepathy Project." We have cults, courses, gurus, too, sometimes with little science and less art. Some fear we're sliding back down the slippery slope into unreason and superstition.

Like most who have looked into it, Dr. Lozanov doesn't think so. A Sofia reporter asked him if psi rather than being an emerging talent might instead be a throwback ability best left with primitives.

"On the contrary," Lozanov replied, "it is the most cultivated, artistic types of personalities, the writers, painters, and artists who have this ability. With modern man, it is more a question of an artistic inspiration in realizing the telepathic connection."

Rather than a throwback ability, such people as the eminent psychologist, Dr. Carl Rogers, might perhaps call psi a "throw ahead" ability. Rogers thinks we may be in an evolutionary transition, as major as the one that urged creatures from the sea up onto expanded life on land. "Are we evolving into new spaces, new ways of being?" he asks. "Will we discover new energies and forces?" Rogers suggests that by using right-brain abilities, psi abilities, we may come to know directly a different universe, a non-linear one like the universe our physicists are describing.

If there is a danger to the superstitions weaving around the psi field, it may lie less with the psychic yoyos and more with the holdover thinkers looking through nineteenth-century eyes at a mechanistic world in which psi cannot exist. Today, this is superstition. Physicists have long since dismantled the "machine" and gone about dematerializing matter. Psi inhabits the realm of the possible.

Fear stayed the authorities of the day from looking through Galileo's telescope at the solar system. Ironically, some now fear looking through the other end of the telescope, inside ourselves, where perhaps science, religion, and the humanities are coming together again. It might not matter too much if it only concerned those superstars who "cloud men's minds" or chase a saltshaker around the table by staring at it. But the promise of psi lies in more than such dazzlers. Communist investigators, including Dr. Lozanov, were the first in our time to view psychic abilities as widespread human abilities, abilities that many people might learn to use. That's the real news of the last ten years. While going about their everyday concerns, men and women have been exercising and using these other ways of knowing, integrating them into the whole self, not to replace reason, but to work with it.

Section One dealt with the learning of facts. This section covers briefly a few techniques to help you make the most of facts, to help set creativity and intuition humming. They may also give you new entrees—sensuous and mind provoking—into the vast, intimate world beyond facts where most of life is lived.

Chapter 14

The Well-tempered Hunch: Professional and Personal

"A feeling, that go-ahead intuition often nudged me into action," explains hotel man Conrad Hilton. Sometimes "Connie's hunches," as competitors called them, almost seemed like an unfair advantage. Take the case of the Stevens Corporation. Trustees put it up for sale and called for sealed bids. Hilton made his first bid in a hurry, $165,000. "Then somehow that didn't feel right. Another figure kept coming—$180,000. It felt right. I changed my bid on that hunch. When they were opened, the closest bid to mine was $179,800." On a hunch, Hilton won by a slim $200. "Eventually," he reports, "the assets returned me 2 million."

But you don't have to be a tycoon. Ask Lawrence Tynan. In the summer of 1971, he looked over his auto agency in Middletown, New Jersey, and wondered why he'd set himself up for bankruptcy. That spring he'd bought five times more cars than usual. He'd done it with a hunch. Then, President Nixon announced his rebate plan for new-car buyers. Soon, instead of cars, Tynan had five times more profits than usual. "I couldn't have gotten these extra cars after Nixon's speech," he points out.

Early on, most of us were imbued with a very strong suggestion from parents, teachers, and the culture around us not to go
with a feeling, not to act on a hunch like Hilton and Tynan did.
Responsible people didn't act that way. It wasn't sensible, we
were told directly and indirectly. In effect, we were being told
to be half-witted. People who use all their wits blend two ways
of knowing; the rational-analytical with the intuitive-creative.

This chapter is about making the most of your intuitive mode
of thinking and responding. Strengthening intuitive ability is in
itself a realization of more of your potential. It is becoming clear
that the Age of Enlightenment only lit up the rational side of
our natures, leaving half of us in the dark. At the same time, it
has also become clear that highly successful people have always
been adept at being whole-witted even though they often make
up "rational" explanations to cover their intuitive tracks. One
man who has certainly used both ways of thinking to a renaissance shine is Buckminster Fuller. "Everybody has this intuition very, very powerfully," Fuller says, "but most of us today
are so quickly frustrated about things, that we learn not to listen
to our intuition."

You might expect to find intuition sparking in the arts or in
love affairs. You might not expect it to be on the job in the
tough, top-level decisions of heavy industry. Yet, that is where
we found it when we interviewed for *Executive ESP*, a book
about decision making. We talked, too, to teachers, consumer
advocates, newspeople, salespeople, weather forecasters. Those
at the top almost always said, "Sure, I use it." "It" was called
hunches, gut feelings, intuition or, sometimes, outright ESP.

Intuition can lighten the load in whatever you do from ar-
chaeology to xerography. Chester Carlson, the lawyer-inventor
of Xerox, was indeed interested in intuition and psi. Why? Because he used them. Carlson was so interested that in the early
sixties he funded ESP research at the New Jersey Institute of
Technology, our fourth largest engineering school.

Working at the college's Psi Communications Project, Dr.
Douglas Dean and Dr. John Mihalasky asked themselves, when

everything is totaled up—education, intelligence, experience—
what is the X-factor that makes the difference between good
and superlative performance? They had a hunch the answer
might be ESP—ESP generally, and in particular *precognition*,
literally the ability to pre-know.

They tested over seven thousand executives for precognition.
"We want you to pick a one-hundred-digit number," they told
them. "*Later*, a computer will select a number for each of you.
See if you can outguess it." Education, reason, experience were
no help. Many men and women, however, apparently could
summon precognition. They scored above chance. Most intriguing was the performance of thirty-six company presidents. The
box score went like this:

Twenty-one presidents who had more than doubled their
firm's profits during the last five years:
nineteen scored high on precognition
two scored at chance

Fifteen presidents of firms that had not done as well:
five scored high on precognition (These turned
out to have increased company profits from
51 to 100 percent)
two scored at chance
eight scored below

Janitors were also tested at the New Jersey college. "Those
ranked most successful by their peers," Dr. Mihalasky says,
"turned out to be the good guessers on the precognition test."
Intuition, it seems, is part of the whole person. We are endowed
with it for a reason—to help us create more successful lives for
ourselves and others no matter where we are. In any of life's
decisions, decisions from rearing kids to buying a house, it
makes sense to use all of our abilities to make better choices.

Intuition is a magnetic word that pulls together a number of
factors, only one of which is ESP. Probably the reason Conrad

Hilton could come up with straight ESP in a pinch was because he was used to acting on an everyday basis with the intuitive part of his mind. Before trying to nurture pure precognitive ability try exercising your intuition. It will help in those decisions. It also is the stuff of creativity. Bucky Fuller tells of a study of famous scientists' diaries in which all of them recorded that the single most important item connected to their great discovery was intuition. The next most important was a second intuition that flashed about thirty seconds after the first and showed how to prove and implement their discovery.

How to Prime Intuition

Be aware of it. Intuition is a human ability and you possess it. In a sense, in using and strengthening this part of your mind, you are strengthening the integrity of your nature as a human being. Examine your feelings and ideas about intuitive action. Do you genuinely trust your intuition? If only in some things, why not in others? What sort of cultural suggestions about intuition have you been saddled with? Track them down and make a list. Where you find negative suggestions, try to work them out. If necessary you may use neutralizing resolutions. (See page 102.) Finally, try to remember a time when intuition worked for you. How did it feel?

When you've gotten your thoughts and feelings straightened out, begin trying out your intuition in small matters. Play games with yourself. For instance, guess the best route home in rush hour or the best corner to catch a cab. Use it to find a parking spot. Can you guess the color of the car you'll park next to? If you're waiting at an elevator bank, guess which one will get to the ground first. What about the weather forecast, do you really think you should change plans because of a predicted blizzard or do you have a feeling it won't materialize? Relying on intuition in relatively unimportant matters gets you used to reaching into this part of your mind.

Once you feel your intuition is flowing, determine how it works for you. Do you get a feeling in a part of your body, do you get mental images or voices, does it wake you up at night? Or, do your hunches work in reverse? Some people almost invariably turn right when they should turn left. You can use such a cussed intuition, once you know how it operates.

Become aware of what disrupts your intuitive thinking. Drs. Mihalasky and Dean found that heavy stress—pain, exhaustion, emotional crisis—tends to skew it. You can release stress with autogenic or other relaxation exercises. Testing thousands, the New Jersey researchers also found a curious, unexplained quirk. Being a part of a very definite minority in a group tends to blank out your intuitive ability *in that group.*

Basic research by Dr. Manfred Clynes affords other clues to priming intuition. Clynes, called one of the most creative and keenest multidisciplinary intellects working in science today, talks of getting into a specific state that allows us to be "catchers" of new ideas. We are not consciously aware of the vast amount of work going on under the surface when we're in this state. New, creative ideas appear whole. After they've come, we can use our conscious faculties to test them. But, Clynes warns, we must not reject ideas before they're born. Rejection occurs when we don't provide the state in ourselves suitable for their birth.

Psychologically, the condition is one of openness, waiting-readiness, and most of all, trust. There must be no fear, and one must genuinely feel the ideas that will come will be good, valuable, and worthy of treasuring. Physically, Clynes has found that when people are in this open creative state, the "head tends to be tilted slightly to the right and upward, the body feels light, and there is a characteristic sensation of expanding pressure in the forehead between the temples. Inhalation takes place slowly and steadily, while exhalation is rapid." This is a genetically programmed state, Clynes discovered. And he says, once it is consciously recognized, it can be learned and cultivated. (For further information, see the Appendix.)

Using Intuition

The how-to of intuitive decision making and problem solving cannot be laid out in laboratory experiments or in hard and fast recipes. But some pointers can be drawn from successful people who make intuition a partner in their ventures. The following technique has worked well for a great many of them.

Get all the information you can about your problem. Dig out data, soak up information, turn it over in your mind, then forget it. Do your relaxation exercises and take yourself on a mental trip to some favorite outdoor spot. Imagine yourself stretching out, watching the clouds slowly forming and dissolving. Sometimes, the solution will suddenly appear as you lie there, but don't worry if it doesn't. The main point in this technique is to short circuit the circling rational mind and let the problem rest. Many people find they're able to come up with an answer most easily when they have switched focus to something else. The full-blown hunch, the intuitive solution, tends to pop up at unlikely times, when you're about to ladle the soup or step off the bus.

For another approach, if you meditate regularly, Jack Schwarz has a suggestion. State your problem before going into meditation, then tell yourself you will look *at* the solution, not for it. If the problem already exists, so does the other side of the coin—the solution.

Autogenics offers a long-tested avenue to intuition and creative problem solving. In the last and crowning autogenic exercise, you "climb the mountain and speak to the wise one." In other words, using deep relaxation and guided imagery, one attempts to contact resources of consciousness not normally in communication. In autogenics this technique is used after you've mastered the rest of the program. However, you might try it simply from a state of deep relaxation. (See page 290 for instructions.)

The idea of personifying and holding a dialogue with "knowing" has long been used in business motivation courses, particularly by such durable success mentors as Napoleon Hill and W. Clement Stone. Andrew Carnegie commissioned Hill to find and make available to the public practical, down-to-earth methods for leading a successful life. As you might imagine, learning how to use the full resources of the mind was one of those methods.

Hill speaks of calling on the teacher-scientist-inventor Dr. Elmer Gates. His secretary told Hill that Gates was busy and she honestly couldn't say how long he'd be—a few minutes, or a few hours. He was, she said, "sitting for an answer." Later, Gates explained to Hill that whenever he had to make a difficult decision or come up with the answer to a problem, he shut himself into a dark, soundproof room, sat down, cleared his mind, and focused on a single point. Then he just waited for the answer to appear. He didn't question or think or figure, he just waited. Sooner or later the answer would appear. Then he switched on the lights and wrote it down.

"Where are these answers coming from?" Hill asked. "From three sources," Gates said: first, from his own accumulated experience and knowledge; second, from the knowledge of others picked up telepathically. And finally, Gates said, "from the great universal storehouse of Infinite Intelligence . . . which may be contacted through the subconscious section of the mind."

Dr. Gates held a great many patents. Over two hundred of these were for inventions started by others who gave up when they couldn't solve a crucial point. Gates brought their concepts to fruition using the intuitive technique of "sitting for an answer."

Al Pollard, Arkansas business consultant and former chairman of the Eighth District Federal Reserve Board, is well known for his management workshops. In the area of problem solving, he emphasizes that one must know what the problem really is. Often it is not what we think it is. To find out, Pollard advises, ask your subconscious. While in a relaxed, meditative state, ask, "I *wonder* what the problem is or will be?" The important word Pollard says is *wonder,* "which triggers a chain reaction to get our intuitive processes going." If intuition is ignited, make a list of the thoughts that come. Pollard also helps top executives use intuition in a different direction. "We try to probe the future and bring back answers, realizing that in the realm of mind there is neither time nor distance."

Intuition can also serve as a self-correction system to help you keep on course and spot errors once a decision has been made. New York businessman-lawyer Richard T. Gallen speaks of using his intuition this way. Millions of TV football fans enjoy the high-stepping razzle-dazzle of the Dallas Cowboy cheerleaders. They've become a celebrity team themselves. Gallen, who heads his own corporation, decided to put together a calendar featuring large color pictures of the Dallas cheerleaders. Necessary business contacts were made. Soon Gallen's photographers arrived back from Dallas and spread hundreds of pictures on his desk. They were good color photos with a Norman Rockwell flavor—one cheerleader playing with a dog, another fixing a car. Yet Gallen began to get an uneasy feeling as he looked through them. He was looking at well-designed, expertly shot pictures, easy to reproduce. At the moment he couldn't think of anything to say against them.

"A few days later, I woke up in the middle of the night. Something was wrong with the cheerleading project. When that sort of thing happens, I know my intuition is trying to tell me something. That's when I have to switch from my right brain to my left brain and sort out logically where the problem lies."

He went down a check list of the project. When he got to the pictures, the uneasiness was there. The problem was in the pictures, but what was it? Finally, Gallen realized that what the public was interested in, what he was selling, was cheerleaders in full regalia going through their performance, not good-looking young women in down-home scenes no matter how appealing. With that thought, the uneasy feeling disappeared. Gallen was able to send his photographers to Dallas again to catch the cheerleaders in action and keep his project on center. It's a good example of how reason and intuition work together to create a successful outcome. They could do so because Gallen, like Hilton, acted on the promptings of his intuition.

Intuition can help you get the idea for a project, make decisions, solve problems and it can also alert you to mistakes along the way. Expert decision makers aren't afraid of making some mistakes, they expect to. But they try to use all the resources of their minds to make more good decisions than bad ones. John E. Fetzer, owner of the Detroit Tigers and Chairman of Fetzer Broadcasting Company, is another executive who speaks of the help he's gotten from ESP and intuition in his business life.

"Success is a thing that I've always taken for granted," he told the editors of *New Realities*. "And I should suspect it's because I do trust intuition to the point that I don't make enough wrong decisions to undermine a successful rhythm."

Making the Most of Dreams

Joseph was the provider because he paid attention to dreams. Seven fat cattle paraded through Pharaoh's dream followed by seven lean ones. As with his own dreams, Joseph acted on the information, laid up supplies, and saved Egypt from famine. Probably long before Joseph, and certainly ever since, people in every culture have maintained that they've caught a glimpse of the future in their dreams.

Precognition is the most enigmatic extrasensory experience, yet researchers find it the most commonly reported one. It seems to happen most often in dreams. Drs. Montague Ullman and Stanley Krippner of the Division of Parapsychology and Psychophysics at Maimonides Hospital, Brooklyn, devised ingenious, controlled experiments to see if they could capture precognitive dreams in the lab. They weren't looking for self-fulfilling prophecies. They wanted to find out if a person could dream of a future experience, one that would be chosen for him by chance the day *after* the dream. They, too, found that people can, on occasion, get a handle on the future in their sleep.

We can learn about ourselves and our relationships in dreams. We may also pick up extrasensory information. Dreams have historically proved a good place to come up with creative ideas and solutions. Further afield, traditionally, Buddhists have said that if you learn to control your dreams, to be a conscious dreamer, you'll be way ahead in the next life.

Catching Dreams

To catch your dream, have pen and paper or a tape recorder by your bed—a material suggestion.

Before going to sleep, repeat at least fifteen times, "I remember my dreams tonight." Also reinforce the idea during the day when you think of it. Anticipate, look forward to the adventure.

Immediately upon waking either at night or in the morning, jot down your dreams. Don't roll over and snooze thinking you'll remember. Most people don't. Make notes at least.

As soon as is practical, fill in your notes. Mention the feel of the dream, the emotional colors as well as images, voices, plot. Include seemingly trivial details.

If at first your dreams elude you, try making one up each morning, the first thing that pops into your mind. This can prime the pump. As a memory jog, dream researcher Patricia Garfield in her *Creative Dreaming* suggests resuming the position you were in when you awakened. You can also assume other favorite sleep positions to see if they bring back other dreams.

Some part of us seems to be impressed by ritual. You can try such old tricks as drinking half a glass of water before you go to sleep telling yourself you'll remember your dream as you drink the rest on waking.

If it appeals to you, eventually train yourself with suggestion to wake up after each dream.

Using a Dream Collection

You can use a growing dream collection in a variety of ways. Every few weeks or so review your dreams. Did you pick up a fragment of the future? As writer J. B. Priestley puts it, these future glimpses are usually of the trivial or the terrible—with the trivial predominating. You may catch sight of a strange name you'll actually see painted on a truck as you go through the day, or get a preview look at a long-lost acquaintance you're going to bump into.

If you find a piece of the future in your dreams, ask yourself what, if anything, was different about that dream. Precognitive dreams are often vivid. Who else was in the dream? Eventually you may be able to recognize precognitive dreams as they happen and, like Joseph, when necessary act upon them.

Don't put a time limit on precognition. At the University of Freiburg, Dr. Hans Bender documented vivid dreams that came true five, fifteen, even twenty-five years later.

Keep an eye out for other kinds of extrasensory information. Here, too, controlled experiments and good case histories show you can pick up other people's thoughts in dreams, or tune in accurately on a distant place.

Problem Solving in Dreams

As with intuition, to solve a problem in your dreams learn all the facts you can about your problem. Before sleep, suggest repeatedly that you'll dream of so and so. *Ask* for a solution. Keep trying. Have confidence. After all, your dreams don't really come from Morpheus. You do create them.

Most successful people have developed the knack of routinely jotting down ideas that come in their dreams. Napoleon Hill once saw just how strong and valuable this habit can become. R. G. Le Tourneau invited Hill to accompany him on his private plane. Le Tourneau built heavy earth-moving equipment and was engaged in such projects as the Hoover Dam. Shortly after they were airborne, Le Tourneau went to sleep. About half an hour later, Hill noticed he suddenly opened a notebook, jotted something, then seemed to go on sleeping. When they landed, Hill asked him if he remembered putting down the note. He didn't, and he quickly pulled the pad from his pocket.

"Here it is!" Le Tourneau exclaimed. "I've been looking for this for several months." It was the answer to a problem that had kept him from completing a new piece of equipment.

When noting your dreams, pay attention to the details—a dream detail gave us the sewing machine. Elias Howe sweated over the problem of how to connect needle, thread, and material. One night, exhausted from false starts, he fell asleep to dream he'd been captured by cannibals. Trussed up in a kettle, the fire laid, Howe knew he'd be eaten if he couldn't come up with the sewing machine. An anxiety dream—with a twist. As the cannibals danced around him, he looked up at their spears. He saw holes at the tips. Howe woke up and realized that if he threaded the needle at the point instead of at the opposite end, the sewing machine would work. He did and it did.

Dreaming with a Friend

Recently dream groups have started up. If you want to explore dreams with friends, first study the subject together. Then compare dreams, being sure always to date them. It appears from reports from dream groups as if friends sometimes are in the same dream "place" or even communicate in their sleep. Things can crop up that for one reason or another aren't stated outright in waking life. Some groups try to dream about a specific subject, sometimes about the group itself, on a particular night.

The idea of exploring dreams is to push back limitations. Don't let it become a limitation. Most dreams are *not* precognitive, particularly death dreams. And we all know about the self-fulfilling prophecy. If you must indulge, only do so with your good dreams.

Precognition

Precognition may sound formidable, but it's an ability you're at least trying to use every time you say, "I bet . . ." One of the best ways to learn anything is play. You can play precognition games alone or with a friend. Steer clear of the "I bet you can't do it" sort of friend. Negative suggestions can freeze learning ability generally. They can be even more lethal when you are trying to develop a new, or sixth, sense. As in all learning, confidence and conviction are important. Remember, strange as it may seem, precognition is the most common psi experience. And, according to new theories put forth by quantum physicists, we live in a universe where precognition is not only possible but also probable. The future, it seems, does cast its shadows into the present, and some of us can sometimes sense them.

This section is not intended as a primer on psi research, detailing the many solid scientific excursions into the field. If you're not familiar with them, follow up some of the books listed in the Appendix. The techniques included are not designed as scientific experiments. Their purpose is to help you learn and help you get a feeling for certain ways of knowing and responding. In anything else, from arithmetic to piano playing to swimming, first you learn, then if you wish, you test yourself. There's no reason to reverse it for psi.

Screening the Future

Not just games, but a great many situations in life involve trying to guess the future. You might find it handy to have a "future screen," a mental visual aid to help give those guesses more shape. Many people like to imagine a TV screen in their mind's eye, a screen that will bring them desired images. Some imagine an antique mirror, a pool, or even a personal fog bank as their screen. In a relaxed, tranquil state, ask, "I wonder on what sort of screen I can best glimpse the future?" Wait until your future screen appears in your imagination. If you like it, use it from now on.

The classical laboratory precognition experiment involves asking a subject which one of five known objects or symbols will later be chosen by chance as the target. If it appeals you can do this at home. Gather together a set—say, five distinctly different, vivid pictures. Number them one through five. Relax body and mind, imagine your future screen and ask yourself which picture will be chosen later by a roll of a die or spin of a spinner. Take your time until something appears. When you're beginning, it helps to roll the die after each guess so you can have quick feedback. If you made a hit and part or all of the correct image appeared, consider how you felt mind/body as it came to you. Try to reproduce that state when you try again. See if there are any qualitative differences between wrong and right images.

Some people do better with numbers, names, colors. Some don't "see" but get a "voice-over" giving the answer. Many see symbolically. This can yield interesting insights into how your mind works, but if possible try to train yourself to "see" literally. Interpretation has muddled prophecy since the days of Delphi.

In the lab, boredom is the greatest stumbling block to studying precognition. As monotony increases, ESP decreases. Practice precognition with anything you enjoy. You can adapt part of regular games like cards or bingo. Or play horseracing by checking the paper before a race and guessing win, place, show. By devising your own games, you'll learn more about the wiles of precognition than if you followed rules in a book.

Reading Tomorrow's Headlines

A noted English economist, Juliet, Lady Rhys-Williams, on two occasions somewhat to her chagrin, read news stories before they were printed. The world's oldest scientific psi society, the one-hundred-year-old Society for Psychical Research in London, documented her case. Once she "heard" in detail a Voice of America news report before it was broadcast. Lady Rhys-Williams wasn't even trying. Some people have tried and find it a satisfying way of trying to flex their ESP.

If you want to get a preview of the news, first do your usual relaxation exercises to get into the proper state. Before beginning the experiment, if you can, reexperience in your imagination a time when you did glimpse the future. Then take yourself on a mental trip. In your mind's eye, follow your normal route to the morning paper. Settle down in your usual spot. Unfold the paper and imagine it whole before you.

Take time, visualize the name of the paper, the date, then slowly focus on the full page. Afterwards write down what rose up in your imagination—pictures, headlines, subjects. You can start with a day ahead, but soon, to avoid too much suggestion from other media, try for at least a week ahead.

You certainly can fool yourself if you wish and say, "See, I predicted a story on the Middle East," but, if you want to, you can also tell the difference between catching a glimpse of unexpected or one-shot events and ongoing news.

Lottery

Dr. Milan Ryzl is the first parapsychologist we know of who mated a real game and lab research. He's good at being first. Ryzl was the first link between parapsychology, East and West. He was the first to embark on a major psi training program. And he was one of the first to realize that the sober side of lab life should be balanced by some zesty experiments. That's why when we met him shortly after he landed in the United States, he asked, "What's the lottery like in New York State? In Prague, we had one where you could pick the numbers. It's perfect for precognition experiments. This is the kind of thing that could get people into the lab!"

Unfortunately at the time, New York did not have that kind of lottery. Now, along with some other states, New York has a legal pick-it lottery with winners announced daily and weekly. If there's one near you, it is a ready-made setup for practicing precognition. Obviously, you don't have to bet to make this a good ESP exercise.

In Prague, Ryzl used a group of people he'd trained to be psychic. He translated numbers into symbols that they were used to working with. Then he asked them to foresee the six winning numbers in the lottery. Ryzl combined their guesses— that is, if a majority got "2" in a particular slot, that seemed a likely number.

Most state lotteries have three- or four-digit winners. Try this alone or, like the communal Czechs, in a group. If you don't have a feeling for numbers, assign each a symbol you like. Ryzl's group improved with practice and finally won "a good sum." By both chance and, it seems, ESP, you are most likely to get the right numbers but the wrong order.

"If you're so psychic, why aren't you rich?" It's beginning to look as if a lot of "psychics" are—only they call themselves things like director of research or chairman of the board. Others are rich in different ways, excelling at what they most want to do. The idea isn't really to start flexing your precognitive abilities to set up as a store-front reader or to break the bank at Atlantic City.

When Dr. Ryzl was teaching people to be psychic, he was aiming at equipping them with a real sixth sense—if not in biological fact, at least by close analogy. He wanted them to be able to interact more consciously with the wide world beyond the five senses. The idea of precognitive exercises is to bring attention to and to stimulate this sensing of the future, to give you a feeling for the varied textures of time—a sensing that could flesh out and strengthen your intuitive way of thinking.

But what if you do get a Day-Glo-bright glimpse of the future —a disaster. People have foreseen the plane would explode or the chandelier would fall on the baby's crib. As a rule of thumb, if you do get an apparent forewarning, treat it as another piece of information to be balanced in with other factors. *Extrasensory talents are extra channels of information.* If however, you get a profound, overwhelming premonition, the odds say, act on it. You may end up looking silly but you'll be around to mull it over.

The more you get into the swing of intuitive thinking generally, the more you realize many of us were saddled with a misconception. The intuitive does not oppose the rational, it complements it. By putting all our attention on the rational, we have developed, as someone has said, a lop-headed culture. The answer is not to become lop-headed in the opposite direction, but to nurture a harmony, a balance between the two, so that we may function as whole people with more flags flying.

Chapter 15
"Second Sight"

"Careful! You don't want to raise false hope for the blind," friends and interviewers would caution when we publicly mentioned successful Soviet experiments with eyeless sight. But now and then, we did mention this ability to perceive colors and geometric figures without the use of the eyes. Practice in eyeless sight sometimes proved a royal way of opening a broad range of psi abilities, at least for the sighted. As for the blind, some days we did regret bringing it up, because there was no place to refer them for training.

That was before something quietly extraordinary began to happen in Buffalo, New York—something that today is lighting up the world of the blind, literally. Where it counts, in everyday experience, blind men and women are learning to use these reserve abilities. Right now, the blind are leading the "blind," making inroads for the rest of us. None of us would have been so sure five or six years ago.

Beware of false hope . . . there probably was a little of that beating like a reflex in Bill Focazio's thoughts one evening in 1973 when he assembled with nineteen other blind people for a new program: Project Blind Awareness. A sturdy, dark-haired man in his early fifties, owner of a men's clothing shop in Niagara Falls, Focazio qualifies as a solid citizen. He was an officer in a local association for the blind, and that's why he'd come—to learn exactly what, he wasn't sure. He found himself answering questionnaires, then picking his way through a chair maze to test his ability to maneuver. At least, there seemed to be some scientists involved: Dr. Sean Zieler, psychologist from Buffalo Veteran's Hospital, Samuel Lentine, a physicist who himself was blind, and Dr. Douglas Dean, electrochemist and parapsychologist at the New Jersey Institute of Technology.

Finally, Focazio sat at a table with a sighted volunteer. She said she was putting sets of colored construction paper in front of him: black and white, red and green. She guided his hands a few inches above the sheets. Could he tell any difference? Was it black? Was it white? Focazio realized by guessing he should get about half right. That's exactly what he felt he was doing, guessing. What made his skepticism jump a number of notches were the words of the teacher, Carol Ann Liaros. Quietly, persistently, in her flat upstate accent, this woman assured the group they could activate a new sense. They could be right about those colors most or even all the time. They could also learn to be aware of many other things, near and far, Liaros said, and become comfortable in the world again.

Bill Focazio wasn't the only one with escalating reservations when he encountered Project Blind Awareness. "The loss of my eyesight hit me at the core of my existence," Lola Reppenhagen admits. Could she again experience the rainbow of colors? Could she really know what was in front of her—a cube, a ball? It wasn't an easy idea to handle. A small, dynamic woman, mother and housewife, Lola Reppenhagen enjoys people and had served as an officer in a Buffalo association for the blind. Typically, she'd come to this group "because I like being involved with new things." Now she was confronted with more than she'd bargained for. "Needless to say, I was very skeptical."

We can talk about awareness and de-suggestion, and overcoming limitations that have been suggested to us. But if anything seems like a four-square limitation, it is to have the world blotted out, to be told you are blind, forever. The living room becomes an obstacle course, curbs and steps loom in the unknown. Is your hair combed, do you have crumbs on your chin? You can't glance in a mirror to find out.

There are more subtle changes, says Father Schommer, a Jesuit priest at Canisius College. "The difficulty is mostly in the emotional line, the depth of one's feelings, as well as your identity as a person." This is particularly true if, like Father Schommer, you go blind as an adult. "I felt as if I were in a closet and couldn't get out. You immediately feel you don't belong—that you did, but now you don't. I was sight oriented. . . . People can tell you, 'Oh, I love you, we want you.' You say, 'Yes, thank you very much,' but inside you are not convinced. . . . Until you get a tool so you feel you really are in contact with the whole world, including the material world, the love and goodwill of others seems to have a thud. It's almost like a piano with a bad bass note, no resonance at all."

The old primrose path. It's one thing to get together for an evening to try telepathy games. It's another to cheerfully assure a roomful of people like Father Schommer, Lola Reppenhagen, and Bill Focazio that they can activate new kinds of abilities to help overcome their troubles—even most parapsychologists would cringe. But Carol Liaros did just that. If she had doubts, they didn't communicate—just that calm assurance. A good-looking woman, now in her early forties, Liaros wears her blond "mane" short; still there's a leonine quality to her. You'd expect her to lead a meeting; you'd expect her to be first on the floor at a disco. She's a take-charge sort of person.

The first person she took charge of was herself, when Hugh Lynn Cayce, writer and son of the psychic Edgar Cayce, told her she was a "natural" with genuine psychic talent. Liaros closed her hairdressing shop, turned from her other business interests, and began to train in earnest. By 1973, many in Buffalo knew Carol Ann Liaros as a psychic and teacher. She'd worked with some of the best scientists in the field, had hosted a local TV show on psi, and taught courses at such places as the Human Dimensions Institute at Rosary Hill College.

Yet, unless they had heard of Liaros, the blind who gathered for the pilot study got no clue that they were trying to awaken psychic abilities. Liaros went over her ESP course and eliminated all mention of psi to keep prejudice from getting in the way. She also rounded up twenty sighted volunteers. Once a week she instructed them how to teach relaxation techniques that seem to enhance psi. A second night each week they worked with the blind.

Feeling some trepidation, with a good grip on their skepticism, Bill Focazio, Lola Reppenhagen, Father Schommer, and many others stuck with Liaros and the volunteers. They kept practicing relaxation, visualizing the bio-fields of energy around the body, sensing colors—to gradually become part of a grassroots revolution, or perhaps the word is *evolution.* The paranormal began to grow amid talk of the blind bowling team and reminiscenses of what had happened to the horseshoe match during the downpour at last summer's cookout. As they came to realize that even their limitations might not be as real as they thought, these blind men and women started to do things that they all readily admit "sound incredible."

Some started to recognize colors far across the room. The world began coming back into "sight" in a way they found very hard to express—they were connected again, but in a new way. There seemed to be a light in their heads, some said, where before there had been only darkness. One man retired his white cane, for he was somehow aware of lamp posts, jutting storefronts, steps, and curbs. A completely blind woman "saw" a photograph. "It's a female, but what's that round thing on top of her head?" The photo showed nutritionist Adelle Davis, who wore her hair in a large, round bun atop her head. As relaxation and training continued, these solid citizens started learning how to travel in their minds' eyes to distant rooms, houses, offices—places they'd never been to—yet they were able to describe the layout. In ESP lingo, theirs is clairvoyance pure and simple. Yet it's hard to square these people with the usual "psychic" image. They never thought of themselves that way either.

Lola Reppenhagen, for instance, after eight months of learning, wrote, "I find it difficult to believe the things that are happening. I have not yet learned to tell each color every time and some not as well as others, but it is coming. I've had some success with mind travel. My awareness of my energy field is developing. I feel as though I can see my hands working, I see my body, I see images and shadows and seem to be able to almost see what is in a room. It seems that I really see it, although I don't, I am totally blind."

Written, taped, photographic records are kept of Project Blind Awareness sessions. Bill Focazio was right when he said he was just guessing that first night. To no one's surprise, statistics showed that the blind picked the colors at a chance level. Then they began training in deep relaxation, in visualization, and in sensitivity techniques. Again and again the blind held their hands over black and white, red and green. After seven sessions, they took more tests. Dr. Zieler reports, "The more they did it, the better they performed—65 percent to 70 percent accuracy with some getting a perfect score."

Dr. Dean, former president of the professional Parapsychology Association, checked two thousand tries at distinguishing between black and white and two thousand between red and green. Odds were ten thousand to one against the blind doing as well as they did by chance. Results were also promising in attempts to distinguish objects and photos. Overall, Dean said, "As an experiment to see if ESP can help the blind, it was fabulous." Dr. Zieler reports, "Some of the things that happened were mind-boggling."

What boggled the scientists' minds went even nearer the nerve with the students as those "incredible sounding" things began to happen. Continuing with the project, Bill Focazio sat, one afternoon, in his men's shop. "All of a sudden, I realized I could 'see' things. Not clearly, of course, but the blurred outlines of a doorway and the desk." Was he possibly getting his sight back? He put his hands over his eyes; the scene stayed. "The images seemed to be coming through the side of my head."

At home, Lola Reppenhagen glanced up when her teenage daughter, Robin, came into the room. She began to remark on the looks of the red slacks and white top Robin had on. Then she remembered she hadn't been able to see her daughter or an outfit for years—and still couldn't with her eyes.

Barbara Engels came into Project Blind Awareness with "traces of bitterness." In her early twenties, she was teaching school, building a life, then she went blind. Now she was a student again, this time with Liaros. She worked on the new techniques. One night, Barbara Engels was dazzled—by an impossibility. She suddenly saw her entire bedroom lit up in a soft chartreuse glow. "I could see the outlines of the bed and the dressers, and the rest of the furnishings." Again it didn't seem involved with eyes. "It was coming through my head." She sat enjoying the sight for the half hour the glow lasted. This lighting-up happened again and then a third time. "Great hope" is what this former teacher has for the PBA course. "It could lead to something that will help us make our way in the world."

Carol Liaros and her students did not discover eyeless sight. It's been around a long time, which, paradoxically, makes their achievement all the more remarkable. In the 1920's, French writer Jules Romaine grew so enthusiastic about eyeless sight, he took time off from his novels to write a landmark study. It could help the blind. Criticism was so virulent that Romaine wasn't heard from again on the topic until the sixties when the Soviets let it be known that at a couple of their teachers' colleges they had been training students, both sighted and blind, in eyeless sight. It had all begun with a simple young woman, Rosa Kuleshova. Living in a factory town in the Ural Mountains, Rosa led a life as plain and utilitarian as the dresses that covered her dowdy frame. About the only glow in her week came from helping the blind at a local center. She learned to read braille.

One day, Rosa got a quirky idea. It occurred to her that *without* braille, she could sense colors and shapes with her fingers—and even with her forehead. Then, she had a simple idea. This ability could help her blind friends.

But Rosa got sidetracked to become a prized exhibit at scientific conferences from Tagil to Sverdlovsk, winding up at the Academy of Sciences in Moscow before she suffered a total nervous breakdown.

Still, the idea that Rosa's ability could help the blind kept Soviet scientists experimenting. As you might expect, Dr. Lozanov, with his ever-persisting emphasis on opening the reserves of the mind, began to explore eyeless sight in 1964. He worked with sixty children who'd been born blind or had lost their sight in infancy. Even so, to keep to the scientific protocol, he blindfolded them and put a screen between their eyes and hands when he asked them to do eyeless sight.

Lozanov got a surprise. Three children were able to distinguish color and geometrical figures right away. "But the most important factor is the remaining fifty-seven children could be *trained* to learn skin sight. . . . Little by little, these blind children were trained to know colors, geometrical figures and even to read," Lozanov reported in a scientific article. These children, too, demonstrated their new-found parapsychological abilities for doctors and psychiatrists.

"Parapsychology can be applied in pedagogy," Dr. Lozanov said. "It can overcome defects of speech, hearing, sight, and can be used in psychology and medicine. It can give us new and very rich material for familiarizing ourselves with secret and unknown possibilities of the human personality."

Since then, in France, in particular, and in many other countries including the United States, scientists have tested and tinkered with eyeless sight. Yet somehow in the academic raveling something kept getting sidetracked.

Finally, Carol Ann Liaros and the volunteers took the promise in hand, and they are turning it into practice on a widening scale. As it grows, Project Blind Awareness is becoming known nationally and internationally. It is attracting increasingly favorable attention from doctors and other professionals. The summer of 1977 saw the first instructor program to train people to begin projects in other cities and states. (Bill Focazio was among the graduate instructors.) In the same year, Project Junior Blind Awareness for children began with, it's reported, rollicking success. Through the years, PBA has stuck to its original concept of offering free programs to the blind. Contributions from Liaros and her volunteers and now from the broader community cover expenses. (For further information, see the Source Section.)

Project Blind Awareness continues to accumulate scientific data. And, it's doing something else. "It opened up the world," for Father Schommer. "Project Blind Awareness opened the door for me to get out of my closet. I felt that I was just as much a part of human society as before, but in a different status." It helped him reconnect with the whole world, very much including the material world.

"It was a new approach to life. . . . You discover things different from ordinary cerebral things; it gave me a sense of awareness." And it helped in relationships. "You are no longer behind a wall or a curtain. It is immediate contact with people. You learn how to come in contact with things and respond to them, finding there is a certain element of living you never thought could be yours."

To meet Lola Reppenhagen is to feel an immediate contact, as strong as if she looked you square in the eye. She seems to have developed a special kind of rapport. "The Blind Awareness course made the whole universe known to me in a form which I never thought possible. They aim at a fantastic relaxation and a lightened sensitiveness for one's own feelings and emotions. For me, a whole new world has opened up. I feel a strong affinity with the whole material universe. I am no longer discouraged with my blindness."

There is something striking in the experience of these New Yorkers. Except for their blindness, they are people like most of us. They didn't yearn to develop strange esoteric powers or to prove a point about the nature of reality. What's striking is not so much that they, on occasion, know a color, see an aura, catch a clairvoyant glimpse of what's happening somewhere else. Something else stands out. As they learned to develop those other, so-called psychic ways of knowing, their mesh with the world and each other shifted. It enlarged, became richer, they were able to act and respond in more satisfying ways. This is the promise inherent in psi that so many people in parapsychology have been talking about for such a very long time. The trouble is that it's hard to exemplify. The Project Blind Awareness people are exemplifying it, at least a little bit, because they approach psi as an integrated part of themselves. A whole new world, that's what they keep saying. What might becoming more aware of these other ways of knowing do for the rest of us? The following section can help you find out.

Learning Eyeless Sight

As experience shows, gaining some sense of eyeless sight often opens the switches to many other abilities. Starting with the material, the close-at-hand, one can move to perceiving the not-so-close-at-hand such as the bioenergies surrounding another's body; or one can move to the distant, seeing what a room looks like across town.

Loosely, psi is of two kinds: energetic abilities like aura seeing, dowsing, healing, PK, or mind over matter; and classical ESP including precognition, telepathy, clairvoyance. People who go in for either find eyeless sight a good lift-off point.

One key to Project Blind Awareness's success is good training in relaxing mind and body. If you don't know how, learn how with some of the exercises mentioned in this book. Whenever you are going to try to learn eyeless sight, do relaxation exercises beforehand.

We know what suggestion on all levels can do. Needless to say

PBA surrounds people in a warm, positive, assured atmosphere. Approach eyeless sight as you do other forms of superlearning. When you're relaxed, just before starting eyeless sight, give yourself a few positive affirmations of success. Then take a few moments to experience the joy of learning. At first, recall any instance of successful learning. Once you've had some success with eyeless sight, reexperience that feeling. As much as possible, remove strain from learning sessions. Go at it in a spirit of high play.

Sensing Bioenergies

One of the first things Liaros has her students do is to try to become aware of bioenergies, of a sort of force field surrounding the human body. One of the ingredients of this energy surrounding the body is heat. Scientists preparing to put humans in space had to investigate fields around the body—they are real.

With your eyes closed to avoid distraction, stand in front of another person. Slowly move your hands down his or her body about three inches away. Can you distinguish any differences, particularly changes in temperature? Do this slowly a number of times, imagine the person's body—throat, chest, stomach— as your hands move. With a little practice many people are surprised to find they can sense something palpable as their hands move.

Visualizing Bioenergies

When you are in a relaxed, contemplative state, visualize your own body. Enlarge the picture and imagine a sort of aura of energy about your body. Imagine it as light. Watch it, enjoy it. Feel it, if you can.

Then imagine yourself with someone you love. Imagine his or

her energy field. Imagine yourself moving toward the person. What is happening to both of your energy fields?

Now visualize color in any form that appeals—squares, circles, or a vibrant red tulip, a sea of daffodils, a bright blue velvet robe. You know that colors are really light pulsing at different frequencies. Imagine you can see those different color waves as you can see heat rising from the highway in summer.

Imagine your hand again, with the energy moving around it. See your hand moving toward one of the vibrant, pulsing colors. Imagine your bioenergies interacting with the color waves. Feel it. (See also color and energy exercises, pages 268, 272.)

Eyes Open

At first, with open eyes, it's easiest to see this bioenergy against a dark background. When lying in bed at night, hold your hands up in front of you. Relax your eyes. Can you make out a dim edging of light around your hands? Point your fingers at each other. Can you make out anything streaming between them? As you move them slowly apart, can you see a sort of jet trail of light against the darkness?

Practicing Eyeless Sight

To practice with color, it's easiest to work with a partner. Start with two sets of colored paper: black and white, red and green. Wear a blindfold—a sleep mask is good—and try to avoid having any light seep through. Since you are trying to activate another system of "seeing," it doesn't help to keep switching back and forth to regular sight between attempts.

Before starting, of course, use your techniques to become deeply relaxed and pay particular attention to relaxing the eyes. Give them a vacation during these sessions.

Your partner puts down the black and white set and guides

your hand to a position a few inches above. Try to sense a difference. Guess, then have your partner immediately say whether you're right. He also records hits and misses. Mix the sheets, try again.

Stop before you get bored or overtired. Remember, the people in Buffalo only got chance results when they started. It takes practice.

You can also try moving your hand to various heights. Soviet students found colors seemed to "radiate" to different levels. Blue waves rose higher than red waves, for instance.

Sticky Fingers

The Soviet method for training both the sighted and blind is to put the person's hands directly on the color surface and then to move them gently over the sheet. (Obviously, sheets of the same material are used, so there is no difference in texture.) After some practice, Soviet students reported definite and different color feelings. These "tactile" sensations remained even when glass was put over the colors.

The consensus is that colors divide into smooth, sticky, and rough sensations. Light blue is smoothest. Yellow is very slippery and not quite as smooth.

Red, green, and dark blue are sticky. Green is stickier than red, but not as coarse. Navy blue is even stickier, yet harder than red and green.

Orange has a very rough, coarse, and braking feel. Violet gives a greater braking effect that seems to slow the hand and feels even rougher.

Black is the most sticky, viscid, and braking of all. White is smooth, though coarser than yellow.

If you want to try this, start with a set of yellow and navy blue.

The Foos Technique

The late Reverend William A. Foos developed a simple yet effective method of learning eyeless sight. Reverend Foos noticed that some children seemed to do consistently better than others in blindfold games. An experimenting man, he devised games to test and train this talent and eventually helped his daughter Margaret and his niece to remarkable eyeless-sight ability. Reverend Foos also had his students tested by scientists and tried to bring this system to the blind.

Do these exercises daily for ten or fifteen minutes. As with autogenics, you recapitulate in short form the preceding steps before starting a new one. If possible, work with a partner who talks you through the exercises. Get relaxed, receptive before starting.

1. Blindfolded sit at a table. Put your palm a few inches in front of your face. Imagine it, feel it, see it. Move your hand from side to side in front of you; sense that hand, visualize it as it moves. Try the other hand.

2. Hold hands with your partner, a minute or so, palm to palm. Your partner holds your hand by the wrist and again moves your palm from side to side before your face. She encourages you to sense, imagine, see your hand.

3. Hold hands with your partner. Then, your partner places her palm in front of your face. Sense it. See it. She moves her hand back and forth. Occasionally, she stops her hand. She asks you to turn in the direction of that hand and smile. Continue imagining, visualizing her hand as it moves back and forth.

4. Stand up, hands at your sides. You're going to play a game. Your partner brings your hands up to waist level at your sides, then brings them together in the middle of your body. Waist level from side to side, she tells you, is the area of the game. Repeat the procedure. Then she puts her hand in front of your forehead. Visualize it. Slowly she moves her hand down. Like a control tower talking down a plane, she

tells you to see her hand, that her hand is moving down, that it's by your chest. Finally she stops, her hand palm up, at the waist level, somewhere in the game area, and says, "Touch!" Without thinking, slap her palm. If you don't hit, so what? Keep practicing.

5. Play the game at a table. Your partner puts your hands at the sides of the table, brings them together in the middle, puts them back to show you the game area. Repeat the procedure. Talking to you, she moves her hand from your forehead down to some spot on the table between your hands. When she says, "Touch!" slap her hand.

6. When you've had some success with this new perception, you prepare to move from hands to objects. The Foos system suggests soft, colorful objects like household sponges. Your partner puts a sponge on the table. She lifts your hand palm down. Holding it by the thumb side, she slowly sweeps it over the table edge, over the table, over the sponge, over the other side of the table, talking continuously, telling you where you are, asking you to perceive differences. All the while, try to sense what your hand is passing over. Visualize it.

7. Always telling you what she is doing, your partner moves the sponge back and forth in front of your face. She holds it before your forehead, moves it down, and puts it somewhere on the table. She says, "Pick it up."

You can go on with more than one sponge and then go on to other objects and patterns. (This account of the Foos system was based on *Eyeless Sight: A How To Manual,* Simone Publications, Stanton, California.)

Sexing a Photo

In the old days, canny country people claimed to tell the sex of a bird-to-be by holding a pendulum or their hands over the egg. In this exercise, you use a photo of a woman and one of a man. With your eyes blindfolded and the pictures turned face down, try to sense a difference. Practice as you did with color. Add new pictures periodically.

Circle, Square, or Eureka

Many of the PBA people said there came to be a light in their heads where before there had been only blackness. Eventually they said light and, later, images seemed to be coming through their foreheads. The forehead is used in initial attempts to sense objects.

For this exercise, take a cube, a marble, and a light bulb. Blindfolded, gently rub each object on your forehead a couple of times. Then have your partner hold one of the objects one or two feet in front of your head. What is it? With all these exercises, remember, use your favorite method to get in a relaxed, positive state before you start.

Traveling Clairvoyance

Extrasensory perception, clairvoyance, the ability to see across time and space—are they really going to make any reverberating difference to humankind? One answer comes from an unusual quarter, Charles Lindbergh. Lindbergh helped begin and faithfully supported the American rocketry program. As men were preparing to step out on the moon, *Life* asked Lindbergh to write his thoughts about the future of rocketry and space travel. He replied, he couldn't. His reasons why were so intriguing, *Life* printed them instead. What he had to say may surprise some people. Yet, Charles Lindbergh, more than any other individual in this century, carried the pioneering spirit of millions up and over into a new age. He was used to carrying the future with him.

Because of the travel time, it now seems our space trips will dead end at the nearer planets. There is an automatic boundary to what we can do. Will this restriction force us to break through into a new age, Lindbergh asks, one that goes as far beyond the age of science as science exceeded superstition. He sees us moving out on adventures "inconceivable by our 20th Century rationality—beyond the solar system, through distant galaxies, possibly through peripheries untouched by time and space."

We can leap more quickly to this era, Lindbergh says, if we apply our science not to vehicles but to life, "to the infinite and infinitely evolving qualities" of humankind. This study, he believes, is not just for future adventures but for our very survival in that future. Considering what may be the unbounded potentials of human beings, Lindbergh says that as we claim these for our own and awareness grows on awareness, humanity "can merge with the miraculous . . . And in this merging, as long sensed by intuition but still only vaguely perceived by rationality, experience may travel without need for accompanying [physical] life.

"Will we discover that only *without* spaceships can we reach the galaxies; that only *without* cyclotrons can we know the interior of atoms? To venture beyond the fantastic accomplishments of this physically fantastic age, sensory perception must combine with the extrasensory . . ." By moving in such paths, Lindbergh believes, we will find the grand adventures of the future.

Perhaps the adventure has already begun. In March 1974, space probe Mariner II was en route to Mercury. Two American psychics, Ingo Swann and Harold Sherman, tried a psychic probe; they would attempt to travel clairvoyantly and report back on Mercury. The experiment was monitored by psychologist Janet Mitchell, consultant to the American Society for Psychical Research. Mitchell and other researchers involved were a little surprised. Though Swann was in New York and Sherman was in Arkansas, the reports of the two agreed on major points, yet they disagreed with what astrophysicists expected to find.

Two and a half weeks after the psychic reports had been

filed and sealed, Mariner II began signaling the first data from Mercury. It was unexpected data. It supported the accounts of the clairvoyants, not the educated guesses of the scientists.

Fly-bys of Mercury, trips past the curve of the galaxy, probably seem rather far afield. The blind people in Buffalo worked on a more down-to-earth kind of clairvoyance. Yet, the most successful of them said, "I came into a whole new relationship with the material world." What does that mean? Finding out is a good reason for spending a little time exploring the clairvoyant ability to know places and objects at a distance. The negative of a holographic 3-D picture can be cut into small pieces, yet each piece carries the whole picture. As individuals, we're separated from much of the world by walls and miles and a host of other apparent barriers. If you get a clairvoyant experience of "elsewhere" you begin to wonder.

And, of course, if you're psi gifted and willing to practice, it would be helpful, not to mention alluring, to be able to turn on clairvoyance. Scan the insides of your car for trouble, check what's at the bottom of the lake. Did you leave the stove on? Are they really roller-skating in the apartment upstairs? The seductive thought of being a fly on the wall is the lifeblood of daydreams and stories. Maybe that's why some beginners do surprisingly well imagining they're elsewhere. Lola Reppenhagen tried this sort of guided daydreaming. What's unusual is that her imagining sometimes turns out to be real. Signed testimonials attest to it: one from Jeff Kaye, a long-time interviewer on WBEN in Buffalo; another from Steve Wilson of Eyewitness News WKBW-TV. Testimonials from members of the media aren't too usual either.

Wilson asked Reppenhagen to mind-travel to a house where a meeting was scheduled. He filmed her description. "She had not been to the home previously and I accompanied her there immediately after our interview. We filmed her entering the home, then filmed what turned out to be exactly what she described to us previously. I know she has also exercised that "sense" for others in the media in the Buffalo area and I know of no one who remained skeptical after witnessing the event for themselves."

Jeff Kaye was "staggered." Reppenhagen was to mind-travel to his home before an interview. "Her accuracy in placing objects in their proper place in the various rooms was nothing short of incredible. There was a picture of a thistle she thought had a special meaning. It does. It's a pen and ink drawing done by one of my children and presented to me on a birthday some years ago. It, by the way, is one of several pictures hung on that wall.

"I . . . quizzed my wife to determine if any strangers or even friends had been in the house and commented on that picture and the answer was negative. I'm totally convinced her impressions were genuine and not gathered in any clandestine way."

Teaching mind-traveling, Carol Ann Liaros seems to have sparked Lola Reppenhagen into a genuine talent. Most of the other blind students aren't having such spectacular success. Yet, they are getting some information and developing a feeling for new places. It's helping them move out in the world with more assurance.

Traveling clairvoyance may sound too hard for a beginner, yet when Dr. Milan Ryzl first developed an intensive program to train people to be psychic, he, too, had success guiding students across Prague in their minds' eyes. At Stanford Research Institute, the famous think tank in California, experiments are continuing on this sort of mental TV. Physicists Dr. Hal Puthoff and Russell Targ at first thought that only those with known psi ability would have a chance to see what was going on somewhere else. They found that regular people, even skeptics, when put in the right surrounding could look in on things at a distance—at least a little bit.

How to Take a Clairvoyant Trip

For immediate feedback, it's best to do this with a partner. Can you describe his home? If you've been to his home, have

him give you the address of some place he's very familiar with
but that is unknown to you.

Become deeply relaxed in body and mind. Then, get beside
yourself—in a calm way. Imagine that you have moved out of
your body and are standing next to it. Look at yourself. Check
your clothes, hair, position. See your body resting comfortably,
safely.

Now imagine that you are traveling upward through the ceiling, out the roof. Look down at the building you've just left.
Then, imagine that you are projecting yourself, willing, desiring
yourself to the target address. Take time for a bird's-eye view
of the neighborhood. Are there gardens, parking lots, are there
stores, does it seem to be country, how about traffic? Absorb as
much as you can. Don't just look, try to bring all your senses into
play. Do you hear shouts from a playground or dogs barking?
Take your time, soak up the feel of the neighborhood.

Then, imagine you are at the front door. Look at that door.
What color is it, does it have any ornament, what's the handle
like? Are you standing on steps, are there shrubs beside you?
Again, take enough time to look carefully.

Go inside. Are you in a foyer, a hall? Does the door open
directly into a room? Look around slowly, carefully, then go
into the living room. What are the predominant colors, what
style is the furniture, how is it positioned? Check wall decorations and windows. Is there a piano or fireplace? Are there
bookshelves or flowers in the room, and what sort of atmosphere does it have? Is this a quiet home, an uproarious one?
Check for particular smells in the house. Try to get a feeling
of how many rooms there are and how they lie in relation to
the living room. Do you get a feeling of pets or people in
the house? Don't rush. See if there's anything that seems
special in the living room. If so, take a closer look. Remember where it's positioned.

When you've soaked up as much as you can, go back out the
door and take a last look at the house. Then return to where
your body has been resting comfortably. Feel your feet, your

legs, trunk, arms, head. Take a few deep breaths; slowly open your eyes. Describe or write down all the information you can about where you've been. Sometimes it helps to make a sketch. Don't leave out seemingly silly or incongruous details like a bathtub in the kitchen—not uncommon in old sections of Manhattan, for instance.

Some people prefer to describe the sights as they go, others find this distracting. Some people find it helpful to be guided as they travel. You can have a friend ad lib, loosely following the above instructions, or you can pretape it yourself. Either way, be sure there are pauses, lots of pauses so you have enough time to absorb before moving on to the next thing.

Variations

Carol Ann Liaros suggests that after you've checked out the living room, "Let your mind loose." Let it be drawn, magnetized to your partner's favorite room (if it's his house). What's this spot like? Can you sense why it's special to him?

Dr. Ryzl sometimes guided students on mental trips to places they knew, even their own homes. He would have them mentally travel through the streets from his office to the spot. Inside, he would ask them to look around and observe what was happening. Who was home, what were they wearing, what were they doing? Was anything cooking in the kitchen, was someone talking on the phone, if the TV is on can you see what's on the screen? On occasion, he also used this technique to help a student find something she'd mislaid around the house. He asked her to see where it was, to go there and look at the object.

This kind of mind-travel is, of course, harder to verify, but it can be done. If you don't practice with a partner, you can try mentally to drop in ahead of time at some place to which you've been invited but have never seen. Or try a public place and later compare your impressions with the real things.

There are genuine clairvoyants in the world—and more are lighting up from Rio to Tokyo to Buffalo. Our first five senses give us a lot of good information. Yet, as we activate more of our circuitry, will space and time join that growing list of limitations that are more suggestive than real?

Chapter 16
Bio-Rapport

Music, rhythm, pulsing beats underscore techniques to open the reserves of the mind, including telepathy. The idea that music can swing us into connection with larger being wouldn't have been strange to Pythagoras or today, perhaps, to Dr. Charles Muses. "All things in the universe were ultimately created by standing waves," mathematician Muses points out. To give us a feeling for what that means, he says we can translate these waves to sound waves and find "it is thus literally true . . . that all natural forms were generated and are maintained by—music or song, in the most profound sense."

In the rarified society that thinkers like Muses inhabit, the idea has been getting around that the universe is a musicosm. They are saying that the ways of music, rather than of mechanics or chance, best describe the working of our cosmos and our own linkings to it.

Keeping in mind the elements of music—rhythm, harmonics, resonance—can help one get a feeling for bio-rapport. Bio-rapport is a Soviet term for telepathy, and telepathy, as almost everyone knows, is thought transference, communication without the use of the five senses. Today it's increasingly apparent that telepathy involves a great deal more than a pear-shaped thought lighting up in one mind and then in another.

This "something more" has to do with the reemergence of an idea that was widely held when philosophers found meaning in the "music of the spheres." It is the idea that all is one, that somehow, somewhere, deep down, everything is connected, communicates, resonates, communes. Such new studies as transpersonal psychology and parapsychology are beginning to unearth the outlines of this connection. In the broadest sense, it seems to run in telepathic veins. This resonating connection can show itself in surprisingly intimate ways, even in the rhythms of our bodies.

It appeared one night, for instance, when a group of spouses filed into a laboratory at the University of Montana to take part in an experiment. Instead of telling them what it was, George Rice hooked the wives to machines that measure changes in galvanic skin response (often used in lie detecting). Meanwhile, husbands were shepherded into a distant room. Rice separated them into two groups. One group only had to watch. The others were asked in the name of science to plunge their feet into buckets of ice water. A man drove his feet into the shocking, cold water. At the same time, in another room the meter registering changes in his wife's skin shifted. Women whose husbands got cold feet showed significantly greater response than those whose didn't. It seems that the couples activated another sort of connection.

A similar thing happened at Rockland State Hospital in New York, only volunteers didn't bring mates, they brought their dogs. When a master in a separate room was "attacked" (surprise ice cubes down the neck) instruments showed the dog's body processes revved up. Apparently the tie that binds extends beyond the human network.

At the New Jersey Institute of Technology, Dr. John Mihalasky, like many others since, discovered he was telepathic. He was hooked to a machine that records changes in blood volume in the hands. Mihalasky knew that someone in another room was trying to project to him names of people—some he knew, some were strangers. Either way, he wasn't getting the message. But his body was. The graph showed when the experimenter focused on someone Mihalasky loved or feared, there was a change in his body—the blood volume in his hand changed. And no change appeared in Mihalasky when unknown names were considered. It was as though blips of pertinent information were picked up on a sort of unconscious radar screen. Dr. Douglas Dean, who designed the tests, has witnessed this gut telepathy occur not just from room to room but from continent to continent, and even when the projector was a skin diver thirty feet underwater.

These instances, and the many others on record, seem to show that on occasion we are already giving off and picking up telepathic messages. Dr. Rex Stanford at the University of Virginia Medical School worked out an ingenious way to see if anything is behind the lapse when we forget to mail a letter, or behind the call we surprised ourselves by making—when they unexpectedly turn out to our advantage. He's concluded we are sometimes prompted to behave in a certain way by unconscious telepathic information.

Communist researchers have a point when they call telepathy bio-rapport. It seems that not just the mind but the whole person is involved in this living link. Considering that it goes on anyway, it is not surprising that telepathy can be learned to one degree or another. As to why you might want to develop some finesse with bio-rapport, the father of Soviet parapsychology, Dr. L. L. Vasiliev, had perhaps the best answer.

Vasiliev, an internationally known physiologist, worked on some weighty, pragmatically oriented psi projects for his government, yet the promise of telepathy that excited him most had little to do with mass reactions. Conscious telepathy, he believed, can gift us with the direct experience of another person. It can bridge not just miles, but the distance between psyches and the barrier of bodies. It can add new dimensions of rapport.

Thinking of the more public world, an even more famous Russian, Dr. K. Tsiolkovsky, founder of the Soviet space program, long ago asserted that we would have to develop telepathy, not only to explore space but also to keep up with the information overload of the space age on earth.

Telepathy or bio-rapport is another channel of information. Awareness of it can give us second thoughts about how our own thoughts go out on the network. It can also make us more aware of subtle suggestions coming to us from the environment. Some have specialized reasons to explore the area. Governments are interested in psi communication systems to use in emergencies in space or in submarines; and they investigate how the psi network might be used in spying or mind control.

On a more mundane level, a mental message can prompt your sister to phone. And records abound of the telepathic SOS that gets through in time of dire need. Whether or not you wind up flashing messages, getting a feeling for telepathy can give a sense of that root-rapport. For some, it eases the static of alienation so they can play their parts more harmoniously in the musicosm.

The Telepathic Beat

The steady beat is the core of superlearning. Pulsing the message can make learning telepathy easier too. We heard this repeatedly talking with Russians. In keeping with the idea of rapport, they tried to turn telepathic partners into "twins." They tried to synchronize the beating of body rhythms to enhance communication. And they used rhythm in less subtle ways. At Moscow's Popov Institute, Vladimir Fidelman, for one, was training people to mentally transmit numbers. Music might interfere with the message. For his beat, Fidelman went electric. He put a number, say three, on a light, flashing it over and over at the sender. "Chant three, three, in rhythm with the light until you can visualize "three" with absolute clarity on an imagined screen in your mind," he told senders. In one series, Fidelman found that out of 134 numbers, his pulsing senders successfully got across 100 to a person almost a mile away. It's a high score.

Many innovations of Soviet parapsychology have been taken up and expanded here. But the beat, the idea of the power of rhythm has been overlooked. Before the Soviet work, the American neurologist Dr. André Puharich did use pulsed lights. He flashed a strobe on the closed eyes of psychic Peter Hurkos. Hurkos could adjust the strobe to any speed that "pleased him." With the bright pulsing light, Hurkos experienced "verifiable heightened telepathy and clairvoyance," Puharich reported. (It's not a good idea to try this experiment on your own, the wrong speed may produce fits.) Puharich no doubt knew of work showing that in some sets of identical twins, if light pulses changed the brain rhythms of one, those of the other shifted simultaneously even if he or she were in a separate room. But like Lozanov, Puharich also had an early interest in shamans and yogis to whom the rhythm of mind linking is old, old knowledge.

Yogi Ramacharaka, for instance, in the *Hindu Yoga Science of Breath,* writes, "Rhythm will augment the sending of thought by several hundred percent." Send after rhythmic breathing, he advises. This involves breathing to your own pulse. (See page 186 for instructions.) Yogis also long ago devised special candles that give a fast flicker effect to change states of consciousness. Western esoteric groups have also always emphasized rhythm—raising your own voltage with rhythm, and getting in rhythm with someone you want to touch at a distance.

Learning—What Helps

More is known about learning telepathy than any other psi talent. Interestingly, independent work on what is conducive to telepathic rapport came up with almost the same conditions as those required for rapid learning and developing supermemory. Perhaps it isn't so strange when one remembers that Dr. Lozanov, moving from the root of Western hermetic tradition and yoga, branched first into telepathic or bio-rapport and then into rapid learning. Telepathy and supermemory are just two of a large set of abilities that tradition maintained could be developed with the same practices.

As with any superlearning system, before beginning telepathy it is important to bring your mind and body into a relaxed, serene state. Rhythmic breathing also helps. In telepathy, too, the ability to visualize well is an asset, particularly if you're going to be the sender of images. Pulsing out information in a rhythmic way appears to increase reception. As with supermemory sessions, the atmosphere should be positive. Try to capture the feeling of play, the joy of adventure and learning. And it helps if you think you can do it. That may sound obvious, but regarding telepathy, there were years of scientific tests to prove that one point. Some people find that role playing helps with psi as it does in rapid-learning classes. If that appeals to you, make up another identity, someone who would be expert in the subject. You can fly in a close encounter or on a star trek. Or be a member of Merlin's troupe casting a mental number on someone. That way you don't have to worry about owning your mistakes.

Before trying a telepathic session, always take two or three minutes to become relaxed in body and calm in mind. Affirm that you can learn and for a moment try to reexperience the good feeling that comes when you do learn successfully.

Getting the Feel

By definition, telepathy involves more than one mind, so you'll have to find a partner. As you are trying to realize a direct connection with another human being, choose someone with whom you have a strong rapport—bio or otherwise. At first, take turns sending and receiving telepathically. You may find you're better at one than the other.

There are many ways to start out in telepathy. Paradoxically, it seems one of the easiest routes is to try to communicate information about a very complex subject—another person. Frances Brown Zeff, former president of the Southern California Society for Psychical Research, teaches parapsychology in the adult extension program at Cyprus College. Apart from studying research, students like to get a feeling for telepathy. Zeff, like other teachers, finds beginners in her course often do well trying to get telepathic impressions of an unknown person. To do this, the sender simply thinks of someone he knows well. He concentrates on him, and attempts to pulse out an image of him. The receiver tries to describe the person, his physical characteristics, and anything else about the person that comes to him.

Again like others, Frances Zeff finds that beginners often do well communicating tastes telepathically. The sender chooses something with a distinctive taste—a sweet piece of candy, a fresh wedge of lemon. Out of sight of the receiver, he tastes the candy, for instance, experiencing the sweet, sugary sensation in his own body as he tries to transmit taste, texture, aroma to the receiver. Zeff finds people do best at this when they're hungry, and they don't seem to pick up tastes quickly when they've come to class immediately after dinner.

Another approach at the beginning is to try to communicate one unknown picture. Works of art are good because they have distinctive line, emotion, and, often, mythic content. The sender simply holds the picture before him out of sight of the receiver. He looks at it, visualizes it clearly, trying to bring as many of his senses into play as possible as he pulses it to the receiver. He tries to pick up whatever he can about the picture —theme, dominant colors, a distinctive shape or line, emotional quality, or whatever. He may find it helps to sketch impressions. It can be interesting to see what elements do get through.

Sooner or later many people want to try the classical ESP test, which involves communicating one of five known objects, symbols, letters, numbers, or pictures. With your partner, choose five of something. If you like letters try B A Z O W. If it's numbers try 4 5 6 7 8.

After the two of you have taken a few minutes to do relaxation and breathing exercises, the sender chooses by chance (dice or spinner) one from a set of five—say a wine glass from a group of five different objects.

As sender, look at the glass, visualize it vividly in your mind, try to bring other senses into action, touch the glass, feel its curve and the cool glass, as you pulse the image to your partner. As for rhythm, you might want to take a tip from yoga and pulse around the rate of your own heartbeat. Some people prefer sending once a second, sixty beats to a minute. You can use a metronome or flashing light to reinforce the beat and try variations in speed to see if they make any difference in your ability to communicate. Eventually, imagine that you are seeing the wine glass through your partner's eyes. Project a minute to a minute and a half.

If you are the receiver, get into a comfortable position with your eyes closed. What you want is a state of "relaxed awareness." Don't file through the choices in your mind. If images flicker across your mental screen, wait until one stabilizes.

Correction

In this basic setup, you should get one out of five right by chance. Don't be too concerned about that at first. Try to distinguish how you felt, what you saw, sending and receiving, when the message gets through. Can you tell the difference between a guess and ESP? Often only a part of the target gets through—why that part? Does it have more emotion, action, color, more definite shape? Try to change sets before you get bored.

To repeat: relaxation, visualization, practice are the keys. Unfortunately, many people first try ESP in a test situation to see if they "have it." If after one or two sessions, telepathy isn't apparent, they give up. With this approach, you never would have learned to read, swim, do multiplication, or "have" any other talent or ability.

Clocks

Though there are more choices, many beginners do well with a clock face, perhaps because we're used to visualizing and responding to clocks. If you want to try this, use a real clock. By chance, choose an hour—one through twelve—set the hands and transmit mentally, *focusing on the angle.*

If you want to make a game of this, use a point system adapted from a famous British experiment: twelve points for the exact hour; six for a mirror image—for example, nine o'clock instead of three o'clock; four points for the hour on either side of the target time. It's common to get the feeling of the correct side of the clock, right or left.

Kinetic Rapport

People who aren't able to link well with images are often able to get together when they try to communicate body movements. The receiver goes into another room where she can act out a motion. Try something rhythmic like an Indian war dance, or a skating motion, swaying from side to side, imagining you're skating, skating.

If you have some success with this sort of communication, you might want to try guiding your receiver's motions. For this, you are both in the same room. Have your receiver walk around a piece of furniture, like a bridge table, for instance. Sometime after the first go round, as he circles, mentally command him to stop at a particular side. Try guiding him around the room, having him go forward, left, reach up, bend down. Try guiding him to an object hidden somewhere in the room. This treasure-hunt approach works well for some beginners, and at first, you can give him feedback as you go.

As receiver of this sort of kinetic rapport, close or semiclose your eyes to avoid distraction. Feel your body, relax and go with the tide, let the wave take you. If there's a feeling of undertow pulling you back, stop.

As sender or projector, mentally command your partner to move forward or left or to stop. Visualize and try to bring your own muscles into play. Feel it in your body.

Rhythm and rapport were the pivotal points on which Dr. Lozanov built his most successful, demonstrable telepathy system, one that drew a lot of attention in the Communist world. A telepathic receiver has a telegraph key placed to the right of him, and another one placed to the left. The sender, in a distant room, sits beside a clicking metronome. Pulsing in rhythm with the clicks, he telepathically suggests, "Press right, right, on the key." Or "left, left" according to a coded dot-dash message. He repeats each command ten times. The receiver must record six out of ten for the symbol to be considered received.

With this rhythmic form of kinetic ESP, the Bulgarians consistently got seventy to eighty percent accuracy in thousands of telegraph code tests. They were able to accurately transmit long segments of information. "Telepathy can be used practically," says Lozanov. "Telepathic and clairvoyant ability can be cultivated and trained by suggestology."

If you want to try this muscular ESP, you might use a metronome with a rhythm of sixty beats a minute, seventy-two beats a minute, or your own pulse rate. Lozanov didn't reveal the specific rhythm used. Instead of telegraph keys, even a piano keyboard divided in two could be used. Instead of press right, strike a high note; for press left, strike a low note.

Dream Rapport

"I'll see you in my dreams," may mean more than you think according to over a decade of work in dream laboratories. It seems it's possible to be a dream maker and send a dream to someone.

To try this exercise, find a willing partner, preferably someone who already keeps a dream log and is used to remembering dreams. In the lab, subjects are awakened immediately after each dream to record impressions. You'll have to rely on the discipline and desire of your dreamer.

Choose ten pictures, ones with strong emotional content, and some with action. Experimenters find, not surprisingly, that erotic and violent themes transmit best.

Don't tell your partner what pictures you've picked. If you're not living in the same house, wait until you're sure she is asleep. Then note the time and begin pulsing your dream theme. Immerse yourself in the image, the emotions. Can you feel the tactile sensations? After a bit, act it out; if there's dancing, dance, if there's a prizefight, shadowbox.

Immediately on awakening, the receiver records everything about her dreams. When you next meet, show her the pictures and ask which, if any, relate to her dreams. Go over her records and check for various levels of possible correspondence.

An older, more simple way to practice late-night telepathy is to attempt to wake someone up. When you're sure your partner is asleep, note the time and start trying to rouse him mentally; command, call, picture, and so forth. Note the time you finish, and the receiver is to note whenever he wakes during the night. In this, once a night is probably enough.

Once on a trip, all three of the authors got involved with a mental wake-up. Jack Schwarz had promised to phone to wake us for an early morning appointment. Instead, at the appropriate time, Nancy, who worked with Schwarz for some years, came wide awake with a dream. In this dream, Jack was telling her wake up; you're going to miss Jack; meet at the hotel. It turned out that the phone was out of order, and Jack could not phone so he decided to put in a mental call while someone was driving across town to knock on the door. If it was a coincidence, it was more handy than most.

Name That Tune

"Why that was just going through my head!" You can sometimes get that response when you start to hum or whistle a tune. With its movement, rhythm, melody, emotion, music would seem to be a very good way of getting minds together, but there's been surprisingly little exploration of it.

Try it yourself. Choose five distinctive musical phrases you and your partner know well—"Yankee Doodle Went to Town," Tchaikovsky's Romeo and Juliet theme, "Jingle Bells." Pick one by chance and start singing mentally. If you can conjure a whole orchestra in your head, hear it and send it.

Parents and Children

If there's rapport anywhere, it exists between parents and their offspring. And it's a connection of many notes. There's a deep-down biological rapport that can cause a baby's body to react at the moment her mother, in another wing of the hospital, is in sudden pain. There's emotional rapport across distances, usually sustaining, sometimes not. In one interesting case, a patient of psychiatrist Dr. Bethold Schwarz developed a sudden, nasty toothache. He rushed to his dentist. The dentist could find nothing wrong, even though the man was clearly in pain. Finally, the ache left as abruptly as it had come. That night, the man's mother phoned from another state. She'd had a painful, infected tooth pulled that day. It was the same tooth. Dr. Schwarz tracked down a number of cases where sympathy pains and emotional bursts pulsed on the underside of consciousness between close relatives and friends. A father himself, he eventually wrote a book about parent-child telepathy.

A Family Log

Some mothers and fathers find it enlightening to keep a small journal to note seeming spontaneous telepathy between them and their children. Schwarz and others find small children may suddenly verbalize your thoughts or even act them out. You might be at your desk hunting for a stapler you haven't used in two months. A little while later, your child may appear with it in his hand and ask you what it is used for. These are small instances, but once you collect a few, you begin to get a feeling of how thought circulates in a family, how perhaps we influence and are influenced beyond the realm of words or action.

Children seem to have more natural psi ability than the rest of us probably because it hasn't been suggested away. A teacher in California became interested when two boys in summer camp remarked they knew he was mad because they noticed the change in the energy or aura around his body. He started to make discreet inquiries with his school children. A number said they'd had experiences we would call psychic. Most commonly mentioned were such things as seeing auras, knowing what was going to happen ahead of time, and strangely, because it's just beginning to be explored by parapsychology—the feeling of floating out of one's body. The children usually didn't talk about these experiences for one of two reasons. They'd gotten the suggestion that such things weren't quite "right" or else they simply assumed such things happened to everyone and weren't worthy of remark.

If you're interested, talk to children about psi. Don't suggest they ought to be having psi experiences. Just treat it as something natural that may or may not happen. You might want to play psi games with them to try to get the "future abilities" of the future citizens humming. Here are some to get you started.

Children's Games

SOMETHING FISHY

Objective:
To enhance concentration and telepathy

Required:
Slips of paper for each member of the group. Draw a fish on two of them; a four-leaf clover on each of the rest.

Instructions:
Children are seated in a circle.
Shuffle the slips of paper.
Each child is dealt one slip of paper, which he holds picture side facing him.
The objective of the game is explained to the children: The clover represents good luck; the fish something fishy. They must try to determine telepathically which person has "something fishy" about him.

Sender:
Each child in turn concentrates and tries to send the thought both by picture and by saying, over and over mentally, the name of the symbol on his card. They must try to pulse the picture rhythmically.

Receivers:
As the sender is doing this, the children in the rest of the circle close their eyes—take a deep breath—become still—turn on their mental screens and wait for one of the two symbols to appear on the screen. They try to tell telepath-

ically if there's "something fishy" about the person, and note it down on the back of their papers.

Winning:
When all have been senders, players show their slips of paper. Points can be awarded to winners.

PSYCHIC DETECTIVE

Objective:
To enhance concentration and telepathy

Required:
Paper slips—one per person
Mark one slip—Happy Face—Witness
Mark one slip—Sad Face—Culprit
Rest of slips will be blank

Instructions:
Children sit in a circle.
Children are each handed one slip of paper, which nobody sees but the person to whom it is given.
Objectives of game are explained. There is only one Happy Face—Witness. There is only one Sad Face—Culprit.
The children write their names (or a given number) on the bottom of their slips of paper.
The child with the "Witness" slip identifies himself or herself to the rest of the group.
All the rest fold up their slips and give them to the Witness.
The Witness unfolds the slips and finds the name of the person who received the Culprit slip.

Sender:
The Witness or sender now concentrates on the name of the person who received the Culprit slip, visualizing the person

as clearly as possible and mentally repeating the name over
and over rhythmically.

Receivers:

As the sender is doing this, the rest of the group close their
eyes, become relaxed and still, and wait for the name of the
Culprit to pop into their minds.

Winners:

Write down the names. Winners can be given points.

PSYCHIC MUSICAL CHAIRS

Required:

Number a group of chairs.
Put slips of paper with matching numbers in a hat.
Each player has a slip of paper and pencil.

Instructions:

Players sit on the chairs and choose a sender.

Sender:

Plays music. He or she draws a number from the hat and
projects the number mentally to the group.

Receivers:

Each player writes down a number received telepathically.
When the music stops, all show their numbers.

Winners:

Players with the correct numbers leave their chairs.

Repeat until there's only one person left in the "psychic hot
seat."

Mental Semaphore and Metaphor

Sending and receiving—those terms come from the early days of radio, when "mental radio" or telepathy was first being examined. If you have a certain bent you can deepen your feeling for psi by making a list describing what you think you're doing when involved with telepathy. Can you come up with more contemporary terms, words perhaps that better describe what's happening than do sender and receiver? Is the message really traveling along from here to there like radio? Do we somehow get into a different space, another state of conscious- ness and just know? Is it more like a composer and performer with the receiver helping to recreate the impulse? Has this anything to do with the idea of creating our own reality? What about this very root sort of telepathic rapport that research indicates extends to animals and possibly even to plants? Is there an energy involved? Do yin and yang apply? And what about resonance?

Fe Fi Fo Fum

There is one experiment, simple as a parable, that can make that idea of being truly connected with life come alive—as crisp and alive as a beanstalk heading toward the sun.

Get simple seeds—bean or barley are good. Plant ten in each of three pots. Label them *Love, Control, Hate*. During the next few weeks all will be treated alike physically, getting the same amount of water, light, and so forth.

Five or ten minutes, twice a day, communicate or commune with your Love pot. Mentally or aloud feed these plantlings positive, encouraging thoughts. Pray for them, bless them if you wish. Tell them they are the best seeds in the world, they can't help growing into beautiful, big plants. Try to feel a rapport and love this wonderful unfolding freshness. Visualize them grow- ing healthy and strong as you speak.

Do nothing with the control pot. Use the hate pot to let loose the frustrations of the day. Aim your angers at those seeds. *Discourage* them. Tell them, "You're no good, you won't amount to anything. Nobody wants you. The world's no good, you won't like it out here. There's no use trying . . ." Sound familiar? Visualize them as puny, stunted.

After a few weeks, compare pots. Check for height, fullness, root system. Do you find any differences? Many kinds of people, from school kids to church congregations to scientists, by using this simple approach, find that somehow or other, their thoughts do have a tangible influence.

Groups

When two or three get together on a thought, voltage seems to increase geometrically. Have a group send to a single person in another room. Try to act as one. This is a particularly good time to use rhythm. Tap sixty beats a minute while everyone sends in concert. During one experiment, a group concentrated on a wall. Nothing was getting through, so they were asked to describe their visualization and everything came up from the papered dining room wall to the great wall of China. If it's visual, have a picture everyone can look at as they pulse.

When sending *to* a number of people, keep an eye out for two who often get the same wrong answer, as if it bled through from one to the other. They may be natural telepathic twins, people on the same "wavelength" who'll do well as a team.

Just how intimately bio-rapport intermingles in our relationships was demonstrated by Dr. A. Esser at Rockland State Hospital. In an experiment with couples, he hooked the wives to physical monitoring machines. In a distant room, their husbands looked through a batch of photographs that included some pictures of ex-girlfriends. A husband looked at a former love, and his wife's body registered a change on the instrument graphs. She wasn't consciously aware that her husband was concentrating on an old attraction—but her body was.

With group telepathy try sending names or faces of people the receiver is strongly involved with. Try pictures or colors, symbols, commercials, emotions, or tastes. Your group can also try getting together mentally when each is in his own home.

Charisma

We all ought to know by now that when you walk into a roomful of strangers, they'll treat you the way you expect to be treated. And, as the Russians put it, bio-rapport is behind that sudden click or clunk you get with certain people. Try experimenting, putting out different attitudes, emotions, thoughts on the telepathic network when you meet somebody new or when you're in a group, business or social. You can try it with people you know, too. See if what you send outward mirrors back.

The reality of bio-rapport came home to actress-author Naura Hayden when she was studying mental acting techniques to help her project the feeling of characters. In particular, she worked on the expansive, open-to-the-world, joyous feeling of an outgoing ingenue and also the folded-in, damped-down feeling of a repressed young woman. The mental techniques didn't seem to be giving her quite the reality of character she wanted. She came across a book on physical exercises for acting and began doing stretching, reaching exercises and also ones where she folded up, curling in on herself like a fetus.

"After practicing my exercises for about a week, I had a friend of mine sit on my couch and I stood with my back to him. Without moving a muscle, I mentally and emotionally opened up and closed up and he 'felt' every one I did. He guessed twenty-five out of twenty-five, so I proved to myself it works." Hayden says in her *Everything You Always Wanted to Know About Energy but Were Too Weak to Ask,* "I began to see that the mind, emotions, and body are one." Bio-rapport, messages pulsing in widening circles out of the whole person, probably lies at the heart of charisma. This is the between-the-lines communication of powerful artists and leaders, and of great teachers. It makes the message take, it reaches and moves us, even to the barricades.

It's beginning to appear that underneath the separate surface of things, there is a connection, a dynamic network, flashing countless messages everywhere, anywhere, perhaps faster than the speed of light. Time and space do not seem to affect these life signals. We are just beginning to realize how we influence and are influenced by thoughts and feelings pulsing along the network. Certainly this is something to be explored by those of varied expertise, but it isn't for experts only. Like the old telephone system, this is a party line and we're all on the line. Or perhaps we can use a more embracing image than a line. As Donald Hatch Andrews remarked, "In shifting the basis of our ideas about the universe from mechanics to music, we move into an entirely new philosophy of science"—and a fresh way of looking at things for the rest of us. In that sense, we form the resonance, we are the music and the message.

SECTION IV
EXERCISES

Chapter 17
Mental Yoga and Concentration Exercises

"Students need to realize that the proper picturization and belief in what they want to do and understand is a powerful agent in helping them achieve their goals." So maintains Al Pollard of Little Rock, founder of a very successful management consulting firm. An internationally recognized pioneer in the development of export trade for his state, Al Pollard is committed to helping businesspeople get in touch with their intuition, creativity, and so-called extrasensory capabilities. He is also working to bring mind-opening techniques into education. "We have to realize that people are looking and hungry for new experiences." He says, "Learning is the only continuum that enables us to have new experiences. So the educational system is a learning, moving experience that has a tremendous potential for giving students and teachers the dynamics to achieve what they want, which should be both rewarding and enjoyable for everyone." One of the dynamics that helps you achieve what you want is the ability to visualize it.

Visualization and concentration, the nerve and muscle that powered the mental feats of such people as Nikola Tesla or the physical feats of Jack Nicklaus can be learned at any age. They can help you unfold new ability in education and sports, pain control and intuition. They can free new strengths across the board from scientific discovery to business, from fiction writing to politics.

Raja Yoga, or mental yoga, is often called the "science of concentration." Its practitioners assert that through graded steps in visualization, it is possible to improve concentration, enhance mental abilities, and develop a photographic memory.

Some of the following exercises are drawn from the classic Raja Yoga visualization exercises for improved mental capacities.

Better Concentration Through Breathing

This exercise uses breathing as a means of developing a communications link between mind and body. It helps aid concentration and visualization skills by focusing attention on the energy interplay involved in breathing. It may also help develop concentration, according to Eastern theory, by charging up bioenergies through increased oxygen intake and increased prana.

This classic exercise, known as "polarization," is also said to be a boon for worriers. Yoga practitioners maintain it can help break up the "worry circle" and relieve anxieties by increasing nerve-energy supply.

You can sense whether or not you're getting somewhere with this concentration exercise after you've practiced it awhile, by noticing whether or not you feel a kind of tingling energy current running through the body with each *in* and *out* breath.

All exercises for the mind must always be done gently.

1. Find a secluded spot where you will not be disturbed. Lie down face up on a couch, bed, or on the floor with your feet pointing south and your head north, so you're lined up with the earth's own magnetic field.

2. Put your feet together and place hands, palms up, touching the sides of the body.

3. Take a slow, even, deep breath (through the nose), and visualize warm, golden *yellow* sun energy being drawn through the top of your head, sweeping through your body, and going out the soles of your feet. Think of this incoming yellow energy as a positive current.

4. As you slowly, and evenly, breathe out, visualize cool, *blue* moon energy being drawn up through the soles of your feet, sweeping through your body, and going out through the top of your head. Think of this outgoing blue energy as a negative current.

5. For about fifteen minutes, continue to breathe *in* yellow; *out* blue. Try to imagine these polarized energies sweeping through the body like an electric current. Let the yellow *in* breath vibrate through you from head to toe. Let the blue *out* breath vibrate through you from toe to head. Try to keep breath, visualization, and inner sensing of energies "in synch."

6. Your concentration ability is considered to be intensified when you feel a definite sensation of being "charged up" with an energy current running through your body with each *in* and *out* breath.

Interior Decorating for the Mind

Visualization, mental imaging, and memory stimulation have a lot to do with focusing the mind. Focusing should be done very gently and delicately, just as you gently adjust a high-powered microscope into focus. Prior to doing a concentration exercise, use one of the relaxation exercises first to get into a tension-free state. Forcing or "willing" just blocks the mental state required for concentration.

MIND DESIGNS

These exercises that help concentration skills are done with several geometric patterns that you can make from paper or poster board. Some people keep these designs pinned up on their walls, or even frame them. The pattern pictures then have a double bonus: they are decorations as well as mind boosters.

In Eastern lore, these geometric patterns are called yantras, and some of the elaborate ones are available as transparencies to be used as window decorations.

HOW TO MAKE DESIGNS FOR THE MIND

Pattern 1: Cut a square of black poster board 15 by 15 inches. Cut a square of white poster board 2 by 2 inches. Glue the white square exactly in the center of the black square.

Pattern 2. Cut a square of black cardboard 15 by 15 inches. Cut an 11-inch-wide five-pointed star from white cardboard. Glue the white star in the middle of the black square.

Pattern 3. Cut a square of white cardboard 15 by 15 inches. Cut a circle of royal blue cardboard 5 inches in diameter. Glue the blue circle exactly in the middle of the white square.

Concentration Exercise 1

This exercise is for (a) concentration skill and (b) visualization skill—through learning to transfer outer patterns to the inner mind's eye.

1. Attach Pattern 1 (black and white squares) to a light-colored wall. Put it at a height that will center the white square at eye level when you are seated in a chair. Be sure there's enough light to see the pattern clearly.

2. Sit in a chair facing the pattern about three feet away from it.

3. Get into a relaxed or centered state through your favorite relaxation method.

4. Close your eyes and, for two minutes, picture a screen of warm, velvety blackness. If distracting images pop up, let them float past and again imagine your black screen, just like a TV screen before it's turned on.

5. Open your eyes and look at the center of the pattern diagram for about three minutes. Keep looking at the diagram intently. Try not to blink, but don't strain. Keep gazing at it until you begin to see an edge of color forming around the white square.

6. Slowly move your eyes away from the diagram and look at the blank wall. An after-image should appear on the wall (a black square). Gaze at the after-image as long as you can see it. If it starts to fade, imagine that it is still there.

7. When the after-image has completely gone, close your eyes and recreate it mentally in your mind's eye. Try to hold it as steadily as possible on the screen of your mind.

8. Repeat the whole procedure.

Exercises 1 and 2 can be done for up to fifteen minutes. Practice for about a week before doing the photographic memory exercise.

Concentration Exercise 2

1. Attach the star pattern to the wall.
2. Sit in a chair three feet away.
3. Get into a relaxed state.
4. Close your eyes and imagine a black screen in your mind.
5. Look at the star pattern. Gaze at the pattern for two minutes.
6. Move your eyes to the wall and gaze at the after-image of the star.
7. Close your eyes and try to see the star pattern on the screen of your mind.

This same type of concentration exercise can also be practiced with your shadow either outdoors or indoors. Stand or sit in the light so that you cast a shadow. Gaze at the neck of your shadow for two minutes or so, then look at a light-colored wall (if outdoors, at the sky), and see the after-image of your own shadow. Close your eyes, and see your shadow in your mind's eye.

Once you've had some practice with this concentration technique, you can try it for making "memory snapshots" of diagrams or pages of books. Try to see the entire diagram clearly with the eyes closed on the screen of your mind.

Size, Color, Motion Exercise

The ability to create vivid mental images is one of the keys to memory power and improved sports performance. Just as in ads or movies, three basic elements make images vivid: size, color, and motion. It's like putting things you have to remember on a huge billboard in vivid colors and with flashing lights.

1. Attach pattern 3 (white square with blue circle) to the wall at eye level.

2. Get into a relaxed, meditative state.

3. Close your eyes for a minute and imagine a black screen.

4. Open your eyes and gaze at the pattern diagram. Focus on the blue circle. Now, imagine seeing it through the zoom lens of a movie camera. Zoom in on the blue circle until it is enormous and fills the whole screen of your mind. Zoom out again until it's normal size. Zoom in and out on the image several times.

5. Now add still more motion to the visualization. Move your eyes around the outer edge of the blue circle clockwise. Do it about five times. Now move your eyes around the blue circle counterclockwise about five times. Do the circling again and gradually increase speed until the circle seems to be spinning like a top, and the image almost seems 3-D. Then slow it down again.

This exercise can be done for about five minutes at a time. The star pattern can also be used for focus, zoom, and circling practice. Look at the star's points for four counts each. Circle around it first clockwise and then counterclockwise. Then increase the speed, then slow it down.

Size, Color, Motion practice can be done with objects, too. Look at a match, for instance. Close your eyes for a moment and mentally see that match as large as a telephone pole. Sense its enormous size. Next, imagine this huge match being ignited and visualize the giant red flame flaring up.

Any sport that involves objects and motion can benefit from practice in size, color, and motion visualization. For instance, a trap-shooting expert who practices mind training applies it to shooting at clay pigeons. He gets into a relaxed, centered state of mind. Then he visualizes his target, the clay pigeons, in every detail.

He uses the zoom-lens visualizing technique so the clay pigeons appear very large and very close and very easy to sight. Then he uses the slowed-down motion technique so they seem to move slowly and lazily into his line of vision and he has plenty of time to sight them with his rifle. He reports he improved his score at the very first try and has now helped others to do the same with these easy visualization techniques.

Photographic Memory Exercise

This exercise is designed to develop concentration and visualization, and after a certain amount of practice, yogis say, it may help develop photographic memory. It can also be used to help you recall material you have forgotten by stimulating communications links to your memory bank.

Before beginning on this exercise, you should have practiced with the picture pattern technique for at least a week.

1. Find a secluded spot and turn the lights very low. Lie down, face up on a couch, bed, or floor.

2. Do a relaxation or centering exercise.

3. Close your eyes and create a mental screen of warm, velvety blackness.

4. Visualize against this black screen a square of white paper about 12 by 12 inches centered about a foot away from your eyes. Try to hold this image steady so it doesn't slide around. (This is the same type of pattern you've worked with previously.)

5. Picturing the white square against the black background, now imagine a black circle the size of a fifty-cent coin right in the middle of the white square. Concentrate on the black circle in the center of the white square against the black background.

6. Suddenly release the entire visualization. Let it go completely. Then watch the kinds of images that suddenly flash through your mind.

This exercise helps relax tension and "unstick" communications between your conscious mind and your memory bank, by setting up a free flow of associations back and forth. Yogis say that if it is practiced, it can be used to help recall things that have slipped your mind—where you've misplaced papers, a name you're trying to remember, items on an exam, and so forth. To use this exercise for recall, close your eyes and give yourself the mental command: "I will remember (name, fact, location)." Then do the memory exercise. Hold the visualization several seconds, release the image, and wait with closed eyes for ten to fifteen seconds to see if the desired item will surface in your conscious mind.

Energy-Field Awareness Exercise

This energy-field visualization exercise is a basic one for developing body awareness and expanded perceptions and is also used in "inner" sports training for body-contact sports or games like tennis to extend control over the racquet.

The body radiates different kinds of energies that are readily measured by modern instruments. First, there's a cocoon of heat around the body that can be picked up by thermistors. There's also an electromagnetic field that's tied in with the beating of the heart. This field can be measured several inches away from the body. There's also a cloud of ions (charged particles) around the body, measured by electrostatic instruments. Aside from these energies, there seem to be additional bio-fields, now being made visible in current research by equipment such as Kirlian photography. Becoming sensitive to these energies radiating from us extends our field of awareness and heightens control.

1. Sit down or lie down in a secluded place and relax by your preferred method or autogenics.

2. In this very comfortable, relaxed state, try to sense or feel energy radiating from your body. As you relax, imagine your awareness is as sensitive as a delicate instrument and can pick up this energy radiating from your own physical body. Just as your physical body is controlled by your mind, this energy radiating from you is also under the direction of the mind.

3. If at first you don't seem to sense this radiant energy coming from your body, think of the energy in metaphorical terms and pretend that you sense it. Imagine or visualize this cocoon of energy all around you.

4. Now, begin to expand this energy surround. Imagine it radiating out about three feet from your body.

5. Next, expand this energy field still more. Let it radiate out nine feet from your body. If you can sense this field, try to actually see the waves of energy coming from you. If you don't sense these energies, visualize them and imagine them spreading out from you. Let them go out nine feet all around you.

6. Now, let your bio-field expand even farther. Let it fill up the entire room. Let it expand out at least fifteen feet away from you.

7. In your mind's eye, begin to pull your energy surround back in toward your body. Try to sense the different feeling involved in expanding and contracting it. Pull it in until it's

twelve feet around you. Sense it and visualize it as a sparkling cloud all around you.

8. Next, use your imagination to pull in your energy field to about six feet from your body.

9. Now, in your mind's eye, pull your energy bio-field in to your body as closely as possible. Try to draw it up around the body until it's as small as possible.

10. Relax and let the energy surround go back to its regular size.

As you practice with this exercise, you'll find you become increasingly aware of the energy system around you and of the energy systems of other people.

Chapter 18
Visualization and Autogenics Exercises

Introduction

The following exercises can be used individually for visualization, mind calming, or concentration practice.

The full sequence can also be used to cover the second stage of autogenics. Second-stage autogenics covers the following progression: (a) visualizing colors; (b) visualizing objects; (c) contemplating abstract concepts; (d) experiencing selected feeling states (self-image changing); (e) visualizing other people and your relationships to these people; (f) visualizing receiving answers from the unconscious.

These exercises can be done quite simply by reading them through and getting the kernel of the technique, then relaxing and taking yourself through them. They can also be put on tape to listen to while you relax, or you can have a friend read them to you. No more than about twenty minutes per day should be spent on any one exercise.

Color Encounters

The objective of this exercise is to practice visualization and mind calming.

Take a comfortable position. Close your eyes and raise them slightly upward. Take a deep breath through your nose and, while slowly exhaling, feel a wave of warm relaxation flow slowly over your entire body from your toes to your head. Use your preferred relaxation method or autogenics to reach a comfortable state of relaxation. One by one, you will visualize dots of colored light suspended in space a short distance away from you. As you focus on each dot of color, it will appear to grow larger and larger, come closer and closer, then become paler and paler, and gradually float off into space.

Mentally visualize a dot of red light in front of you—bright, vivid, red light. See it becoming larger and larger. Picture this red light coming closer and closer. Now the red grows paler and paler. It gradually begins to fade away now into the distance.

Picture the next dot of light. The color is orange. Imagine the deep, rich orange light drawing closer and getting larger and larger like a spotlight. Now the orange is getting paler and paler and slowly becomes like a cloud of light as it fades away into the distance.

Now visualize the color yellow. A yellow dot of light. Just like the beam of a spotlight, it draws nearer and nearer, growing larger and brighter. Take a minute and bask in this golden circle of yellow light. The light gradually gets paler and paler and floats away.

Visualize the color green—a clear, emerald green dot of light. Watch it move closer and closer until all you see is this pure emerald green. Then watch the green light become paler until it disappears from sight.

Visualize the color blue, a pale, soft blue dot of light. See the blue light drawing nearer and nearer, growing larger and larger, and circling around you until it totally embraces you. It lifts you gently up, growing lighter and lighter, getting paler and paler until it forms a buoyant white cloud of light.

Imagine yourself floating up into the sky on this wonderful cloud of white light. Become aware of other clouds as you float past them. Enjoy the tranquil feeling of peacefulness and happiness throughout your whole body.

Whenever you wish, you can remember this relaxed feeling. You can remember this centered, calm feeling before appointments or any special occasion when it would help you. You feel relaxed, calm, healthy, competent.

Now, start to come back gently. Feel yourself slowly returning to your usual surroundings and to a more aware self. Slowly open your eyes, take several deep breaths, stretch, and turn on all body switches. You feel centered and rested.

Concentration Practice

OBJECTS

Use real objects for practice in this exercise. Some athletes use sports paraphernalia for concentration practice. For instance, Billie Jean King uses a tennis ball. She gazes at a tennis ball in her hand and absorbs the details of its seams, matted hair, shape, color, and texture. In this concentration practice, a rock, fruit, and a small transistor radio will be explored. You can explore many other objects in the same way.

Relax in your preferred way or through autogenics.

1. ROCK

Reach out and take a rock in your hand. Turn it over and over, feel its texture. Is it smooth or rough? Hard or porous? Smell it. Does it have a smell? Taste it. Does it have a taste?

Now relax still more, close your eyes, and in your imagination, feel that you are very, very small, tiny enough to crawl inside the rock and look around. Now imagine that you are the rock. How does it feel to be that rock? Do you feel heavy or light, large or small? Now while you are still that rock, pretend that you are lying out in a field of grass. Imagine that a gentle rain is falling down on you. How does the rain affect you? Are there any changes in the ground that you are lying on? Now imagine the rain has stopped. The sun is coming out. Feel the warming rays of the sun shining down on you as you lie in this field of grass. Imagine now, that you are shedding the shell of the rock and slowly returning to your normal size and state. You can recall everything you experienced. Count from 1 to 5 and on the count of 5, open your eyes and feel alert and refreshed.

2. FRUIT (ORANGE)

Relax by your preferred method.

Reach out and take the orange in your hand. Turn it over and over, feel its texture, smell it, and recall how the odor of it affected you.

Feel yourself relaxing still further, and imagine that you are becoming smaller and smaller, tiny enough to be able to crawl inside the orange and explore it. How does the inside of the fruit look and feel. Taste the fruit inside, and remember how it tastes. Is it a fresh orange? Does the color on the inside look the same as it did from the outside?

Imagine now that you are leaving the interior of the orange and returning to normal size. You remember everything you saw, felt, tasted, and experienced.

Count from 1 to 5 and feel yourself alert and refreshed.

3. TRANSISTOR RADIO

Relax by your preferred method.

Reach out and take the small transistor radio in your hand. Turn it over and over, feeling its weight and shape. Notice how it feels. Smell it. How does it smell? Relax still further. Imagine that you are very, very tiny and can get inside the radio to look around. Now you are inside the transistor radio. Look around. What color are the different parts of the works? How does the inside look and feel? Is it crowded? Travel through the different parts of the radio.

Imagine now that you are leaving the interior of the radio and returning to normal size. You remember everything you saw and experienced on your journey.

Count from 1 to 5 and feel yourself alert and refreshed. Some other objects you can use for concentration practice might include a silver coin, a plant, a seed, a fabric, cotton batting, an ice cube.

I Am a Camera

There are visualization exercises for improved concentration and memory. Get comfortable and use your favorite method to reach a relaxed state.

INTRODUCTION TO MENTAL SCREEN

Imagine your head is a camera.
Imagine your eyes are the lens of the camera.
You're going to take some mental pictures.
Concentrate on several objects within the room
   A lamp
   A chair
   A book
   A rug
   A plant
Next center your attention on an open space on the wall.
Pretend your head is a projector.
Those pictures are now in your head.
Project them onto the wall.
This is done with the eyes open.

SUGGESTION

Each object should be done separately at first to absorb more detail. Then do the exercise with two objects and gradually add others. Work up to bringing in a whole tray loaded with objects and take a quick mental snapshot of it. Project it on the wall to try to recall all the objects in detail.

Now shut your eyes and imagine a large, white screen in front of you. This is a mental screen.

Open your eyes and look at several objects again. Close your eyes and project the images of the objects on the mental screen. Start with one object, and increase the number of objects.

Experiment with this technique on your own. Take a picture of a friend—in your home, or in your friend's home. You can take pictures this way anytime—you can practice while standing in lines or waiting in traffic. It will enhance both memory and concentration.

Waking Dream

Combining relaxation and visualization, this exercise helps open the creative part of your mind and helps you sense and feel such abstract concepts as peace and serenity.

Take a comfortable position. Close your eyes and raise them slightly upward. Take a deep breath through your nose and, while slowly exhaling, feel a wave of warm relaxation flow slowly over your entire body from your toes to your head. Use your preferred relaxation method or autogenics to reach a state of relaxation.

Imagine yourself walking along a winding path in a lush, green wooded area. Ahead of you is a small, grassy hill. Slowly and easily, start climbing the hill. Notice the wild flowers nestled in the long grass along the path. Hear the pebbles crunch as you walk over them. Pause as you reach the top of the hill. Below, at the bottom of this hill, you can see a small, winding

stream. Climb slowly down the hill toward the stream. You feel
the cool, soft grass under your feet as you walk. Follow the path
sloping down the hill to level ground again and on to the edge
of the stream. Look along the bank and see the slender willows
bending over the water. See the rich, brown mud of the banks.
Watch the eddies of sunlight reflecting in the clear, cool water
as it flows along. As you reach the edge of the stream, you notice
a raft.

Examine this raft. It is constructed of thick wood—its surface
is polished smooth. The raft is blanketed with a soft, cushiony
moss. You are aware that this is a safe, secure raft. Walk over
and climb on the raft. Push away from shore. Settle back and
feel a wave of warm relaxation enfold you as you float along.

Feel the gentle rise and fall of the waves. Become aware of
the easy, rocking motion as you drift slowly on and on. Listen
to the gentle slapping of the water against the sides of the raft.
Enjoy total relaxation as you float downstream toward a small
tunnel, a familiar, safe tunnel where for a while you can be
shaded from the sun. As you enter the tunnel, you can see the
light on the other side of it sparkling on the water. This is a
dream tunnel. As you enter the comfortable darkness of the
tunnel, let yourself dream. Look into the darkness. Take your
time, and let whatever will, come and play itself out in your
mind.

As you pass out of the tunnel, feel yourself being bathed in
the warm, bright sunshine. Feel that sun bringing you energy
and happiness.

Smell the fresh country scents of stream and grass as a gentle
breeze passes over you. Open all your senses, all your pores to
the nature around you. Look over the side of the raft and see
many different-colored small fish swimming by the side. Notice
the various colors and shapes as the fish gleam and dart. Then
look at the banks and see the leafy branches overhanging the
river and glimpse birds moving in the leaves. Then look at the
sky above. Feel contentment and serenity as you peacefully
drift on and on, drifting like the small, white clouds in the sky,

gliding effortlessly high up in the blue. Feel the quietness around you. Take a moment to contemplate tranquility, harmony, and peace. Other abstract ideas you can contemplate: compassion, faith, justice, mercy, etc.

Feel the warmth of the sun engulf your body. Become fully aware of being within this experience, the flowing motion of the raft, the warmth, the smells, the sounds of just drifting along the stream. Let yourself become one with the sensations around you.

Come away from this experience gently. Count from 1 to 5. Slowly become aware of your present surroundings. Feel your body switch on as you very slowly open your eyes and look around the room. Stretch and take a few deep breaths. You feel centered and rested.

Health Spa for the Mind

You are going to create a special place, a nowhere space, in your mind. This is to help focus attention for visualization and concentration. This is your own creative space, a private spot where you can go to relax, to work out problems, to make decisions. In the midst of our many activities, we often don't have time to get away. But anyone can create a mental "getaway" place for himself. It is living space for you, where you can think and feel clearly, insulated from the distractions and rhythms of the world around you.

You can create this get-away space anywhere you want—a favorite fishing spot, a beach, the mountains, the bottom of the sea, in this world or out of it. You are going to mentally design a room, or several, if you wish, and put things in the rooms to be used later.

Take a comfortable position. Close your eyes and raise them slightly upward. Breathe slowly and deeply through your nose. Now take a deep breath and while slowly exhaling, feel a wave of warm relaxation flow slowly over your entire body from your toes to your head.

Follow your preferred technique for relaxation or autogenics.

When you feel completely relaxed, mentally visualize yourself walking in a garden, a park, or a field. Notice the trees and clusters of bushes along the path on which you are walking. Ahead of you is a small clearing and one very large, very old tree. As you walk closer, you see the thick, strong, old arms of the tree. Hanging from one arm is a sturdy swing. Walk up and sit down on the swing.

Slowly start swinging, back and forth, back and forth. Take a deep breath as you swing backward. Let it out as you swing forward. Swinging back and forth, back and forth, with every breath, gently swinging higher and higher, you feel lighter and lighter. Take another deep breath as you swing higher and notice a big, white, feathery cloud floating directly in front of you. Take another deep breath and as you swing forward, float up onto this soft, billowy cloud. This cloud will carry you safely anywhere you want to go. Go high up in the air, then begin to settle down slowly, in a great, slow arc, until your feet are again on the ground in the spot you've chosen to construct your get-away place. (Pause.)

When you're working mentally, construction is as easy as saying 1,2,3. Tell yourself that when you've counted to 3, the room(s) you want will appear. They can be any shape, style, color, or decor. When you've counted 3 and your room has appeared, look around, make sure you like everything about it. Make any necessary changes.

Next, you're going to add some specific objects to this private place. Again use the 1,2,3 method. At the count of 3 you're going to create a carpet—any size, shape, or design you like. Make sure it's properly placed on the floor. Sit down on it. You can sit on this carpet any time you want and immediately feel relaxed. When you sit on this rug it will automatically bring enough energy to work on any project.

Now, you also need several comfortable chairs. Pick a couple of chairs you like. When the chairs appear at the count of 3, make sure they're just what you want. (Pause.)

Using your 1,2,3 construction method, create a desk. It's a

large, attractive, well-organized desk. Install a large TV screen which you can see from the desk. Conveniently located near your desk is a control panel for the TV screen, consisting of three buttons—*on-off, clear,* and *change.* Visualize all clearly.

Place a row of bottles and one large glass on the desk. They will be used later. Next create a special door in your private room, one through which, when you wish, people can enter to help you with a project. Then create a full-length mirror of any style. Hang it on the wall.

Look around your room once more, making sure you've put everything in it you'd like. Walk around in it, begin to feel at home. Sit down and tell yourself a few times that whenever you wish to come to this place on your own, you can do so by becoming relaxed and slowly visualizing the colors: red, orange, yellow, green, blue, indigo, and violet. When you complete the rainbow, you imagine yourself on the carpet in your get-away place, and you will be there. Always leave this place from your carpet too.

When you are ready, return to your regular surroundings on your own. Count from 1 to 5. As you count, feel yourself slowly returning to your usual surroundings, and to a more aware self. At the count of 5, slowly open your eyes, take several deep breaths, stretch, and feel energized and rested.

Improving Your Self-Image

In this exercise you take an honest look at yourself to see who and what you really are. You then create an improved self-image with all the things you would like to be.

Take a comfortable position. Close your eyes and raise them slightly upward. Breathe slowly and deeply through your nose. Now take a deep breath and, while slowly exhaling, feel a wave of warm relaxation flow slowly over your entire body from your toes to your head.

Follow your preferred technique for relaxation or autogenics.

When you feel completely relaxed, visualize yourself on a beautiful beach. Feel the warmth of the sun brightly shining down on you. Walk along the beach and down to the edge of the water. Feel the warmth of the sand under your feet and the fine sand as it trickles between your toes as you walk. As you walk along the edge of the water, feel the waves gently lapping up around your ankles. In the distance you can hear the seagulls calling to each other. A little ahead of you, half buried in the sand, is a brightly colored object. Walk up to it and pick it up. You see that it's a beach ball—a large, round, multicolored beach ball. Throw the ball into the air and catch it. Each time you throw the ball up in the air, it will go higher and you will feel more and more relaxed. Throw the ball again. Watch how the colors sparkle in the sun. Notice how the colors spin as the ball sails through the air. Inhale deeply each time you throw the ball into the air. Exhale as the ball descends and you catch it.

Do this several times. Take another deep breath and throw the ball one more time—high, high into the air, so high that it disappears into the clouds. Lie down in the soft, warm sand and just relax. The more you relax, the lighter your body will feel, more relaxed and lighter and lighter with every breath. Lighter and lighter until you feel light enough to float upward into the air.

To become still more relaxed, visualize a rainbow of seven colors. Mentally trace each of the color bands of the rainbow one by one. When you complete the rainbow, you will be in your special "get-away" place. Red . . . orange . . . yellow . . . green . . . blue . . . indigo . . . violet. You are now in your special room in your "get-away" place.

At this time, sit on your rug and become relaxed and comfortable. Think about yourself—what kind of person do you think you are? Begin to examine any of your present attitudes that you consider to be negative or restrictive. See the effect you have on other people. Begin to see yourself as others see you, not how you *think* they see you or how you would *like* them to see you.

Being honest with yourself is a step in adjusting negative attitudes, experiences, programming, so your unobstructed self can manifest. You can use a "mental TV screen" technique to rework any experience you'd like to unblock—whether in personal life, sports, performing, or school—incidents of fear (sports, exams), embarrassment (auditions), lack of confidence (learning), shyness, and so on. Select a few each time you do the exercise. Spend only a few minutes on each. The following are samples.

Now get up from the rug and walk over to your desk. Sit down comfortably. Think back to a time when you felt angry. Press the *on* button on your panel that operates your large TV screen, and this scene will appear as a movie before you. Relive the effect being angry had on you for a moment. Then see the effect it had on the people around you.

After you have done this, press the *clear* button, instantly erasing this picture from the screen and from your mind. Cleanse yourself of the negative feeling. Press the *change* button and bring the scene back, this time reliving it as it should have been. Instead of feeling angry, give love and understanding. Press the button and clear the screen.

Put another experience up on the screen—one in which you felt jealousy or envy for a friend. Remember how you felt inside when you were jealous of someone else. Think about how your feelings affect the people around you. After you have done this for a moment, press the *clear* button, erasing these experiences from the screen and from your mind. Cleanse yourself of any of these negative feelings. Press the *change* button and bring the scene back, changing this experience, and reliving it as it should have been. Instead of jealousy or envy, feel joy and support for another's happiness. Let yourself be trusting.

Put another movie on your screen. Recreate a time when you were insulted by another person. Relive this experience and feel the effect it had on you. For a moment, examine the effect it had on the other person. See how other people reacted toward that person. Press the button to clear the screen. Erase the experience from your mind and cleanse yourself of the negative feelings. Press the *change* button. Bring the scene back and change the experience, this time reliving it as it should have been. See yourself confident, non-attached, and not accepting the insult.

Review any time when you felt sorry for yourself, or felt left out, or when you blamed someone else for your wrongdoings or shortcomings. Press the *on* button and put that experience on the screen. Remember how you felt when you did this. See how the people around you reacted to your actions—your family, friends, associates. Press the *clear* button. Erase these negative, unpleasant feelings. Press *change* and recreate the scene introducing a sense of belonging, well-being, and harmony to the situation in the picture. Turn off the screen.

Go over and sit down on the rug. Imagine that there's a funnel shape going from the top of your head all the way to infinity. Cleansing, purifying energy is pouring into your head through that funnel shape. As this pure, white energy pours into you, through your head and down through your body, it washes away the dead energy of old hurts, old angers, old jealousies, old negative reactions, old programming. Feel the energy pour into your head, down your neck, through your chest. It flows down your arms and into your hands and through every finger. Feel the energy flow through your torso, and down through your legs, feet, and toes. This purifying energy cleanses the entire interior and exterior of your body, and as the negative energies are transformed into positive energies, you feel your real self becoming clearer and clearer.

Feel yourself full to overflowing with this purifying energy. It is now radiating from every pore of your body. Whatever the type of negative sensation, whether fear, anger, guilt, loneliness, or negative thoughts and emotions of others directed toward you, this energy can neutralize it. As if you were watching a movie, see this energy flow through you, cleansing and purifying. If any part of your body is not at par, imagine this energy flowing into that area. Watch it change, and visualize that area of the body as whole and well.

When you feel completely clear, notice a feeling of freedom, joy, and power as it spreads over you. You can use this energy technique any time you wish to get clear of negative feelings or impressions.

Now go over to your desk and sit down in front of the row of small bottles and the drinking glass. These bottles symbolically contain all the things that you would like to be. There are such characteristics as self-acceptance, self-confidence, love, understanding, honesty, joy, beauty, kindness, freedom, friendliness, assertiveness, power, security . . . For a kind of mental cocktail, mix the characteristics you desire into the glass and drink the liquid. As you are drinking, feel all the characteristics you have put in the glass flowing through your whole body. Feel them soaking into your skin all over your body and becoming you. When you have finished drinking from the glass, stand up and go to the full-length mirror.

As you look at yourself, see and feel yourself becoming the person that you would like to be and realize that you are now that person. Know that you will be successful at anything you want to do. See and *believe* that you now are the person you want to be.

If you want to adjust your weight, see yourself at your ideal weight. If you want to stop smoking, see yourself enjoying yourself without a cigarette. If you want to be free of money worries, picture yourself enjoying abundance and security. If you lack confidence or feel powerless, claim your own power and see yourself confident and assertive.

Feel yourself becoming a totally balanced person. Let yourself become the person that you want to be. And now *know that you are* already that person.

Realize that, afterward, the drink you drank will still be taking effect within you and all the things you desired will continue to become a part of you.

When you are ready, return to your regular world on your

own. Count from 1 to 5. As you count, feel yourself slowly returning to your usual surroundings, and to a more aware self. At the count of 5, slowly open your eyes, take several deep breaths, stretch, and feel energized and rested.

Communications: Relationships

This exercise can be an aid in improving your communications with your family, friends, and other people you are involved with in your daily life.

Take a comfortable position. Close your eyes and raise them slightly upward. Take a deep breath through your nose and, while slowly exhaling, feel a wave of warm relaxation flow slowly over your entire body from your toes all the way to your head.

Use your preferred relaxation method or autogenics to reach a comfortable state of relaxation.

Now, mentally visualize yourself in a park. It's evening, and there's going to be a fireworks display. You spread out a blanket on the grass and lie down on it. You feel very relaxed and comfortable. You look up at the clear night sky. There's the sound of the first fireworks and a rocket of red shoots up into the black darkness. A fountain of brilliant red color cascades across the sky. You enjoy the vivid display. Another rocket takes off. A display of luminous orange fireworks showers down bright sparks.

With each color, you feel more and more relaxed. There's the *whoosh* of a roman candle, and cascades of golden yellow ripple against the blackness. You feel steadily more calm and centered. Now there's a green rocket. It spirals up into the heavens lighting up the entire sky with rich emerald green. You feel very, very comfortable and relaxed now. A blue rocket takes off. The sky lights up with streamers of shimmering blue color. A roman candle shoots up. Fountains of purple color fill the sky. You feel very relaxed, breathing deeply and easily. The last fireworks display of the evening shoots up into the dark sky. It's a beautiful violet-pink color. Galaxies of violet light up the night. You watch the last sparks of violet color fade into the darkness.

Feeling very, very relaxed, you count from 1 to 3 and imagine yourself resting on your rug in your own get-away place—in your own room. You get up and sit in one of the chairs.

At this time, you are going to select a person with whom you want to develop more effective communication. It can be a friend, family member, instructor, co-worker, or boss with whom you might be having a disagreement. It can be anyone with whom you wish to establish more effective communication and understanding.

Count from 1 to 3, and the person whom you have selected will walk through the door into your room. The door opens and the person enters your room. He/she closes the door and comes over and stands in front of you.

Look at this person. Begin to see him as a fellow human being with feelings, attitudes, and emotions. Focus in on every detail of the person—the face, hair, forehead, cheeks, lips, eyes, ears . . .

Now both of you walk to the desk and sit down on chairs facing each other.

At this time, in your own words, tell this person what you feel is the cause of the lack of communication or understanding between the two of you. Be clear and complete and honest in your description of this problem. Take your time. (Pause.)

Now have the other person tell you in his own words what he feels is the problem. Listen carefully to what he has to say. Try to understand and feel what the person is feeling.

If you would like some help, ask a third person to come in as a fair witness. This person will come through the door into your room. Ask for his opinion.

Now turn to the other person and, this time, acting as a completely objective third party, express the situation as you now understand it. Be as clear and as honest as possible. (Pause.)

You and the other person stand up. Face each other and mentally see yourselves having the kind of communication and understanding that you are capable of having. See yourselves having complete understanding, and feel the feeling of hurt or anger or misunderstanding dissolve as you smile at this person. If you are having any problem becoming friendly with this person, ask another person or expert for advice.

In the future, any time you wish to develop further communication with this or any other person, simply bring the person into your "get-away" place. Look at and appreciate that other person. Become more sensitive to his feelings and attitudes. Try to understand his point of view and know that he also wishes to develop more effective communication.

Now, say good-bye. When you next see or think of this person, this experience will help you have a better understanding or communication between the two of you. The person now leaves your "get-away" place.

Now, count slowly from 1 to 5. As you count, feel yourself slowly returning to your usual surroundings and to a more aware self. You may draw from these energies and sensations that you now feel any time in the future. At the count of 5, slowly open your eyes, take several deep breaths, stretch, and feel energized, centered, and rested.

Any time you wish to increase your knowledge or understanding of any relationship or problem, mentally have the person enter your get-away place and have an expert come in as well. Communicate with them and ask them any questions you wish.

At night, just before going to sleep, make a practice of reviewing your day. In a relaxed, non-attached way, review each incident of the day and if you are pleased with any action or reaction which you exhibited, dwell upon it and impress it strongly upon your mind.

If you reacted in a way that you are not pleased about, then review the incident thoroughly. After reviewing your negative action, erase it from your mind. Then relive the experience the way it should have happened. See yourself behaving the way you would like to in the future. This nightly "accounting" of the day will have a profound effect on your life.

Communications: Solving Problems; Getting Answers

The objective of this exercise is to tap the resources of the inner mind to get information, solve problems creatively, receive answers to questions.

Take a comfortable position. Close your eyes and raise them slightly upward. Take a deep breath through your nose and, while slowly exhaling, feel a wave of warm relaxation flow slowly over your entire body from your toes to your head.

Use your preferred relaxation method or autogenics to reach a comfortable state of relaxation.

Mentally visualize yourself in a favorite place of relaxation—in your room, sitting on the beach, or wherever you feel most comfortable. Now as you are sitting or lying on the floor, feel your body slowly becoming as light as a balloon. Feel it becoming lighter and lighter, and as it is becoming lighter, feel yourself begin to rise slowly off the floor. Become still lighter as you begin to float around the room. Now float still higher until you pass out of the room, still higher until you pass out of the building. You now are floating above the building. You can look around and see other buildings. You can see cars passing on the streets below, you can see people walking on the sidewalks. Experience a feeling of freedom, comfort, and safety as you float. You can be anywhere you want to go simply by thinking about it.

Now float still higher until you no longer can see the city below. You can project yourself anywhere in the past, present, or future. All you have to do is make yourself as light as a balloon, then rise into the air. Keep rising until you no longer can see the ground below you. Then in your mind, decide the time and place that you would like to visit. You can then come down to earth in that particular time and location. After you have collected the information that you wanted and wish to return to the present time, simply allow yourself to become as light as a balloon again. Float up until you no longer can see the ground below. Set your destination to come back to the present. Slowly come back down to the ground and you will find yourself back in the present time and place. As you are gently floating, mentally look around and notice anything you are attracted to. Now slowly come back to the room.

You now feel very, very relaxed both physically and mentally. Whenever you have a specific problem that you are working on, mentally create and project an image of this problem situation onto your mental TV screen, and then examine it. Examine it one time only. After you have examined the problem thoroughly erase it from the screen of your mind, and from that point on try not to think of this problem. In its place, using the *change* button, mentally create and project the image of your desired end result on the screen. Always let this be your final image. Energize and visualize this desired end result for at least several minutes, three times a day. Feel that the goal is already accomplished. This technique will stimulate the inner mind to find creative solutions to reach your goal. Solutions may suddenly just seem to pop into your mind.

Constructive thoughts *energized* by concentration lead to actualization of desired results.

Possibly your problem or question is one needing the advice of an expert or a wise advisor. You are now going to meet someone who has the kind of answers you need. This "wise being" may be a living person or someone from history. It may even be an animal or bird. Some people picture this helpful advisor as a "wise old man" or "wise old woman." It's a way of picturing the "inner source" of your own mind.

Imagine being out in nature. It can be in a lush garden, or on a hillside or in a forest clearing or on a mountain top. Or you may find you are drawn to an ancient temple, an undersea location, or even a space-age data center to meet your wise advisor. Some people like to wait for their advisor at their "get-away" place. Take a moment to find your spot. (Pause.)

Someone is coming to meet you. Wait for that person or being. As she or he nears, look clearly, and see what this person looks like. Speak to the person. Converse with the person. Ask your question. Expect that this person will work with you in all ways to help solve whatever problem you are working on. She will give you all the information or guidance that you desire. She will stay with you as advisor until the project is completed. Expect an answer. Wait for an answer. (Pause.)

If you need clarification, ask for someone else to come to speak to you who can aid you further. Wait for the answer. The answers may be spoken or they may be in the form of visual symbols. They may illuminate a problem or bring new under-standings. (Pause.)

Now, you are going to return to your regular world as you count from 1 to 5. As you count, feel yourself slowly returning to the room and to a more aware self. At the count of 5, slowly open your eyes, take several deep breaths, stretch, and feel energized and rested. Note down any answers or symbols received during the session.

Chapter 19
Children's Exercises

Introducing Muscle Relaxation to Children

For younger students, muscle relaxation can be introduced in the following way:

This is an exercise that lets us relax our bodies and minds. We tighten up and relax our muscles from toe to head. Once we learn to feel what it's like to be relaxed, we don't have to lose energy through muscle tension. Anytime something happens that makes us feel tense or anxious, we can use this way of relaxing to help us feel calm. That way, we don't ever have to feel nervous before an exam or an appointment, or a special event.

Sit down or lie down and get very, very comfortable. Close your eyes. Begin to relax your whole body. Think about your toes—think about the bones and muscles inside them—feel their weight. Now, tense up your toes as tightly as possible. Hold that tense feeling in your toes to the slow count of five. . . . Now, relax your toes. Relax them completely. Notice the difference.

(Continue with the rest of the body, following the exercise on page 96.)

Introducing Breathing Exercises to Children

Younger students, under the age of ten, may need a bit of practice in breathing exercises before attempting to do any rhythmic breathing. It's helpful to start out with a discussion about how people breathe.

Let's take a look at how we're breathing now. Let's experiment. Place your right hand over your heart. Take a deep breath. Hold your breath for a few seconds. Then release it with a sigh. Can you feel your heartbeat? Do you notice any other sensations?

Bend down and put your palms on the floor. Stretch way up now and raise your palms toward the ceiling. Do this bending and stretching a couple of times.

Now stop and check out your breathing. Do you notice your heartbeat? Do you notice anything else?

Imagine it's a cold day and you can see the puff of your breath on the air. Is it a big puff?

Now try breathing using your tummy. Try to picture your chest as a big accordion that opens and closes.

When we breathe in (inhale), the accordion opens.

When we breathe out (exhale), the accordion closes.

You push your tummy out when you breathe in.

You bring your tummy in when you breathe out.

Try this a few times. Try to breathe through your nose. Put your hand on your stomach. Notice the way your hand moves up and down as you breathe in and out.

Practice: inhale—exhale (repeat several times). Practice: inhale—hold—exhale (repeat several times).

ALTERNATE BREATHING

Practice: Inhale through left nostril gently, while blocking the right nostril by pressing it lightly with your thumb. Count —1, 2—

Put your third finger over your left nostril and press it lightly while you release your thumb, and exhale through your right nostril. Gently release all the air as you count 1, 2, 3, 4.

Do the reverse movement, breathing in through the right nostril and exhaling through the left nostril.

Repeat several times.

RHYTHMIC BREATHING

After some practice in exploring breathing, see if you can practice breathing in time to a count. When you breathe in, say "in"; when you breathe out, say "out."

(If you have a metronome, set it ticking at sixty beats a minute. If not, use a watch with a second hand, and count the seconds aloud.)

Practice: Breathe: *in*—2, 3, 4; *out*—2, 3, 4. Repeat many times.

If children have no problem breathing in time to a count, try the count of: *In*—2; *hold,* 2, 3, 4; *out*—2.

Note: Dr. Allyn Prichard found in his experience teaching breathing practice to young children in Georgia that it was difficult for children below the fifth-grade level to breathe in the *In*—2; *hold*—2,3,4; *out*—2 pattern.

Up to third- or fourth-grade level, they focused mainly on having children try to breathe rhythmically using the *In, 2,3,4; out, 2,3,4,* pattern.

All breathing practice must be done gently and never forced.

Practice this rhythmic breathing to a count a few minutes a day for several days before trying to practice breathing to a count while the music is being played.

Mental Relaxation and Mind Calming

The objective of this exercise is to increase visualization and practice mind calming and relaxation.

Sit down or lie down and get very, very comfortable. Close your eyes and take a deep breath. Let your body and mind relax completely. Breathe in again and as you breathe out, feel more and more relaxed. Turn off all your body switches except your ears. Continue to breathe deeply as you now feel completely relaxed, as though you were a soft, feathery cloud floating along in the air. Everything feels very pleasant and relaxed and peaceful. Take a moment to become very still inside.

Now, you are going to create in your mind's eye a country scene.

Visualize a bright red barn. See yourself, as if you're in a movie, walking toward this barn. As you grow closer to it, mentally examine the whole building. Is it a large or small barn?

Become aware of the walls. Are they brick or wood, smooth or rough? Look up above the red walls to the roof. Is it flat, or pointed? Is there a hayloft?

Walk closer to the barn. When you reach the entrance, open the door and go inside. What's in there? Is there hay on the floor? What's the floor made of? Take another deep breath and become aware of the smell of the barn. Take one final look around—then as you walk back out the door, you notice a thick bed of pink flowers planted a short distance away from the barn. Walk over to these flowering plants and examine them carefully. Are they all one shade of pink? Do they differ in size? Take a deep breath and smell the perfumed scent of the flowers. Feel the softness of the petals. Take one last moment to enjoy these lovely pink flowers.

Walk a little farther along and notice how green the grass is around you. Remove your shoes and walk through this grass. Feel the soft, cool grass become like a velvet sponge as you walk on it. Feel the blades of grass between your toes. Lie down on your stomach in the grass and smell the clean, fresh grass beneath you. Roll over on your back and stretch out in the grass. Feel the cool, soft blades of grass against your skin.

Take a deep breath and see the warm, yellow sun. Feel it beaming down on you. Feel the sun warming your arms and legs. Feel the sun's warmth over your whole body.

Still lying there, look up into the clear, blue sky. Take a deep breath and breathe in the refreshing, clean air. Feel it travel from your head right down to your feet. As you look at the sky, notice if any birds are flying in the air, or if any clouds are drifting by.

As you lie there, the sun is setting and the sky gradually becomes a deeper and deeper blue. Take a deep breath and notice that the daylight is almost gone and the sky has become a deep purple blue. Stars are beginning to appear. Notice the patterns of the stars. Gaze at the full sweep of the heavens.

Feel peaceful and serene and happy through your whole body. You're completely relaxed in this comfortable place in your mind. It's going to be fun to come back here again. Anytime you wish, you can remember this centered, calm feeling. You can remember this calmness before a school test, or a doctor or dentist appointment, or whenever you want to.

Now, start to come back gently. Become aware of your position and your surroundings. Become aware of your feet, knees, hands, head. Turn on all body switches. Stretch, open your eyes —you will feel centered and calm.

Note: To avoid monotony, visualization and mind-calming exercises can be varied from time to time. Visualization sequences from other exercises in this and other books can be used.

For mind calming, Iowa teacher Charles Gritton highly recommends a set of records called *The Environment.* Instead of having to read a visualization exercise to children, the records do it for you. These environment records are great favorites with his classes. They cover visits to such places as a country stream, the ocean, an aviary, and so on. He found that the children especially liked imagining a trip to a swamp.

Mind Calming and Visualization

Sit down or lie down and get very comfortable. Close your eyes and take a deep breath. Let your body and mind relax completely. Take another deep breath and as you breathe out feel more and more relaxed.

Continue to breathe deeply as you now feel completely relaxed, as though you were floating on a big, fluffy white cloud. Everything feels very pleasant and very calm.

Picture in your mind a shopping mall or district. Imagine that you are there right now. You are walking along past different store windows filled with colorful toys and ahead you see an ice-cream store. You walk in. There are huge pictures of ice-cream cones on the walls. There's a jolly little man all dressed in white with a big, white cap behind the counter. He's the ice-cream man and he's going to make a very special ice-cream cone just for you. It's going to be a giant ice-cream cone with seven scoops of ice cream. You go over to the counter to watch.

The ice-cream man picks out a giant cone, and a metal ice-cream scoop. He opens the first container of ice cream. It's bright, *red,* cherry ice cream. Watch that scoop of red ice cream as he puts it on the cone. He opens the next container. He digs deep. It's *orange* ice cream. He puts the orange ice cream on top of the scoop of red ice cream.

He opens the next ice-cream container. The ice cream is *yellow.* It's lemon ice cream. There goes the scoop of yellow, lemon ice cream right on top of the cone, right on top of the orange ice cream.

You move in closer to see what's in the next round container. Cool, lime *green* ice cream! Think of its tart taste. The ice-cream man swirls around the whole container as he scoops up that lime green ice cream. He puts the green scoop right on top of the yellow scoop on the very top of the giant cone.

What's next? He slides back the lid of the next container. He digs into it, and comes out with a scoop of juicy, *blue,* blueberry ice cream. There are blueberries mixed all through the ice cream. You watch the blue, blueberry scoop stick on top of the lime green ice cream on top of the cone.

Now he's digging in the next container. He pulls out a scoop of—*purple* ice cream—refreshing grape ice cream. The purple, grape ice cream goes right on top of the blueberry scoop.

Here comes the final topping on this amazing cone. He opens the container. He digs in. It's pale *purple-pink,* raspberry ice cream. He puts a scoop of the raspberry ice cream right on the very top. What a combination! Seven scoops of seven colors piled up on a giant cone. It's a rainbow ice-cream cone. Picture it for a moment. Imagine tasting all the different flavors.

You now count slowly from 1 to 5 and open your eyes. You are back in your regular surroundings. Stretch, and turn on all body switches. You feel centered and rested.

Energy-Centering Exercise

The object of the exercise is to experience and generate energy.

Sit cross-legged on the floor, hands resting lightly on your knees, palms up. Sit with your spine straight. (If there are several children doing this exercise, it can be done with them sitting in the form of a circle.)

To help center yourself, picture energy flowing smoothly through your body from the lower part of your body (abdomen), which is your center, up through your chest and head, releasing it through the top of your head. Picture light coming through your body and pouring like a fountain out through the top of your head.

A Mystery Box

This children's game is designed to enhance sensitivity to touch and improve mental imagery.

PREPARATIONS: Prepare a shoe box. Decorate the outside and cut a circle in one end large enough for a child's wrist and hand to go through. Place objects one at a time in the shoe box. Replace the lid so that the children can't see the objects. One at a time, have each child put his or her hand into the box and experience what is inside.

In order to keep all the children occupied, have one child act as the "senser." Have this child give a verbal description of what he is feeling. He must *not* name the object even if he thinks he knows what it is. The rest of the children try to make a mental picture of the hidden object based on what the senser is saying. Each child will tell what he thinks the object is. This can be done verbally or by writing it on a slip of paper.

Let each child experience several objects. The same object may be used more than once. Note difference in description.

SUGGESTED OBJECTS: Pinecone; ball of cotton; eraser; stone; metal square; sponge; shell; feather.

Note: Additional exercises for children can be adapted from those in the exercise section.

Chapter 20
The Possible Human— Possible Now?

Learn faster and lose stress while you're at it, swim more powerfully, ski with élan, be free of pain, let intuition enrich relationships—there are a lot of promises in the many systems of superlearning. Pushing the promises further, supposedly as you synchronize and harmonize the forces of mind/body to move out in one direction, the rhythm can carry you into a more boundless life in many areas. There is a new lushness and deepening of the experience of being alive. What is so attractive about the promises of the new learning systems is they connect the drive for inner expansion with the drive for satisfying outward performance. They wed increased awareness and sensitivity with practical results in the here and now. The promises are so attractive that it's hard not to think the claims are far too good and far too many to be true. And they are beyond the possible, unless we accept the premise underlying all the promises in the words of biofeedback pioneer Dr. Barbara Brown, "Human beings possess capabilities of mind that are literally beyond genius."

Scientists have joined the humanists to point to the shimmering possibilities of what it might mean to be fully human. It sounds as though each of us might yet become wizards and make the emerald city of Oz our own. To claim the city we have to get there. An increasing number of people have begun to synthesize the understanding of East and West, the old and the new, science and the arts to give us that needed yellow-brick road. To get on it, however, you have to recognize there's somewhere to go.

A pivotal scientist of international reputation, Dr. Brown has just culminated years of research with a new theory and a new book, *Supermind.* Our highest, most elegant intellectual capacities lie untapped and unrecognized, she says, in what we call the unconscious. According to Brown, such human potentials have gone largely unrecognized because science has not spent its energies exploring what it means to be human.

On the personal level, we haven't explored those possibilities very much either. We've been sold and have sold ourselves a bill of goods about who we are. It's growing apparent that we've bought shoddy goods, an image many sizes too small. While Brown has stirred the world of science—issuing "a kind of proclamation for the Emancipation of the Mind"—the rest of us might try our own "declaration of independence." We might set out for a further point of life, liberty, and the pursuit of happiness and embark on the pursuit of ourselves, our possible selves.

Where that pursuit could carry us, no one knows, but we can have an idea of where we might be in six months or two years if we care to try. The experience of thousands who have tried and become "wizzes" in one field or another testifies to the resources available right now. For instance, from his years of working with students of all ages Dr. Lozanov has come to say that the human capacity to remember and learn seems almost boundless. There is no apparent cutoff point. It seems if we want to break out of our rut, we can learn the basics—the facts we need to know without stress, we can have easy access to other languages, we can have memory control.

Resources, it seems, are available too, for the taking, on the physical level. One would think, for instance, that Vasily Alexeyev, who has already demolished eighty world weight-lifting records, has realized his potential. Yet, a famous Soviet coach, Yuri Sandlov, considering Alexeyev's performance, recently mused that there must be limits somewhere. "But," he concluded, "it's too early to speak of them." In the current Soviet view, a synchronized mind/body approach to sports can expand performance by over forty percent. The records that are possible haven't even begun to be chalked up.

When it comes to the performance of the body, other limits are beginning to dissolve, ones that go to the marrow of us all. "Our society's expectations are so low," Dr. Robert Ornstein, author of *The Psychology of Consciousness,* said to a recent medical conference sponsored by Albert Einstein College of Medicine, ". . . mental control of physical states can show individuals that they have absorbed from their culture a radical underestimation of their possibilities." Experts like Ornstein and Brown agree that it is possible to begin to take command of what happens inside our bodies, down to controlling a single cell. Right now a frontier is open that could eventually bring us into a world sprung from the wasteful limitations of pain and disease.

Delving into untapped reserves, businesspeople found that another sort of apparent limitation—inflation, hard times, uncertainty about the future—could be eased using intuition and making the most of the metaphorical mind. Taking up the same abilities, the blind found, in a very different way, that they too could add new octaves to their lives, they could enhance relationships with the world full of life around them. Right-brain potentials, so long shunned by science, are rapidly coming into their own. Suddenly, to people in a great many different disciplines, this is where the really human action is. This is where the most revolutionary or even evolutionary discoveries await. Many would echo what Charles Lindbergh said as he looked out across the breadth of these potentials, "Through his [man's] evolving awareness, and his awareness of that awareness, he can merge with the miraculous. . . ."

As Lindbergh also points out, every age unfolds its own challenges and these "cannot be met successfully by elaborating methods of the past." The times demand larger theories, more sweeping perspectives. This is what prompted Marilyn Ferguson, the editor of *Brain/Mind Bulletin,* to wonder if the Soviets might have a "weapon" we're overlooking as we worry about the intricacies of electronic surveillance, mind control, and the balance of nukes. This is something we could have too without laying out a penny from the defense budget. "It is a holistic, free-wheeling, interdisciplinary approach to science." This open theoretical view that lets specialties commune with each other lies behind the holistic sort of training used by Russia and her allies for the last two decades in schools, sports arenas, health sanitoriums. As Ferguson points out, American science exceeds the Soviet in quantity and quality of data, but we have defused the understanding that might bloom from our fact-finding by focusing on fragments, by keeping specialists incommunicado and holistic thinkers unfunded. One of the most knowledgeable observers of current research, Ferguson reports that discoveries in "brain research, consciousness research, physics, parapsychology and molecular biology are converging toward a radical, new world-view. At the same time, the most innovative American researchers warn that the politics of science is frustrating the most exciting adventure of this century or any other: the search for what it means to be human." And, she continues, "We will have no one to blame but ourselves if we fail to use the most potent psychic 'weapon' around—imagination."

We are just beginning to learn how to learn. The systems in superlearning are a starter set of tools. Even so, it seems obvious they could help move us from much of the stress and distress of our times. If we bother to try. Some people have told us that such systems might well work in Russia or in Switzerland. But, they say, they're not for America. Americans want instant solutions, magic pills. Many of us do, much of the time. But many of us have just about used up the joys of instant satisfaction. Many of us are beginning to feel squeezed from all directions. We are starting to realize that what is outside ourselves, be it pill or politician, isn't going to make things right for us in the long run. The urge to reclaim the ability to act, the ability to matter to ourselves and others is energizing another American trait—self-reliance. As the historian Kenneth Demarest so rightly puts it, "The only true elite that has ever existed has been the elite of those who genuinely tried. Membership is paradoxically open to all, and its healthy destiny is to become less and less of an elite as more and more people fulfill what human beings can become when they wholeheartedly try."

Superlearning offers nothing you can take to make you feel all-knowing for an hour, to make you suddenly spurt ahead in a race, or even to cure your headache before the commercial ends. There are no magic pills. But there are available, right now, ways to nurture the live seeds within us, to start growing on our own time, in our own bodies and minds toward that larger person, the possible human being. If you want to try.

APPENDIX

Appendix

Recap

Superlearning is an easy, relaxed way to learn that speeds up learning 2, 5, 10, or more times, and has many of the health benefits trumpeted by meditation and relaxation courses. This Westernized, modernized way of accelerated learning taps the reserves of the mind to release better mental abilities, super-memory, and other powers. It mobilizes some of the ninety percent of the brain's potential that we seldom use. It sets up *communications links:* links from body to mind, links from conscious to unconscious. It is a holistic, global way to learn using both right brain and left brain simultaneously and involving the whole person.

Superlearning is learning without tension. It uses body resources economically and efficiently. It is painless learning without stress or tension. "Trying too hard" blocks the free flow of energy needed for the mind's functioning. Superlearning uses "human energy conservation" to get results.

BODY-MIND LINK

How does it work? A very specific kind of music has a psychophysical effect and creates a relaxed, meditative state in the body. Physiological research showed this particular music slows body rhythms to more efficient levels. This music-induced relaxation brings health benefits. It overcomes fatigue and enhances physical and emotional well-being. It's a bit like mantra meditation for it is a mind/body link that helps open up inner awareness. Physiological research also shows this calmed state of the body facilitates mental functioning and learning. The body uses *less* energy, so there's *more* for the mind. This particular music induces alert relaxation—alert mind, relaxed body.

How can you, at will, retrieve what you perceive? The answer is rhythm. The connection is made through synchronizing rhythms. Data to be learned is chanted with intonations in rhythm in time to the music. The person learning breathes along rhythmically in a relaxed state. So data, intonations, music, breathing, and body rhythms are all synchronized to a specific rhythmic cycle. The rhythm, intonations, music, and breathing make links with the unconscious, as the data simultaneously links with the conscious mind. Harmonized rhythms strengthen the information signal. Conscious awareness of unconscious perceptions is opened up through this link so you become aware of what's in your memory bank.

Finally, superlearning is about learning to learn. There is a snowballing effect once you begin to use the techniques. How do you go about doing superlearning on your own? The process is very simple. In advance, get the music, organize your material and tape it, reading it aloud at slow-paced intervals over the specified music.

Then, just relax and listen to your material as you breathe along to the music.

Teaching Elements

Teaching with the suggestopedia system involves a whole complex of methods the Bulgarians culled from many systems. Some elements similar to Montessori methods are used and lessons are presented vividly and dramatically along the lines of *Sesame Street* and *The Electric Company.*

Body language and other nonverbal cues a student picks up from a teacher must be organized to enhance learning rather than interfere with it. The teacher must try to create a warm, positive, pleasant learning environment. To help orchestrate nonverbal communication in teaching, teachers are given background in psychotherapeutic techniques, acting, singing, etc. (see telepathy p. 257). Creating vivid mental pictures and training the imagination and the ability to visualize are important.

Good rapport is basic to good communication, in their view. Because the supermemory sessions tend to expand students' awareness of cues coming to them from teachers—fears, attitudes, ideals—these nonverbal elements have to be taken into account and organized to enhance motivation. For instance, if a teacher genuinely can't stand a particular student, that student is very likely to become aware of it, and it may affect learning. In Bulgarian classes, rapport between student and teacher is considered so important, students are encouraged to change classes to be with a teacher with whom they have good rapport.

Lozanov's theory also points up "infantilization" especially for adults—that is, restoring the ease with which a small child learns, and a child's spontaneity, receptivity, and ability to memorize.

Lessons feature role playing (giving students new identities to diminish worry about making mistakes), playlets, games, songs, and great emphasis on the use of all the arts. Many of the same techniques used in TV ads are used to make lessons attention-getting.

Authority was also found to aid memory. Two groups of students were given the same words to memorize. One group was told the words were from a favorite poet's work. That group learned the most words.

Feedback is another teaching principle. It's used to reinforce confidence in superlearning abilities. Each time we see that we have improved, it strengthens our belief that we really have extraordinary capabilities and we can use them. Feedback of results can be done with frequent check quizzes. Constantly seeing progress reinforces, improves, convinces, and motivates.

Organization of course material has much in common with courses designed for sleep-learning.

Dr. Lozanov's book *Suggestology* outlines his suggestion theory based on scientific findings of Slavic authorities. Rhythm, intonation, music, all come under the classification of suggestion in his theory.

Professionals interested in the theory and in teaching with the method will find information sources in the reference section.

Two of the basic Lozanov teaching procedures involve: 1. self-image therapy for students and 2. organization of nonverbal cues. For Westerners a lot of the other Bulgarian teaching ideas are perfectly familiar and have been used for years over here—that is, games and skits. The trend toward transpersonal and holistic education is also well under way in America. Many of these educational approaches were derived from the work of another psychiatrist, an Italian, Roberto Assagioli, developer of psychosynthesis. These approaches focus on harmonizing physical/sensory, emotional, intellectual, imaginative, and intuitive sides of the personality in the process of learning.

Rudolf Steiner, Austrian founder of anthroposophy, author of *Curative Education* and originator of the Waldorf Schools around the world, also developed teaching techniques designed to enhance "the natural unfoldment of the genius within each child."

The Bulgarian goal is to use these various holistic teaching techniques to help to amplify and consolidate the expanded abilities in students that open up through the supermemory sessions.

The major difference in teaching with the Lozanov system compared to other methods is that after a certain number of weeks or months of supermemory sessions, students actually begin to develop a form of semiphotographic memory, or at least greatly improved memory, so that many of the old forms of teaching involving a lot of repetition are no longer needed. Teaching becomes a creative frontier and can go well beyond information handling.

The supermemory sessions by themselves can lead to a considerable speed-up in learning. If holistic teaching methods are combined with them, they can increase the speed of learning and help expand potentials even further.

For instance, if course materials are designed to follow a specific pattern and progression that enhances visualization, progress will be even better. The Bulgarians have prepared courses in the form of dialogues and scenes that follow a specific sequence. (For more information, contact Superlearning Corp., Suite 500, 450 Seventh Avenue, New York, N.Y. 10123.)

For more on holistic learning procedures, contact Institute for Wholistic Education, Box 575, Amherst, Mass. 01002.

For more on the Waldorf Schools, contact Rudolf Steiner Library, 211 Madison Ave., New York, N.Y. 10016.

Class Procedure

Before beginning a suggestopedia course in Bulgaria, students initially had four days of preparation that included exercises and de-suggestion of limited learning abilities. A course in a particular subject would run about thirty days, four hours a day with one break. Each session is in three parts: 1. a conversational review of previously learned material, using the best elements of oral and audiovisual methods; 2. a presentation of new material in the form of dialogues—real-life situations are acted out; 3. memory-reinforcement session. The memory-reinforcement session is done in two parts: active and passive.

In the *active* part, students go over the text while it is being read to them. They relax and breathe deeply while the teacher reads the phrases in the three intonations in precise rhythm on the eight-second cycle. No music is played during this reading of the material. Students follow the material in the text and repeat the phrases to themselves mentally.

In the *passive* part of the memory session, students relax, close their eyes, and listen to the Baroque music and try to visualize the material while the teacher gives the phrases a very dramatic, "artistic" reading on the eight-second cycle in time to the music.

SIMPLIFIED PROCEDURE

Many American users of the method have compressed the two parts of the memory-reinforcement session into one, and still get a six to one speed-up in learning.

The simplified memory-reinforcement procedure then is: Students relax and breathe deeply and rhythmically in time to the music. The instructor recites or chants the material on either a twelve-second or eight-second cycle in time to the music and uses the three different intonations.

The Westernized procedure for organizing a course starts with a week or so devoted to training in relaxation, visualization, and breathing exercises. They present the material to be learned vividly and dramatically with games, plays, dialogues, oral reading. Prior to the concert session, they spend five to ten minutes on simple, physical, stretching exercises, visualization, relaxation and breathing routines, and positive affirmations for easy, effective learning, academic excellence, good health. Check quizzes are given daily.

Originally, in the Bulgarian version, classes were small (twelve), and they sat in comfortable easy chairs arranged in a circle. The American version has the kids relax on mats on the floor. "If you have comfortable chairs, it's fine," says Lozanov. "If you don't have chairs, it's also OK. The method has to be flexible and adaptable."

BACKGROUND ON THE MEMORY-EXPANSION SESSIONS

As pointed out earlier, because of political considerations, much confusion and cover-up has surrounded the memory-expansion aspects of the Lozanov system. Different countries seem to have been given quite different versions. This applies within Soviet-bloc countries too. One source suggests that East Germany apparently paid for the method and got full details, while others did not.

(As early as 1970, the head of the Mnemology Center at Karl Marx University in Leipzig, Dr. Jenicke, announced that they had already conducted experiments in the Bulgarian suggestopedic method. In a typical experiment, 3,182 lexical units and ideomatic phrases were learned in thirty days with ninety-four percent retention.)

The Hungarian government had not paid for the method as of 1978 and their people were only given certain parts but not allowed to see all the Bulgarian research or have all their questions answered. Even Westerners who paid were not given all details.

In 1978, reports were that the Suggestology Institute in Bulgaria had been taken over by Communist Party members and that the innovative teachers who had developed essential suggestopedic methods and programs had been pushed out. It appeared to many that teachers trained by these newcomers at the Institute were given only partial information. Unless the trainees were already well versed in some of the original systems from which suggestopedia was drawn (Raja Yoga, autogenics, etc.) they were not able to get good results.

Many Westerners at the institute in Bulgaria were given lists of music by nineteenth-century composers and told to read material over it. Not understanding the reason for what they were doing, teachers obediently read course material over whole concertos, shouting at the top of their lungs to be heard over thunderous sections of the music. Even if students had ever actually reached an altered-state of consciousness with slowed-down body/mind rhythms, they would have been knocked out of it by this performance.

The principle behind the music session follows the research on accelerated learning and expanded time perception pioneered in the United States by Drs. Cooper and Erickson decades ago. It involved sixty beats a minute and ten-second activity cycles. The sixty beats a minute slow down body/mind rhythms so that the beats seem to be perceived by a person as being slower than they actually are. Because of this slowed-down time perception, a large number of mental and creative activities can be accomplished in very little clock time, because time itself actually seems to expand.

Research has recently been done on this time distortion principle in learning by Drs. Houston and Masters. They showed that students could improve graphic art skills in a few hours, skills that might normally take a semester of classroom work. Author Gay Luce *(Body Time)* points out, "Studies of time distortion emphasize how limited our cultural view of 'time sense' can be, and may offer us ways of enriching the education of the young by compressing more learning into the early school years."

Slowing down body/mind rhythms to expand time seems to be a biological basis for better learning in animals too. When lab animals had brain-wave rhythms slowed down through electrical induction, they *doubled* their rate of learning performance. (See *The Brain-Changers* by Maya Pines, New York: Harper & Row, 1973.)

In Lozanov's adaptation of this accelerated-learning principle to a regular environment, music with this sixty-beat-a-minute rhythm is used to slow down body/mind rhythms and to literally "expand time."

To be sure that the music will actually accomplish this purpose, we were told that students in Bulgaria are generally tested for sensitivity to music. If people are not responsive to the music, other ways of slowing body/mind rhythms can be used such as breathing exercises or autogenics or biofeedback techniques. (Some few people have been found to respond negatively to music and these people could use a metronome beating at sixty beats a minute instead.)

The Bulgarians have recently issued details of an additional concert session. This is a supplementary concert and does not replace the Baroque concert. It is done ahead of it. The music lists include nineteenth-century composers: Brahms' Violin Concerto in D Major; Tchaikovsky's Piano Concerto in B♭ Minor; Beethoven's Emperor Concerto for piano. The slow movements in each concerto (some of which have a beat of approximately sixty to the minute) can be spliced together for a concert session. The material can be read over the music on the eight-second cycle. The volume must be kept *low* to sustain a reverie-like restful state in the students. Because there are often fluctuating rhythms in more modern classical music compared to Baroque, teachers were given a pattern to follow in reading over this music and told not to read over certain passages. This type of concert session is fairly difficult for the teacher.

This additional concert is followed by the Baroque supermemory concert described in Chapter 8.

Sources
Section I

For further information on suggestology and suggestopedia, the following publications are very helpful.

Suggestology and Outlines of Suggestopedy, by George Lozanov, published by Gordon and Breach (1 Park Avenue, New York, N.Y. 10016) in 1978, is an Americanized adaptation of Dr. Lozanov's thesis published in Bulgaria under the title *Suggestology.*

The Proceedings of the 1971 Conference on Suggestology are available in a 669-page volume, *Problems of Suggestology,* obtainable from the Institute of Suggestology, 9 Budapest Street, Sofia, Bulgaria. It reveals research carried out in both Soviet-bloc and Western countries on suggestology and rapid learning. Summaries are in English.

The Suggestology and Suggestopedia Journal was available from Haemus Foreign Trade Co., 6 Russki Blvd., Sofia, Bulgaria. (Three issues have reached the West so far.)

The booklet by Dr. Jane Bancroft, *The Lozanov Language Class,* reveals many of the basic ideas behind suggestopedia and some of the concealed elements. It also gives "how-to" details. It is available on microfiche from the Centre for Applied Linguistics, 1611 N. Kent St., Arlington, Va. 22209. It is also available in the *Journal of Suggestive-Accelerative Learning and Teaching,* Vol. 1, #1, Spring, 1976.

Two more helpful articles by Dr. Bancroft are: "The Lozanov Method and Its American Adaptations" in the *Modern Language Journal,* April, 1978; "The Psychology of Suggestopedia: Or Learning Without Stress," *Educational Courier,* 42, #4, Feb. 1972 (Suite 315, 207 Queen's Quay West, Toronto, Canada). (See additional articles in the Bibliography.)

Don Schuster, Ray Benitez-Bordon, and Charles Gritton have compiled a manual for teachers: *Suggestive, Accelerative Learning and Teaching: A Manual of Classroom Procedures Based on the Lozanov Method* (1976), available from S.A.L.T. in Iowa.

The *Journal of Suggestive-Accelerative Learning and Teaching,* (S.A.L.T.), and the *Newsletter,* are published by the Society for Suggestive-Accelerative Learning and Teaching, 2740 Richmond Ave., Des Moines, Iowa 50317.

Details of teacher-training programs can be obtained from S.A.L.T.

An insider's view of the Lozanov method by a Bulgarian involved with the system is revealed in *La Suggestologie et La Suggestopédie,* by Dr. Bagriana Bélanger, published in 1978 by Éditions Retz, 114 Champs-Elysées, Paris, France 75008.

Dr. Belanger, married to a Canadian, now lives in Ottawa. Her family and Lozanov's family were long friends and neighbors. Her close friends in college later became pioneers of Lozanov's education techniques, and Dr. Belanger was herself trained in the method in Bulgaria. She was in a unique position to observe the inside elements that helped form Lozanov's concepts and she gives some fascinating insights into Bulgarian parapsychology and the traditions from which it springs.

For more background, see *The ESP Papers* by S. Ostrander and L. Schroeder, 1976 (Bantam Books, 414 East Golf Road, Des Plaines, Ill. 60816). It includes the translations of the original articles from the USSR and Bulgaria about suggestopedia and Dr. Lozanov's work and travels to India

Details of Dr. Lozanov's pioneering research into parapsychology and its role in the development of suggestopedia are covered in *Psychic Discoveries Behind the Iron Curtain* (Bantam Books, 1971). *The Handbook of Psychic Discoveries* (1974, Berkley Publishing, 200 Madison Ave., New York) gives where-to-find-it information on many aspects of Soviet-bloc research into psi and suggestology, and includes make-it-yourself equipment for exploring the effects of music on plants and people, aura photography, psi development, and so forth.

The application of suggestopedia to remedial reading is discussed in articles by Allyn Prichard and Jean Taylor: "An Altered-States Approach to Reading," published in the *Educational Courier*, Feb., 1976 (Suite 315, 207 Queen's Quay West, Toronto, Canada). "Adapting the Lozanov Method for Remedial Reading Instruction" appeared in the *Journal of S.A.L.T.*, Summer, 1976.

Materials on holistic education can be obtained from the Institute for Wholistic Education, Box 575, Amherst, Massachusetts 01002. *A Guide to Resources in Humanistic and Transpersonal Education* lists over five hundred resources, plus where to find holistic and humanistic education organizations. *The Inner Classroom: Teaching with Guided Fantasy and Wholistic Education*, by Jack Canfield and Paula Klimek, covers New Age education.

"Learning, Education, Creativity, Suggestology and Learning Disorders," is a Theme Pack (No. 11) available from *Brain/ Mind Bulletin*, P.O. Box 42211, Los Angeles, California 90042.

Videotapes: A tape of Lozanov classes at the Moscow Foreign Languages Pedagogical Institute shows classes being taught by Galina Kitaigorodskaya in January 1974 and reveals some of the teaching elements involved in suggestopedia.

Interview with Dr. Lozanov, May 8, 1975, Washington, D.C. These and other videotapes are available from: Dimitri Devyatkin, 134 Haven Ave., New York, N.Y. 10032.

Audio and video tapes of presentations and demonstrations

by Dr. Lozanov and his colleagues at the 1977 international conference on suggestive-accelerative learning in Iowa are available from:
The Office of Extension Courses and Conferences
102 Scheman Continuing Education Building
Iowa State University
Ames, Iowa 50011

Sources: Sophrology and Other Expanded Learning Systems

La Sophrologie: Une Révolution en Psychologie, Pédagogie, Médecine? by Drs. H. Boon, Y. Davrou, J.-C. Macquet, published in 1976 by Éditions Retz, 114 Champs-Elysées, Paris, France, covers the development of sophrology in various fields from medicine to sports and education. Retz also publishes *Le Guide Pratique de la Sophrologie* by Davrou and Macquet, which gives fifty do-it-yourself sophrology exercises. In *Le Professeur Caycedo, Père de la Sophrologie Raconte sa Grande Aventure* (Retz, 1978), a personal account of Caycedo's journeys through India and the Orient is given. *Sophrologie dans Notre Civilisation* by Raymond Abrezol, published in 1973 by Inter Marketing Group, Neuchâtel, Switzerland, gives medical background on sophrology. Caycedo's major work is *La India de Los Yoguis* (Barcelona: Editorial Andes Internacional, 1977). Caycedo's memory system is outlined in "Curso de Entrenamiento Sofrologico de la Memoria," Barcelona, Unidesch, 1979. Dr. Jane Bancroft's report showing the similarities between the two systems developed by Caycedo and Lozanov is "Caycedo's Sophrology and Lozanov's Suggestology—Mirror Images of a System." It is available from ERIC Documents on Foreign Language Teaching and Linguistics, 1979 (1611 N. Kent St., Arlington, Va. 22209).

The teaching method developed by Jacques de Coulon involving exercises for concentration and breathing patterns found to enhance learning are covered in *Éveille et Harmonie de la Personalité,* published in 1977 by Editions Signal in Lausanne, Switzerland.

For more on the dramatic form of teaching used in the Dartmouth Intensive Language Model, see *Time,* July 16, 1979.

For more on how students can achieve high marks through superlearning methods, see "Adapted Suggestology and Student Achievement" by Donald A. Vannan, *Journal of Research in Science Teaching,* Vol. 16, No. 3, pp. 263–267 (1979). Also by Dr. Vannan, "Adapted Suggestology and Elementary Science at Bloomsburg State College"—ERIC Resources in Education, Ed 152 520, August 1978, p. 141.

Superlearning Resources

Superlearning® Inc.,
Suite 500
450 Seventh Avenue,
New York, N.Y. 10123

Mail order: tapes, resource materials produced under the direction of the authors of *Superlearning.*

For Superlearning relaxation/concentration exercises PLUS 20 minutes of specially selected (4/4 time) slow Baroque music to aid learning —Tape # 101—"SUPERLEARNING EXERCISE AND MUSIC CASSETTE TAPE."

How-to guide to producing your own Superlearning tape, including a short demonstration lesson; Timer Tape—4-second clicks to help pace material. TAPE # 102—"SUPERLEARNING DEMONSTRATION & TIMER TAPE."

More Superlearning music . . . a full 40 minutes. TAPE # 103— "SUPERLEARNING MUSIC."

"SUPERLEARNING LANGUAGES"—3-hour, 3-cassette program of travelers' phrases with booklet of text. Over 1,000 words of vocabulary. Available in *Spanish, French, German, Italian, Indonesian.*

Other materials available: subliminals, concentration aids, relaxation & children's tapes, autogenics, sports, music, academic subjects and more. *Write or phone for free information.* 212-279-8450.

Tapes: $13.95 per single tape; Language Programs $39.95 *each.* U.S. Funds.

Partial List of Organizations

Society for Accelerated Learning and Teaching (S.A.L.T.)
P.O. Box 1216, Welch Station
Ames, Iowa 50010
(Teacher training programs, research reports, resources)

Lozanov Learning™ Institute Inc.
Suite 1215, 1110 Fidler Lane
Silver Spring, Maryland 20910

World Federation of Sophrology
Carrera 17 No. 95–06
Bogotá 8, Colombia

Relaxation Response Inc.
858 Eglinton Ave. W. #108
Toronto, Ontario, Canada M6C 2B6
(Relaxation training programs)

Holistic Education (degree program)
c/o Interface/Beacon College M.A. Program
230 Central Street
Newton, MA 02166

Instituto Alfonso Caycedo
Balmes 102
Barcelona 8, Spain
(Sophrology programs for education)

ERIC Clearinghouse on Languages and Linguistics
Center for Applied Linguistics
3520 Prospect Street N.W.
Washington, D.C. 20007
(Materials on accelerated learning, suggestopedia, etc.)

Yoga Teachers' Association
Box 11476
Chicago, Ill. 60611

Consulting

Dr. W. Jane Bancroft, University of Toronto, Scarborough College, West Hill, Ontario, Canada M1C 1A4.
(Consulting on Superlearning.)

Dr. Allyn Prichard, Rte. 8, Univeter Road, Canton, Georgia 30114.
(Remedial reading through superlearning techniques.)

Dr. Bagriana Belanger, c/o University of Ottawa, Ottawa, Ontario, Canada.
(Consulting on suggestology. Author of *La Suggestologie.*)

Dr. Win Wenger, Psychegenics,
P.O. Box 332, Gaithersburg,
Md. 20760.
(Relaxation training and rapid learning.)

Some Recent Conferences

1971—First International Conference on the Problems of Suggestology, Varna, Bulgaria. 1974—Conference on Hypnopedia and Suggestopedia in Moscow. 1975—Conference on Suggestopedia in East Germany. 1975—International Congress on the Psychology of Consciousness and Suggestology, Pepperdine University, Los Angeles. 1975—The International Symposium on Suggestology—the Psychology of Suggestion, sponsored by Mankind Research Unlimited, Washington, D.C. 1976 —Conference on Suggestopedia in Budapest, Hungary. 1976—

Premier congrès mondial d'hypnopédie et de suggesto-hypnopédie, Paris. 1976—First International Conference on Suggestive-Accelerative Learning and Teaching and Suggestology, Des Moines, Iowa. 1977 and 1978—Second and Third Iowa Conferences. (Conferences on suggestopedia have also been held in Ottawa, Canada, over the past six years.) 1978— European Congress of Hypnosis and Psychotherapy and Psychosomatic Medicine (Suggestopedia Section), Malmö, Sweden.

Bibliography
Section I

Selected Bibliography

Allen, J. "On Teacher Training Experience at the Research Institute of Suggestology, Bulgaria." *Journal of S.A.L.T.*, Vol. 1, No. 4 (Winter 1976).

A.R.E., "Thought, Concentration and Memory." Virginia Beach, Va., Association for Research and Enlightenment, Circulating File, 1970.

Balevsky, P. "EEG Changes in the Process of Memorization under Ordinary and Suggestive Conditions." *Suggestology and Suggestopedia Journal*, Vol. 1, No. 1 (1975).

Bancroft, W. J. "Progressives and Pedagogues in the USSR." *Educational Courier* (Dec.-Jan. 1971).

———. "Foreign Language Teaching in Bulgaria." *Canadian Modern Language Review* (March 1972).

———. "Civilization and Diversity—Foreign Language Teaching in Hungary." *Canadian Modern Language Review* (January 1973).

———. "Education for the Future: Or the Lozanov System Revisited." *Educational Courier* (June 1973).

———. "The Lozanov Method in Hungary." *Educational Courier* (June 1975).

————. "Suggestology and Suggestopaedia: The Theory of the Lozanov Method." *Journal of S.A.L.T.*, Vol. 1, No. 3 (Fall 1976).

————. "Discovering the Lozanov Method." *Journal of S.A.L.T.*, Vol. 1, No. 4 (Winter 1976).

(See also Sources).

Benitez-Bordon, R., and D. P. McClure. "Toward a Theory for Research of Learning in an Altered State of Consciousness." Unpublished monograph, University of Iowa, 1974.

————and D. Schuster. "Foreign Language Learning via the Lozanov Method: Pilot Studies." *Journal of S.A.L.T.*, Vol. 1, No. 1 (Spring 1976).

————. "The Effects of Suggestive Learning Climate, Synchronized Breathing and Music on the Learning and Retention of Spanish Words." *Journal of S.A.L.T.*, Vol. 1, No. 1 (Spring 1976).

Benson, H. *The Relaxation Response.* New York: Morrow, 1976.

Beal, James. "Field Effects, Known and Unknown Associated with Living Systems." New Advances in Parapsychology IEEE Intercon, 1972.

Block, Alex Ben. "The Sputnik of the Classrooms." *New West,* July 18, 1977.

Brown, Barbara. *New Mind, New Body.* New York: Bantam, 1975.

Canfield, J., and P. Klimek. "Education in the New Age." *New Age,* February 1978.

Carson, Jo. "Learning Without Pain: Doctor Explains Suggestology." *Toronto Globe and Mail,* Mar. 9, 1971.

Caskey, O., and M. Flake. *Suggestive-Accelerative Learning: Adaptations of the Lozanov Method.* Texas Tech. University, 1976.

Cooper, L., and M. Erickson. *Time Distortion in Hypnosis.* Baltimore: Williams and Wilkins, 1954.

Coué, Emile. *Suggestion and Autosuggestion.* New York: Weiser, 1974.

Curtis, David. *Sleep and Learn.* New York: Lancer Books, 1972.

De Sau, G. "Hallahan High Pre and Post Testing." Silva Mind Control International, Laredo, Texas, 1972.

"Dr. Georgi Lozanov, The Man Who Created Suggestology." *Horizons* (Toronto), May 1, 1978.

Eliade, Mircea. *Yoga, Immortality and Freedom.* New York: Bollingen, 1958.

Fano, R. M. "The Information Theory Point of View of Speech Communication." *Journal of the Acoustical Society of America*, Vol. 22, No. 6 (November 1950).

Ferguson, Marilyn. *The Brain Revolution*. New York: Bantam, 1975.

———. "Current Brain Research and Human Potential for Learning." *Journal of S.A.L.T.*, Vol. 1, No. 4 (Winter 1976).

———. "A New Perspective on Reality." *Brain/Mind Bulletin*, Vol. 2, No. 16, July 4, 1977.

Fincher, J. "Education Now." *Saturday Review*, Mar. 18, 1978.

Fuerst, Kurt. "Some Observations of Behavior in a Suggestopedic French Language Class (Ottawa)." *Journal of S.A.L.T.*, Vol. 1, No. 3 (Fall 1976).

Godefroy, C. "L'étrange Voyage du Docteur Lozanov de la Parapsychologie à la Pédagogie." *Psychologie*, Janvier 1977.

Gritton, C. "Practical Issues in Adapting Suggestopedia to An American Classroom." *Journal of S.A.L.T.*, Vol. 1, No. 4 (Winter 1976).

———and R. Benitez-Bordon. "Americanizing Suggestopedia: A Preliminary Trial in a U.S. Classroom." *Journal of S.A.L.T.*, Vol. 1, No. 2 (Summer 1976).

Hendricks, G., and T. Roberts. *The Second Centering Book: More Awareness Activities for Children, Parents and Teachers*. Englewood Cliffs: Prentice-Hall, 1977.

Hittleman, R. *Guide to Yoga Meditation*. New York: Bantam, 1972.

Key, W. *Subliminal Seduction*. New York: Signet, 1974.

Kline, P. "The Sandy Spring Experiment: Applying Relaxation Techniques to Education." *Journal of S.A.L.T.*, Vol. 1, No. 1 (Spring 1976).

Krishna, Gopi. *The Awakening of Kundalini*. New York: Dutton, 1975.

———. *The Biological Basis of Religion and Genius*. New York: Harper and Row, 1971.

Leonard, G. *The Ultimate Athlete*. New York: Avon Books, 1977.

———. "Foundations of Suggestology." Institute of Suggestology, Bulgaria, 1971.

Lozanov, G. "The Nature and History of the Suggestopedic System of Teaching Foreign Languages and its Experimental Prospects." *Suggestology and Suggestopedia Journal*, Vol. 1, No. 1 (1975).

———. "Suggestology and Suggestopedia." Address to the Second International Conference on Suggestive-Accelerative Learning and Teaching, Iowa, 1977. Videotape. Iowa State U., 1977.

———. "Suggestopedia in Primary Schools." *Suggestology and Suggestopedia*, Vol. 1, No. 2 (1975).

Lozanov, G., and P. Balevsky. "The Effect of the Suggestopedic System of Instruction on the Physical Development, State of Health and Working Capacity of First and Second Grade Pupils." *Suggestology and Suggestopedia,* Vol. 1, No. 3 (1975).

————and P. Balevsky and R. Trashliev. "Basic Trends and Methods of our Experimental Suggestological Investigations." Institute of Suggestology, Bulgaria, 1969.

(See also Sources)

Luce, G. *Body Time.* New York: Bantam, 1973.

Miele, Philip. "The Power of Suggestion: A New Way of Learning Languages." *Parade,* Mar. 12, 1978.

Mumford, John. *Psychosomatic Yoga.* London: Thorson's, 1961.

Natan, T., and T. Tashev. "Suggestion to Aid Teachers and Doctors." *Bulgaria Today,* No. 9, 1966.

Ornstein, Robert. *On the Experience of Time.* New York: Penguin, 1969.

————. "The Education of the Intuitive Mode." in *The Psychology of Consciousness.* New York: Pelican-Penguin, 1975.

Pelletier, K., and C. Garfield. *Consciousness East and West.* New York: Harper and Row, 1976.

Philipov, E. "Suggestology: The Use of Suggestion in Learning and Hypermnesia." Unpublished dissertation, U.S. International University, San Diego, 1975. Ann Arbor, Mich., University Microfilm 75-20255.

Pollack, Cecelia. "Educational Experiment: Therapeutic Pedagogy." *Journal of S.A.L.T.,* Vol. 1, No. 2 (Summer 1976).

Prichard, Allyn. "Suggestopedia, a Transpersonal Approach to Learning." *Journal of S.A.L.T.,* Vol. 1, No. 3 (Fall 1976).

————. "Lozanov-Type Suggestion Techniques for Remedial Reading." *Journal of S.A.L.T.,* Vol. 1, No. 4 (Winter 1976).

(See also Sources)

Ramacharaka, Yogi. *Science of Breath: The Oriental Breathing Philosophy.* Chicago: Yogi Publication Society, 1904.

Regush, N. "Ottawa 'Bungling' Language Program: Professor Demands Investigation." *The Montreal Gazette,* Sept. 6, 1977.

Retallack, Dorothy. *The Sound of Music and Plants.* Marina del Rey: DeVorss & Co., 1973.

Robinett, E. "The Effects of Suggestopedia in Increasing Foreign Language Achievement." Unpublished doctoral dissertation, Texas Tech. University, 1975.

Rozman, D. *Meditation for Children.* New York: Pocketbooks, 1977.

Rubin, F. *Current Research in Hypnopedia.* New York: Elsevier, 1968.

Simurov, A., and V. Chertkov. "Is It Possible to Learn a Language in a Month?" *Pravda,* Moscow, July 27, 1969.

Schuster, D. "A Preliminary Evaluation of the Suggestive-Accelerative Lozanov Method in Teaching Beginning Spanish." *Journal of S.A.L.T.,* Vol. 1, No. 1 (Spring 1976).

———. "The Effects of the Alpha Mental State, Indirect Suggestion and Associative Mental Activity on Learning Rare English Words." *Journal of S.A.L.T.,* Vol. 1, No. 2 (Summer 1976).

———. "Proceedings of the First International Conference on Suggestive-Accelerative Learning and Teaching and Suggestology, Des Moines, Iowa, 1976." *Journal of S.A.L.T.,* Vol. 1, No. 4 (Winter 1976).

———. "Introduction to the Lozanov Method." *Journal of S.A.L.T.,* Vol. 1, No. 4 (Winter 1976).

Schwarz, Jack. *The Path of Action.* New York: Dutton, 1977.

Scott, Cyril. *Music: Its Secret Influence Throughout the Ages.* New York: Weiser, 1958.

Seki, Hideo. "Transpersonal Model of the Suggestopedic Class from the Standpoint of Communication Theory." Tokyo: The PS Institute of Japan, 1978.

Shaffer, Douglas. "Suggestopedic Hypermnesia: A Scientific Explanation for the Lozanov Effect." Unpublished. Ferdowsi University, Iran, 1977.

Singh, T.C.N. *Music, The Keynote of Human Evolution.* Santa Barbara: J.A. Rowny, 1965.

Stevick Earl. *Memory, Meaning And Method: Some Psychological Perspectives on Language Learning.* Rowley, Mass: Newbury House, 1976.

Taimni, I.K. *The Science of Yoga.* Wheaton, Illinois: Quest Books, 1967.

Thorstad, H., and W. Garry. "Suggestopedia, An Advanced Simulation Technique." Norfolk: U.S. Atlantic Fleet Training Center, 1977.

Turnbow, A.W. *Sleep-Learning: Its Theory, Application and Technique.* Sleep-Learning Research Association, 1956.

Wenger, Win. "Do Synchronicities in the Suggestopedic Teaching Method Enhance Learning?" *Journal of S.A.L.T.,* Vol. 1, No. 3 (Fall 1976).

White, J., and S. Krippner. *Future Science: Life Energies and the Physics of Paranormal Phenomena.* Garden City: Anchor Press, 1977.

Wolkowski, Zbigniew. "Suggestology—A Major Contribution by Bulgarian Scientists." Monograph No. 10, Oct., 1974. Mankind Research Unlimited, Inc.

Zemke, Ron, and D. Nicholson. "Suggestology: Will It Really Revolutionize Training?" *Training,* January 1977.

Sources
Section II

For further information on autogenic training try:

The Psychosomatic Medicine Clinic
2510 Webster Street
Berkeley, California 94705

Vera Fryling, M.D.
6401 Broadway Terrace
Oakland, California 94618
(Tapes and seminars on autogenics by a foremost expert who trained in Berlin with the originator, Johannes Schulz, M.D.)

For the work of Jack Schwarz—holistic medicine, pain control, training of health professionals, contact:

Aletheia Psycho-Physical Foundation
515 N.E. 8th Street
Grants Pass, Oregon 97526

For information kit and tapes on visualization/meditation adjunct therapy for cancer, contact:

Cancer Counseling and Training Center
Box 281
Scarsdale, New York 10583
(914-723-8534)

Carl Simonton, M.D.
Cancer Counseling and Research Center
Suite 710
1300 Summit Avenue
Fort Worth, Texas, 76104
(817-926-7821)

For biogenics and pain control, contact:

C. Norman Shealy, M.D.
Pain Rehabilitation Clinic
Route 2—Welsh Coulee
La Crosse, Wisconsin

For psychological research; monitoring of internal states; effects of music on the body, etc., contact:

The International Kirlian Research Association,
IKRA Communications
411 East 7th Street
Brooklyn, New York 11218

Bibliography
Section II

Selected Bibliography

Barrat, R. "J'ai Découvert La Sophrologie." *Paris Match*, April 27, 1974.

Boon, H., Y. Davrou, and J.-C. Macquet. *La Sophrologie: Une Revolution en Psychologie, Pedagogie, Médecine?* Paris: Retz, 1976.

Brown, Barbara B. *Stress and the Art of Biofeedback*. New York: Harper and Row, 1977.

Dean, Stanley R., ed. *Psychiatry and Mysticism*. Chicago: Nelson Hall, 1975.

Green, Elmer, and Alyce Green. *Beyond Biofeedback*. New York: Delacorte, 1977.

Grim, Paul. "Psychotherapy by Somatic Alteration." *Mental Hygiene*, July, 1969.

————. "Use Your Body to Control Your Mind." *Fate*, July 1976.

Hendrick, Gay, and James Fadiman, eds. *Transpersonal Education: A Curriculum for Feeling and Being*. Englewood Cliffs: Prentice-Hall, 1976.

Keen, Sam. "Our Bodies, Our Souls—An Interview with Michael Murphy." *New Age*, January, 1978.

LeShan, Lawrence. *The Medium, the Mystic and the Physicist*. New York: Viking, 1974.

————. *You Can Fight for Your Life.* New York: Jove/HBJ Books, 1977.

Lindemann, Hannes. *Relieve Tension the Autogenic Way.* New York: Peter H. Wyden, 1973.

Luthe, W., ed. *Autogenic Training.* New York: Grune and Stratton, 1965.

————. *Autogenic Therapy,* Vols 1 & 4. New York: Grune and Stratton, 1969–70.

Morehouse, L., and L. Gross. *Maximum Performance.* New York: Simon and Schuster, 1977.

Murphy, Michael. *Golf in the Kingdom.* New York: Viking, 1972.

Pelletier, Kenneth R. *Mind as Healer, Mind as Slayer.* New York: Delacorte, 1976.

Rosa, Karl. *Autogenic Training.* London: Victor Gollancz, 1976.

Schultz, J.H., and W. Luthe. *Autogenic Training, a Psychophysiologic Approach in Psychotherapy.* New York: Grune and Stratton, 1959.

Schwarz, Jack. *Voluntary Controls.* New York: E.P. Dutton, 1978.

Shealy, C. Norman. *90 Days to Self-Health.* New York: The Dial Press, 1977.

Simonton, J.C., and S. Simonton. "Belief Systems and Management of the Emotional Aspects of Malignancy." *Journal of Transpersonal Psychology,* Vol. 7, No. 1 (1975).

Steiger, Brad. *Life Without Pain: Komar's Secrets of Pain Control.* New York: Berkley, 1978.

————. *The Varieties of Healing Experience: A Symposium.* Los Altos, California: Academy of Parapsychology and Medicine, 1973.

Sources
Section III

For further information on Project Blind Awareness:

Carol Ann Liaros
Project Blind Awareness
2750 West 29th Avenue
Suite 114D
Hollywood, Florida 33020

Visions Unlimited:
An Awareness Program for the Blind
209 Hartwell Road
Buffalo, N.Y. 14216

For schools offering courses in psi:

Mrs. J.E. Nester, ASPR
Information Services for Psi Education
5 West 73rd Street
New York, New York 10024 ($2.00, but subject to change)

For information and tapes on Sentics, the work of Dr. Manfred Clynes:

American Sentic Association,
P.O. Box 2716
La Jolla, California 92038

Bibliography
Section III

Selected Bibliography

Andreas, Peter Von. "Blind See Without Eyes." *Esotera,* June, 1976. (German)

Braud, William, and Lendell Braud. "Preliminary Explorations of Psi-Conducive States: Progressive Muscular Relaxation." *Journal of the American Society for Psychical Research,* Vol. 67, No. 1 (January 1973).

Brown, Barbara. *Supermind.* New York: Harper and Row, 1979.

Clynes, Manfred. *Sentics, The Touch of Emotions.* Garden City: Anchor Press, 1977.

Dean, Douglas, J. Mihalasky, S. Ostrander, and L. Schroeder. *Executive ESP.* Englewood Cliffs: Prentice-Hall, 1974.

Ehrenwald, Jan. *New Dimensions of Deep Analysis: A Study of Telepathy in Interpersonal Relationships.* New York: G.P. Putnam's Sons, 1974.

"Executive Reports—You Can Profit by Executive Hunches." *International Management,* March 1966.

Goodavage, Joseph. *Magic: Science of the Future.* New York: New American Library, 1976.

Hammond, David. *The Search for Psychic Power.* New York: Bantam Books, 1975.

Harman, Willis W. "The Societal Implications and Social Impact of Paranormal Phenomena." In *Future Science.* J. White & S. Krippner, eds. Garden City: Anchor Press, 1977.

Mihalasky, John. "Extrasensory Perception in Management." *Advanced Management Journal,* July 1967.

———. "Question: What Do Some Executives Have More of? Answer: Intuition, Maybe." *Think,* November-December 1969.

———. "How Extrasensory Perception Can Play a Role in Idea Generation." *American Society of Mechanical Engineers Publication,* No. 72-De-5, 1972.

——— and D. Dean. "Bio-Communication." Conference Record, 1969 IEEE International Conference On Communication, Cat. No. 69C29-COM.

——— and H. Sherwood. "Dollars May Flow from the Sixth Sense." *Nation's Business,* April 1971.

Mishlove, Jeffrey. *The Roots of Consciousness.* New York: Random House, 1975.

Mitchell, Edgar., ed. *Psychic Exploration.* New York: G.P. Putnam's Sons, 1974.

Moss, Thelma. *The Probability of the Impossible.* Los Angeles: Tarcher, 1974.

Muses, C.M., and Arthur Young, eds. *Consciousness and Reality.* New York: Outerbridge and Lazard, 1972.

Ostrander, Sheila, and Lynn Schroeder. "Eyeless Sight." In *Psychic Discoveries Behind the Iron Curtain.* Englewood Cliffs: Prentice-Hall, 1970.

———. *Psychic Experiences.* New York: Sterling, 1977. (For teenagers.)

Peterson, James. "Extrasensory Abilities of Children: An Ignored Reality?" *Learning,* December 1975.

Puharich, Andrija. *Beyond Telepathy.* Garden City: Anchor Books, 1973.

Roberts, T., ed. *Four Psychologies Applied to Education: Freudian, Behavioral, Humanistic, Transpersonal.* New York: John Wiley & Sons, 1975.

Ryzl, Milan. *Parapsychology: A Scientific Approach.* New York: Hawthorn, 1970.

Schwarz, B.E. *Parent-Child Telepathy.* New York: Garrett-Helix, 1971.

Shapin, Betty, and Lisette Coly. *Education in Parapsychology.* New York: Parapsychology Foundation, Inc., 1976.

Targ, Russell, and Harold Puthoff. *Mind-Reach.* New York: Delacorte, 1977.

Tart, Charles. *States of Consciousness.* New York: E.P. Dutton, 1975.

Thompson, William Irwin. *At the Edge of History.* New York: Harper/Colophon, 1972.

Toben, Bob. *Space-Time and Beyond.* New York: E.P. Dutton, 1974.

Tutko, Agatha J. "Teaching the Blind to See." *Fate,* May 1975.

Ullman, M., S. Krippner, and A. Vaughan. *Dream Telepathy.* New York: Macmillan, 1973.

Young, Arthur M. *The Reflexive Universe.* New York: Delacorte, 1976.

Index

For information & Superlearning materials:

Superlearning Inc.
450 Seventh Avenue
Suite 500
New York, New York 10123
212-279-8450